STUDY WORKBOOK

Environmental Science

YOUR WORLD, YOUR TURN

SAVVAS
LEARNING COMPANY

ISBN-13: 978-1-4183-3637-0
ISBN-10:   1-4183-3637-8
4 21

Contents

Study Workbook

Did you know that learning to study more effectively can make a real difference in your performance at school? *Environmental Science Study Workbook* is designed to help you acquire skills that will allow you to learn the concepts of environmental science more effectively. Your active participation in class and use of this workbook can go a long way toward helping you achieve success.

This study workbook can be used to:

- Preview a chapter
- Learn key vocabulary terms
- Master difficult concepts
- Integrate and build on knowledge throughout each lesson
- Review for chapter and unit tests
- Practice 21st Century Skills

Here are some suggestions for how to use this workbook to help you study more effectively.

Start with the Investigative Phenomenon

Each chapter in your workbook begins with the Investigative Phenomenon. Fill in the first column of the graphic organizer before you read the chapter. Fill in the second column after you finish each lesson. Use your responses to discuss the Investigative Phenomenon.

Preview Each Lesson

Go through the Key Concepts before you read a lesson. Use the Vocabulary Preview chart to preview key vocabulary and to develop a strategy to help you remember each term.

Work Through the Lesson

In each lesson, you will find different workbook activities designed to help you understand and remember what you read in your textbook. Completing these activities will help you master the key concepts and vocabulary of each lesson. The questions are written in a variety of formats.

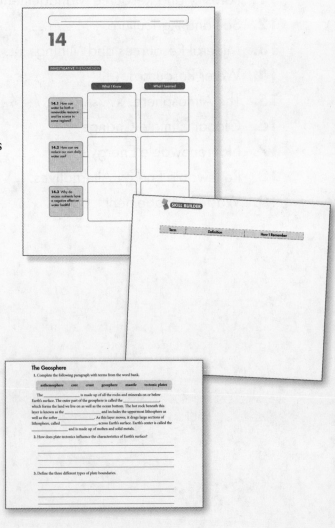

Organize Your Thoughts

A variety of Organize Information activities helps you use graphic organizers to integrate lesson concepts.

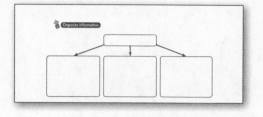

Use Visuals

You will also be able to work with a variety of visuals to reinforce concepts. Skill Builder visuals integrate concepts throughout the lesson.

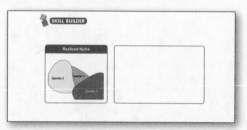

Math Support

Each chapter has a math support page for either the Real Data or Ecological Footprints feature in the Student Edition. This page provides the additional math background and support you may need to answer the textbook questions or perform the calculations.

Central Case Activity

Central Case Activity pages provide you with additional information related to the chapter Central Cases in your textbook. Use this information to help you weigh in on the Investigative Phenomenon. The Central Case Activity pages also give you the opportunity to practice your 21st Century Skills—you might make a multimedia presentation, draft an action plan, or even create public policy statements!

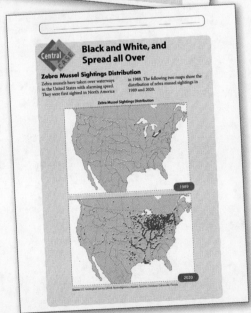

1 An Introduction to Environmental Science

Before you read the chapter, answer each question with information you know. After you complete the chapter, re-answer the questions using information you learned.

INVESTIGATIVE PHENOMENON **Can we reduce the ozone hole?**

	What I Know	What I Learned
1.1 How does environmental science help us understand the natural world?		
1.2 What does it mean to "do science"?		
1.3 What happens to a scientific study after data have been gathered and the results are analyzed?		

1.1 Our Island, Earth

Key Concepts

🔑 Environmental scientists study how the natural world works, and how humans and the environment affect each other.

🔑 In the last several hundred years, both human population and resource consumption have increased dramatically.

SKILL BUILDER Vocabulary Preview

Define each vocabulary term in your own words. Then, write yourself a quick note on how you will remember each. One term has been done for you.

Term	Definition	How I Remember
Environment		
Environmental science		
Environmental-ism		
Natural resource	A material or energy source provided by nature that people need to survive	I think of all the resources in my school library and then think of what that means in a natural environment.
Renewable natural resource		

Term	Definition	How I Remember
Nonrenewable natural resource		
Sustainable		
Fossil fuel		
Ecological footprint		

Our Environment

1. List three examples of nonliving things in the environment.

_____

2. Give two reasons why environmental science is important.

_____

_____

_____

3. Name four of the disciplines that contribute to the study of our interactions with the environment.

_____

4. What is the difference between environmental science and environmentalism?

_____

_____

_____

Population Up, Resources Down

For Questions 5–10, write True *if the statement is true. If the statement is false, replace the underlined word to make the statement true. Write your changes on the line.*

_____ 5. Nature makes natural resources at <u>similar</u> speeds.

_____ 6. Fruit is an example of a <u>renewable</u> resource.

_____ 7. For most of human history, population has been <u>high</u> and relatively stable.

_____ 8. The Industrial Revolution marked a shift from a rural society to an urban society powered by <u>renewable</u> resources.

_____ 9. Our ecological footprint is affected by the number of people on Earth and how much we <u>consume</u>.

_____ 10. The tragedy of the commons refers to the overuse of <u>unregulated</u> resources.

11. In what way is living on Earth similar to living on an island?

_____

_____

12. Why are sunlight and oil on opposite sides of the renewability continuum?

_____

_____

_____

_____

13. What could cause a renewable natural resource to become a nonrenewable resource?

_____

_____

14. How can a nonliving thing have an ecological footprint?

_____

_____

15. What is one way the tragedy of the commons could be avoided?

_____

_____

SKILL BUILDER Think Visually

Use the graph below to answer Questions 16 and 17.

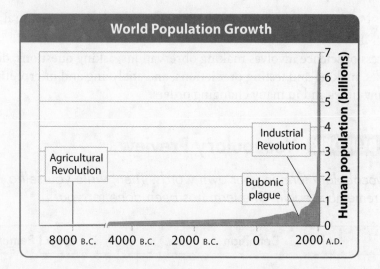

World Population Growth

Industrial Revolution

Agricultural Revolution

Bubonic plague

Human population (billions)

8000 B.C.   4000 B.C.   2000 B.C.   0   2000 A.D.

16. Which event shown on the graph signaled the biggest change in human population growth?_____

17. Explain how understanding environmental science can help people solve problems related to human population growth.

_____

_____

_____

EXTENSION Choose two different organisms or objects. Think about the relationship they have with other organisms or objects in their environment. Compare their ecological footprints by listing the ways they affect the environment.

1.1 ◯ SELF-CHECK

Answer the questions to test your knowledge of lesson concepts. You can check your work using the answers on the bottom of the page.

18. Why is it important to remember that people are part of the environment, too?

_____

19. Why is natural gas considered a nonrenewable resource? _____

_____

18. Sample answer: Because people interact with, rely on, and affect the health of the environment 19. Because it forms much more slowly than humans use it

1.2 The Nature of Science

Key Concepts

- Science is both an organized and methodical way of studying the natural world and the knowledge gained from such studies.
- The process of science involves making observations, asking questions, developing hypotheses, making and testing predictions, and analyzing and interpreting results—often many times and in many changing orders.

SKILL BUILDER Vocabulary Preview

Define each vocabulary term in your own words. Then, write yourself a quick note on how you will remember each. One term has been done for you.

Term	Definition	How I Remember
Hypothesis		
Prediction		
Independent variable		
Dependent variable	A variable that depends on the conditions set up in an experiment	I think of how I am dependent on something. For example, what I wear depends on the weather.
Controlled study		
Data		

SKILL BUILDER Reading Strategy

Fill in the chart to preview the lesson. Then, on the lines below the chart, write one sentence to explain what you think this lesson will be about.

What is the title of this lesson?	
Which vocabulary words are new to you?	
Which key concept can help you understand the definition of science?	
What do the photos show?	
What do the diagrams show?	

_____

_____

What Science Is and Is Not

1. What are the two components of science?

_____

_____

2. What does the natural world include?

_____

_____

3. What is the goal of science?

_____

_____

4. How do scientists examine the workings of the natural world?

_____

5. Explain the following statement: "Nothing in science can be absolutely proven no matter how much evidence is collected."

_____

_____

_____

The Process of Science

For Questions 6–9, circle the letter of the correct answer.

6. Which of the following statements best describes the process of science?
  A. It is mysterious.
  B. It is predictable.
  C. It proceeds in a linear fashion.
  D. It produces knowledge over time.

7. Which of the following plays an especially important role in the early stages of an investigation?
  A. making observations
  B. gathering data
  C. interpreting data
  D. making predictions

8. Which of the following is NOT involved in testing ideas?
  A. making predictions
  B. making observations
  C. making policy decisions
  D. conducting experiments

9. What must scientists do if a large number of tests refute their hypothesis?
  A. repeat each test
  B. publish a report
  C. reject the test results
  D. reject the hypothesis

10. What is the relationship between hypotheses and predictions?

_____

_____

11. What do scientists use models for?

_____

_____

12. Name two methods scientists use to test predictions.

_____

13. What is the difference between an independent variable and a dependent variable?

_____

_____

_____

14. Briefly define *correlation*.

_____

15. Why is it important to control all variables except one when studying cause-and-effect relationships?

_____

_____

16. Why are quantitative data particularly helpful to scientists?

_____

1.2 SELF-CHECK

Answer the questions to test your knowledge of lesson concepts. You can check your work using the answers on the bottom of the page.

17. Give an example of a rule of the natural world that a scientist can assume is always true.

_____

18. What activities make up the process of science? _____

_____

_____

19. What is controlled in a controlled study? _____

_____

17. Sample answer: The boiling point of water is always 100°C at sea level. 18. Making observations, asking questions, developing hypotheses, making and testing predictions, analyzing and interpreting data 19. All variables except the one being studied

1.3 The Community of Science

Key Concepts

 The scientific community, through peer review and replication, helps to verify the accuracy of results and contributes to the establishment of scientific theories.

 Environmental ethics explores how environmental science interacts with, and is guided by, a society's morals and principles.

SKILL BUILDER Vocabulary Preview

Define each vocabulary term in your own words. Then, write yourself a quick note on how you will remember each. One term has been done for you.

Term	Definition	How I Remember
Peer review		
Theory	A broad explanation that applies to a wide range of situations and observations and that is supported by several lines of evidence and broadly accepted by the scientific community	I remember reading about the Big Bang theory in a science magazine.
Ethics		
Environmental ethics		

Community Analysis and Feedback

1. How does peer review benefit the scientific community?

_____

_____

2. What happens to a scientific article that is rejected by a panel of other scientists?

_____

3. Why is the replication of results important?

_____

_____

4. Explain the following statement: "Science is self-correcting."

_____

5. Give an example of a self-correction in science.

_____

_____

_____

6. What is the difference between a hypothesis and a theory?

_____

_____

7. How does popular use of the word *theory* differ from use of the word *theory* in science?

_____

_____

_____

_____

8. Give one reason why an idea is not a theory.

_____

9. **Think Visually** Fill in the diagram by writing three ways the scientific community reviews scientific results.

Scientific Results

Benefits and Outcomes

10. Give an example of how ethics could impact a government's policy on science.

_____

_____

11. Briefly explain the relationship between culture and worldview.

_____

_____

12. What role do a society's beliefs play in an objective process like science?

_____

_____

13. What led to the application of ethical standards to relationships between people and their environment?

_____

_____

14. What does the environmental justice movement promote?

_____

_____

15. **Think Visually** *Anthropocentrism, biocentrism,* and *ecocentrism* are ethical standards in environmental ethics. Think about what they mean. Then, label each of the circles below with the name of the ethical standard it represents and a description of what that standard places the highest value on.

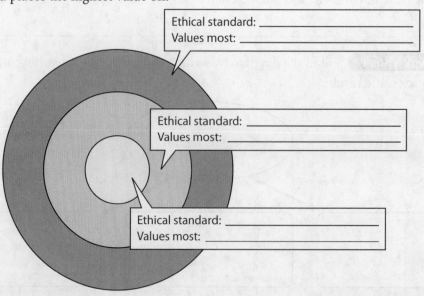

Ethical standard: _____
Values most: _____

Ethical standard: _____
Values most: _____

Ethical standard: _____
Values most: _____

SKILL BUILDER Organize Information

16. Write each term from the word bank in the correct column of the table below.

| build knowledge | develop technologies | inform policy |
| peer review | replication | satisfy curiosity | self-correction |

Analysis and Feedback of Scientific Knowledge	Benefits and Outcomes of Scientific Knowledge

EXTENSION Use the Internet to research a group or organization that works for environmental justice. On a separate sheet of paper, write a short report on the group's recent environmental initiatives.

1.3 SELF-CHECK

Answer the questions to test your knowledge of lesson concepts. You can check your work using the answers on the bottom of the page.

17. How do peer review of scientific articles and replication of test results contribute to the development of scientific theories? _____

_____

18. Give an example of how ethical standards have been applied to a worldwide environmental issue. _____

_____

19. Give an example of an ethical question related to people and their interactions with the environment. _____

_____

20. Name three ethical standards that are applied to environmental issues.

_____

17. Sample answer: Both peer review and replication are forms of testing, and an idea must be rigorously tested before it is accepted as a theory. **18. Sample answer:** In 1987, 93 nations signed the Montreal Protocol, agreeing to control the use and production of ozone-depleting substances. **19. Sample answer:** Does the present generation have an obligation to conserve resources for future generations? **20.** Anthropocentrism, biocentrism, ecocentrism

Chapter Vocabulary Review

Match each term with its definition.

_____ **1.** natural resource

_____ **2.** ethics

_____ **3.** independent variable

_____ **4.** peer review

_____ **5.** environment

_____ **6.** dependent variable

_____ **7.** sustainable

_____ **8.** data

_____ **9.** theory

_____ **10.** environmentalism

_____ **11.** hypothesis

_____ **12.** ecological footprint

a. information gathered from a study

b. all living and nonliving things with which organisms interact

c. a testable idea that attempts to explain a phenomenon

d. the study of right and wrong

e. used at a rate equal to the rate of replenishment into the foreseeable future

f. a factor scientists manipulate in an experiment

g. the environmental effects of an individual or group in terms of resources used and waste produced

h. a social movement dedicated to protecting the natural world

i. formal examination of a research report by the scientific community

j. a material or energy source provided by nature that people need to survive

k. a factor determined by the conditions set up in an experiment

l. a broad explanation for a wide range of situations and observations

Use each vocabulary term in a sentence.

13. controlled study _____

_____

14. environmental ethics _____

EXTENSION Use ten or more vocabulary words to create a poster that explains the study of environmental science. Add images to your poster that illustrate some aspect of the environment.

Ecological Footprints

"Overshooting" Ecological Resources

About 1.8 hectares of functioning ecosystem are available per person in the world. However, the average person has an ecological footprint of about 2.2 hectares. In this activity, you will calculate the percentage by which people in the world and people in various nations are using more than the resources available per person.

▶ To find the percentage by which people in the world are "overshooting" available resources, use the steps shown below.

Step 1	Find the difference between the number of hectares required per person and the number of hectares available per person.	$2.2 - 1.8 = 0.4$ **hectare**
Step 2	Write a ratio that compares the difference found in Step 1 to the number of hectares available per person.	$\frac{0.4}{1.8} \approx 0.2222$
Step 3	Write the ratio as a percentage, rounding to the nearest tenth.	$0.2222 = 22.2\%$

1. For each nation listed in the table below, calculate the difference between the ecological footprint, or the number of hectares required per person, and the number of hectares available per person. Write your answers in the third column.

Nation	Ecological Footprint (hectares per person)	Hectares Required Minus Hectares Available (per person)	Percentage Over Hectares Available (per person)
Bangladesh	0.5		
Colombia	1.3		
Mexico	2.6		
Sweden	6.1		
Thailand	1.4		
United States	9.6		

Data from *Living Planet Report 2006*. WWF International, Zoological Society of London, and Global Footprint Network.

2. Which nations have an ecological footprint greater than the resources available per

person? _____

3. By what percentage are these nations "overshooting" available resources? Round your answers to the nearest tenth and add them to the fourth column in the table.

Fixing a Hole in the Sky

Depletion of Ozone

Ozone is both harmful and beneficial. Ozone near Earth's surface is a damaging pollutant. But in the stratosphere, ozone protects Earth from harmful UV radiation. Depletion of ozone in the stratosphere concerns scientists because it allows too much UV radiation to reach Earth.

Overexposure to UV radiation may harm the body's immune system and cause skin cancer and cataracts. Scientists also believe excess UV radiation reaching Earth's surface disrupts the reproductive cycle of phytoplankton. These single-celled organisms are found in the top 2 meters of ocean water and are the bottom level of the food chain for many other marine organisms. Scientists also believe excessive ultraviolet radiation disrupts the reproductive rates of young fish, shrimp, crabs, frogs, and salamanders.

The Montreal Protocol was signed in 1987, with the goal of phasing out the production and use of substances that deplete the stratospheric ozone layer. Since then, the world's scientific community has met several times to accelerate and adjust its provisions. Targeted substances include CFCs, halons, carbon tetrachloride, methyl bromide, and methyl chloroform. Phaseout schedules differ among nations and for different substances. The ultimate goal, however, is the worldwide elimination of ozone-depleting substances by the middle of the twenty-first century.

Tracking the Ozone Hole

The U.S. Environmental Protection Agency collects data daily on ozone levels near Earth's surface. These data are carefully monitored and studied to determine where and how ozone levels near Earth's surface are changing. But how do scientists collect data high up in Earth's stratosphere—10 to 40 kilometers above Earth?

The United States began monitoring ozone levels in 1920 using ground-based instruments at various places around the globe. The instruments measured the amount of UV radiation reaching Earth's surface. As valuable as these data were, they did not tell scientists if a change in ozone levels in one place meant a global reduction in ozone in the stratosphere. In recent years, NASA and the National Oceanic and Atmospheric Administration (NOAA) have worked together to monitor and understand changes in global ozone levels through images and other data collected by satellites orbiting far above Earth.

Data from satellites provide evidence that stratospheric ozone is definitely being depleted, but scientists are not yet sure how much of the depletion is due to human activity and how much is the result of Earth's natural cycles. Tracking the ozone hole remains an important scientific activity, one that will yield vital scientific knowledge as scientists continue to collect data from afar.

Use the information in **Depletion of Ozone** to answer the questions below.

1. Why are scientists concerned about the depletion of ozone levels in the stratosphere?

   _____

   _____

   _____

2. How were ozone levels monitored in 1920?

   _____

   _____

3. How is information on ozone levels in the stratosphere tracked today?

   _____

4. The data collected over the years clearly confirm a depletion of ozone in the stratosphere. What do scientists still need to learn about the ozone hole?

   _____

   _____

21st Century Skills

Use the Internet to find out more about the ozone hole and how scientists track its status. Work with a partner to research the ozone hole over Antarctica. Create a poster that explains what you learned about the ozone hole. Your poster should include images of the hole when it was first identified and at regular intervals since.

*The 21st Century Skills used in this activity include **Information Literacy, Initiative and Self-Direction,** and **Information, Communication, and Technology (ICT) Literacy.***

2 Economics and Environmental Policy

Before you read the chapter, answer each question with information you know. After you complete the chapter, re-answer the questions using information you learned.

INVESTIGATIVE PHENOMENON **How do economic factors influence environmental policy?**

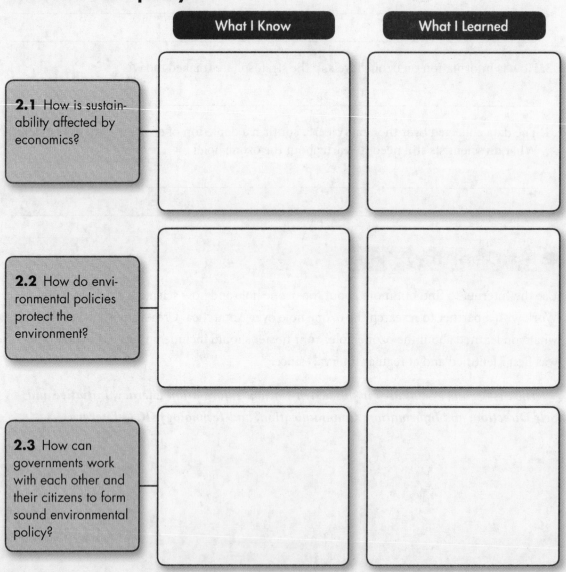

What I Know	What I Learned
2.1 How is sustainability affected by economics?		
2.2 How do environmental policies protect the environment?		
2.3 How can governments work with each other and their citizens to form sound environmental policy?		

2.1 Economics

Key Concepts

 Supply and demand and cost-benefit analysis are two economic concepts that greatly contribute to decision making.

Key All economies depend on the environment for resources and for management of wastes, but these connections are often overlooked.

Key A new trend in economics is the recognition that suppliers of goods and services need to consider how to conserve resources and reduce harm to the environment.

SKILL BUILDER Vocabulary Preview

Define each vocabulary term in your own words. Then, write yourself a quick note on how you will remember each. One term has been done for you.

Term	Definition	How I Remember
Economics		
Supply		
Demand	The amount of a product people will buy at a given price if free to do so	When people demand something, they want it and are willing to pay for it.
Cost-benefit analysis		
Ecological economics		
Environmental economics		
Non-market value		

Term	Definition	How I Remember
Market failure		
Ecolabeling		

What Is Economics?

Match each type of economy with the statement that best describes it.

_____ 1. centrally planned economy

_____ 2. free market economy

_____ 3. mixed economy

a. The government decides what is made, how it is made, and who gets what.

b. Both government and individuals play roles in economic decision making.

c. Individuals decide what is made, how it is made, and how much is made.

4. Is economics only about money? Explain your answer.

_____

_____

5. Compare and contrast goods and services.

_____

_____

_____

6. Explain how supply and demand works.

_____

_____

_____

7. On the surface, cost-benefit analysis seems straightforward. What can make this decision-making method both complicated and controversial?

_____

_____

_____

Economics and the Environment

8. Briefly define *natural resources*.

_____

9. What kinds of "services" do ecological systems provide?

_____

10. Organize Information Fill in the diagram with short descriptions of economic assumptions that have harmed the environment.

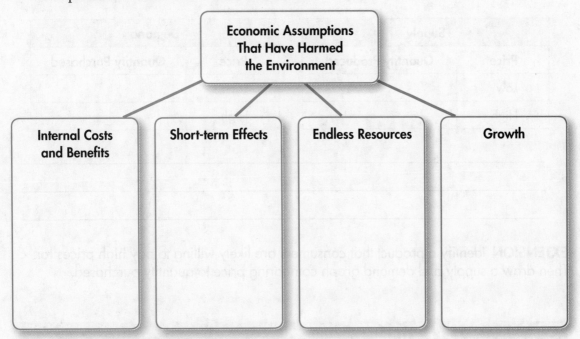

Economics and Sustainability

11. Complete the following paragraph with terms from the word bank.

> ecolabeling   ecological economics   environmental economics
> market failure   non-market value

  Many economists in _____ argue that economies must be stable to be

sustainable. But economists in _____ think growing economies can

become sustainable if they address environmental problems. In particular, these economists are

developing ways to include the _____ of ecosystem services in prices. They are

also finding ways to avoid _____ by acknowledging the positive effects of the

environment on economies and the negative effects of economic activities on the environment

and people. _____ helps consumers push companies toward sustainability.

12. How do companies benefit by offering sustainable products and services?

_____

_____

SKILL BUILDER Organize Information

13. Complete the tables below to show how the quantity produced and the quantity purchased change in a typical market. On the lines below the tables, describe what might happen if consumers were willing to pay a high price for a new sustainable product, such as a very energy and water efficient yet expensive washing machine.

Supply			Demand	
Price	Quantity Produced		Price	Quantity Purchased
Low			Low	
High			High	

_____

_____

_____

EXTENSION Identify a product that consumers are likely willing to pay high prices for. Then draw a supply and demand graph comparing price to quantity purchased.

2.1 ◯ SELF-CHECK

Answer the questions to test your knowledge of lesson concepts. You can check your work using the answers on the bottom of the page.

14. Which kind of economy do most nations have today? Explain your answer.

_____

_____

15. What are external costs, and how do they relate to market failure?

_____

_____

14. Most nations have a mixed economy because both governments and individuals make economic decisions.
15. External costs involve parties other than buyers and sellers. When buyers and sellers ignore external costs in their decision making, markets do not reflect the full costs of actions and are said to fail.

2.2 United States Environmental Policy

Key Concepts

- Environmental policy makes use of science, ethics, economics, and the political process to solve environmental problems.
- Throughout its history, the United States government has reinvented its approach to the relationship between the nation's goals and the environment.
- Modern U.S. environmental policy reveals lessons learned from past misuses of resources and strives for a sustainable future.

SKILL BUILDER Vocabulary Preview

Define each vocabulary term in your own words. Then, write yourself a quick note on how you will remember each. One term has been done for you.

Term	Definition	How I Remember
Policy		
Environmental policy		
Environmental Impact Statement (EIS)	A report that evaluates the impact of new construction on the environment	*To impact* means "to affect," so an Environmental *impact* Statement tells how something will affect the environment.

What Is Environmental Policy?

1. Identify three goals of modern-day environmental policies.

_____

_____

2. Name five individuals and groups that help make environmental policies.

_____

_____

3. What role does science play in making environmental policy?

_____

_____

4. How do environmental catastrophies tend to influence environmental policies in state and local governments?

_____

_____

_____

_____

5. **Organize Information** Fill in the T-chart with short descriptions of how different branches of the U.S. government are involved in environmental policy.

Branch of U.S. Government	Its Role in Environmental Policy

History of U.S. Environmental Policy

For Questions 6–8, write True *if the statement is true. If the statement is false, replace the underlined word to make the statement true. Write your changes on the line.*

_____ **6.** From the 1780s to the late 1800s, people thought the amount of land and resources in the West was <u>limited</u>.

_____ **7.** People <u>overused</u> natural resources in the West from the late 1800s through the mid-1960s.

_____ **8.** The <u>pristine</u> condition of Ohio's Cuyahoga River during the 1950s and 1960s helped make more people aware of environmental issues.

9. How did Rachel Carson's *Silent Spring* help change U.S. environmental policies?

_____

_____

_____

Modern U.S. Environmental Policy

10. **Think Visually** Add labels to the timeline for the following environmental events and laws.

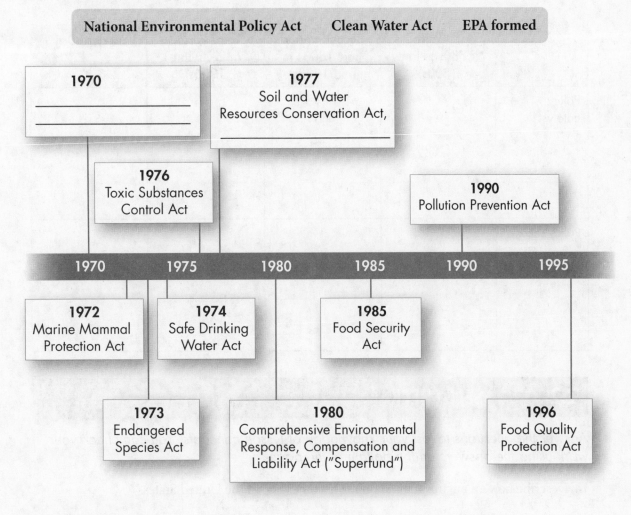

National Environmental Policy Act   Clean Water Act   EPA formed

1970
_____
_____

1977
Soil and Water
Resources Conservation Act,
_____

1976
Toxic Substances
Control Act

1990
Pollution Prevention Act

| 1970 | 1975 | 1980 | 1985 | 1990 | 1995 |

1972
Marine Mammal
Protection Act

1974
Safe Drinking
Water Act

1985
Food Security
Act

1973
Endangered
Species Act

1980
Comprehensive Environmental
Response, Compensation and
Liability Act ("Superfund")

1996
Food Quality
Protection Act

11. After studying the timeline above, what observations can you make about U.S. environmental policy between 1970 and 1996?

_____

_____

_____

12. What is the current direction of environmental policy in the United States? Give examples.

_____

_____

_____

_____

_____

SKILL BUILDER Organize Information

13. Fill in the compare/contrast table with information about the three historical periods of U.S. environmental policy and modern-day U.S. environmental policy.

	First Period (1780s to late 1800s)	Second Period (late 1800s to mid-1900s)	Third Period (mid- to late 1900s)	Modern Day
Policy catalyst				
Policy focus				

2.2 ◯ SELF-CHECK

Answer the questions to test your knowledge of lesson concepts. You can check your work using the answers on the bottom of the page.

14. Describe how an environmental policy becomes law in the United States.

_____

_____

_____

15. Since the late 1800s, how has the United States tried to protect the environment?

_____

_____

_____

14. Sample answer: A policy becomes law when Congress passes a bill and the President signs it into law. Policies and laws also are created at state and local levels of government. **15.** Starting in the late 1800s the United States began passing environmental laws. The EPA was created in 1970 to coordinate efforts to protect the environment. Today, the United States is working on conserving energy and developing renewable energy sources—moving toward sustainability.

2.3 International Environmental Policy and Approaches

Key Concepts

 International organizations, laws, and treaties help governments of the world come to agreement on environmental issues.

 Approaches to environmental policy may include direct laws from a government body or policies with economic incentives.

 Steps of the environmental policy process include identifying a problem, finding the cause, proposing solutions, getting organized, gaining access to policymakers, and guiding the solution to law.

SKILL BUILDER Vocabulary Preview

Define each vocabulary term in your own words. Then, write yourself a quick note on how you will remember each. One term has been done for you.

Term	Definition	How I Remember
Command-and-control approach		
Subsidy		
Green tax	A tax imposed on companies that participate in activities or produce products that are harmful to the environment	I can remember that if a company is not "green," it does not have good environmental practices, so it is taxed.
Cap-and-trade		
Lobbying		

SKILL BUILDER Reading Strategy

As you read the lesson, complete the main ideas and details chart.

Main Ideas	Details
International environmental policy	
Approaches to environmental policy	
The environmental policy process	

International Environmental Policy

1. Why must nations sometimes work together to solve environmental problems?

_____

_____

2. Give an example of a transboundary problem.

_____

_____

3. How do international organizations encourage nations to work on environmental issues?

_____

_____

4. Explain the role played by non-governmental organizations in international environmental policy.

_____

_____

For Questions 5–8, match each organization with the statement that best describes the work it is doing to influence international environmental policy.

_____ 5. United Nations

_____ 6. European Union

_____ 7. World Trade Organization

_____ 8. World Bank

a. Makes current environmental data and analyses available to policymakers in member nations

b. Imposes financial penalties on member nations that do not comply with its directives

c. Promotes research and programs that provide information to international policymakers

d. Funds projects such as dams and irrigation systems

Approaches to Environmental Policy

For Questions 9–12, complete each statement by writing the correct word or words.

9. Using a _____ approach to environmental policy, a government sets rules and threatens punishment for violations.

10. Green taxes let _____ decide how best to reduce pollution.

11. Critics of _____ systems say that giving companies permission to pollute will not solve environmental problems in the long run.

12. A local government that gives rebates to residents who buy water-efficient toilets is using a _____ as a policy tool.

13. How have governments responded to the criticism that free-market competition produces better and cheaper solutions to environmental problems than the command-and-control approach does?

_____

_____

_____

14. Explain how a cap-and-trade system works.

_____

_____

_____

The Environmental Policy Process

15. [Organize Information] Fill in the flowchart with the steps in the environmental policy process. The first step is provided.

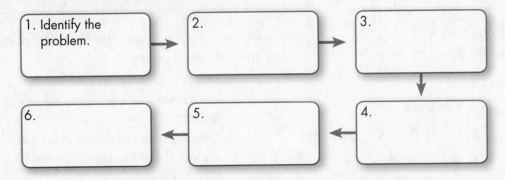

16. Describe ways in which science can help identify environmental problems and their causes.

_____

_____

_____

17. Explain a problem an environmental policy might face even after it becomes a law.

_____

_____

2.3 ⊙ SELF-CHECK

Answer the questions to test your knowledge of lesson concepts. You can check your work using the answers on the bottom of the page.

18. Governments can use taxes both to encourage compliance with environmental policies and to discourage noncompliance. Give an example of each.

_____

_____

19. How can people who are too young to vote influence environmental policy?

_____

_____

_____

18. Sample answer: Tax breaks encourage environmentally sound actions, and green taxes discourage actions and products that harm the environment. 19. Sample answer: Young people can make a difference by lobby-ing for changes in their school's environmental policies, joining a local environmental group, or taking part in international meetings.

Chapter Vocabulary Review

Match each term with its definition.

_____ **1.** supply

_____ **2.** policy

_____ **3.** subsidy

_____ **4.** demand

_____ **5.** lobbying

_____ **6.** economics

_____ **7.** green tax

_____ **8.** non-market value

_____ **9.** market failure

_____ **10.** cost-benefit analysis

a. the study of how resources become goods and services that are distributed and used

b. a tax on companies that harm the environment

c. a comparison of the disadvantages and advantages of a specific action

d. the amount of a product offered for sale at a given price

e. efforts to influence an elected official to support a specific interest

f. a value that is not usually included in the price of goods or services

g. a formal set of plans for addressing problems and guiding decision making

h. the amount of a product people will buy at a given price if free to do so

i. when a market does not reflect the full costs and benefits of actions

j. a giveaway of cash or public resources to encourage an activity or lower a product's price

Write a sentence that shows the relationship between the two terms.

11. command-and-control approach, lobbying _____

_____

_____

12. subsidy, green taxes _____

_____

_____

13. ecological economics, environmental economics _____

_____

_____

EXTENSION On a separate sheet of paper, write a short paragraph describing U.S. efforts to address environmental issues over the last few decades. In the paragraph, use at least one vocabulary term from each lesson in the chapter.

Ecological Footprints

Daily Water Use

The United States used about 349 billion gallons of fresh water per day in 2005. The water use in each of four categories is shown below as a percentage of total water use. In this activity, you will calculate the billion gallons of water these percentages represent. You also will calculate the average amount of fresh water used per person per day for each category.

Daily Freshwater Use in 2005				
Category	Electricity	Irrigation	Public Water Supply	Industrial/ Livestock/ Mining
Total fresh water used per day (percent)	41%	37%	13%	7%
Total fresh water used per day in the U.S. (billion gallons)	143.09			
Average fresh water used per person per day (gallons)	475.38			

Data from U.S. Geological Survey, *Estimated use of water in the United States, 2005.*

▶ To find how much water is used in each category, first write the percentage as a decimal. Then, multiply the decimal by the total amount of water used. The calculation for the gallons of fresh water used per day in the electricity category is modeled at the right:

$$41\% = \frac{41}{100} = 0.41$$

water used = decimal × total amount used

billion gallons = 0.41 × 349

$$= 143.09 \text{ billion gallons}$$

1. Calculate the gallons of water used per day for each of the other three categories shown in the table above. Write your answers in the table.

▶ To find the average amount of fresh water used per person per day, divide each amount by the population. In 2005, the U.S. population was 301 million (0.301 billion). The calculation for the average amount of water used per person per day for electricity is shown at the right:

$$\text{water used per person per day} = \frac{\text{amount used}}{\text{population}}$$

$$= \frac{143.09 \text{ billion gallons}}{0.301 \text{ billion people}}$$

$$\approx 475.38 \text{ gallons per person}$$

2. Calculate the average daily water use per person for each of the other three categories shown in the table above. Write your answers in the table.

Cleaning the Tides of San Diego and Tijuana

Border 2012

The pollution problem in the Tijuana River is just part of a larger environmental situation along the 3100-kilometer (2000-mile) border between Mexico and the United States. Located along this border are 15 pairs of U.S.-Mexico "sister cities." The map below shows the U.S.-Mexico border region and these sister cities.

Rapid population growth in the border region's sister cities has placed stresses on the region's resources, causing many environmental problems. These problems include air and water pollution, overloading of water and sewage treatment plants, and overuse of natural resources. Furthermore, the health of the region's nearly 13 million residents is also at stake. The pollution is causing respiratory ailments, water-borne diseases, respiratory ailments, and other health problems.

The U.S. Environmental Protection Agency (EPA) and Mexico's Secretariat of Environment and Natural Resources (SEMARNAT), along with many other organizations, are working together on an environmental plan for the region called "Border 2012." This binational effort takes into account population, demographics, language, trade, and biological diversity of the various parts of the border. Border 2012's six goals are to: reduce water contamination; reduce air pollution; reduce land contamination; improve environmental health; establish emergency preparedness and response; and to enforce environmental stewardship.

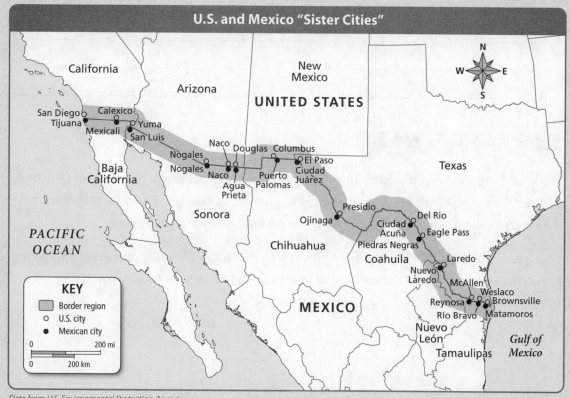

U.S. and Mexico "Sister Cities"

Data from U.S. Environmental Protection Agency.

Use the information in **Border 2012** to answer the questions below.

1. Identify 3 of the 15 pairs of sister cities along the U.S.-Mexico border.

_____

_____

_____

2. Do you think the health of the environment in the border region—and the health of the residents—will improve or worsen in the future? Explain your answer.

_____

_____

_____

3. Why is it important that both nations work together to clean up the pollution?

_____

_____

_____

_____

4. **REVISIT** **INVESTIGATIVE** PHENOMENON   Use the information in the article and the map to explain how two nations can work together to balance their own interests and needs with the health of the environment. _____

_____

_____

_____

21st Century Skills

Find out more about Border 2012. In small groups, use Internet resources to explore the topic on the EPA and SEMARNAT Web sites and on other reputable sites. Brainstorm solutions to the environmental problems in the region, and present your ideas to the class.

*The 21st Century Skills used in this activity include **Critical Thinking and Problem Solving, Creativity and Innovation, Communication and Collaboration, Media Literacy,** and **Information Literacy.***

3 Earth's Environmental Systems

Before you read the chapter, answer each question with information you know. After you complete the chapter, re-answer the questions using information you learned.

INVESTIGATIVE PHENOMENON **How do "dead zones" affect the environment surrounding them?**

	What I Know	What I Learned
3.1 What properties of matter are most important to environmental systems?		
3.2 What types of systems play roles in environmental science?		
3.3 What are the characteristics of Earth's geosphere, biosphere, atmosphere, and hydrosphere?		
3.4 How do nutrients cycle through the environment?		

3.1 Matter and the Environment

Key Concepts

 Atoms and elements are the building blocks of chemistry.

 Proteins, nucleic acids, carbohydrates, and lipids are the building blocks of life.

 Water is a unique compound with several unusual properties that make it essential to life.

SKILL BUILDER **Vocabulary Preview**

Define each vocabulary term in your own words. Then, write yourself a quick note on how you will remember each. One term has been done for you.

Term	Definition	How I Remember
Matter		
Atom		
Element		
Nucleus		
Molecule		
Compound		
Hydrocarbon	An organic compound that contains only hydrogen and carbon	The prefix *hydro–* means "combined with hydrogen," so *hydrocarbon* means "carbon combined with hydrogen."

Term	Definition	How I Remember
Solution		
Macromolecule		
Protein		
Nucleic acid		
Carbohydrate		
Lipid		
pH		

Building Blocks of Chemistry

Match each term with the statement that best describes it.

_____ 1. element

_____ 2. electron

_____ 3. compound

a. the negatively charged part of an atom

b. water, for example

c. its properties cannot be broken down any further

4. Write a sentence that shows the relationship between matter and atoms.

_____

5. Give two examples of substances that contain hydrocarbons.

_____

Macromolecules

For Questions 6–8, circle the letter of the correct answer.

6. The characteristic that best defines a macromolecule is its

   A. size.

   B. function.

   C. life cycle.

   D. chemical makeup.

7. All of the following macromolecules are polymers EXCEPT

   A. lipids.

   B. proteins.

   C. nucleic acids.

   D. carbohydrates.

8. All of the following are part of a carbohydrate EXCEPT

   A. carbon.

   B. oxygen.

   C. hydrogen.

   D. phosphorus.

9. Explain how macromolecules are involved in passing traits from parents to offspring.

_____

_____

_____

Water

For Questions 10–12, write True *if the statement is true. If the statement is false, replace the underlined word to make the statement true. Write your changes on the line.*

_____ **10.** Water molecules adhere to each other through <u>covalent</u> bonds.

_____ **11.** Its <u>cohesion</u> allows water to transport nutrients and wastes in plants and animals.

_____ **12.** A solution with a pH less than 7 is <u>basic</u>.

13. How does water resist changes in temperature?

_____

_____

_____

14. Why is water called "the universal solvent"?

_____

SKILL BUILDER Organize Information

15. Fill in the compare/contrast table below with information about the different types of matter.

	O₂	Hydrocarbons	Protein	DNA
Matter type				
Description				
Function				

3.1 ◎ SELF-CHECK

Answer the questions to test your knowledge of lesson concepts. You can check your work using the answers on the bottom of the page.

16. Is water an element? Why or why not? _____

_____

17. Describe the special properties of water that allow it to support life on Earth.

_____

_____

_____

_____

_____

16. No. It is a compound because it is made up of two elements, hydrogen and oxygen. **17.** Water sticks to itself, which allows it to carry materials in plants and animals. Water is resistant to temperature change, which stabilizes aquatic systems and their climates. Liquid water is denser than frozen water, which allows ice to float and insulate underwater environments. Water is a univeral solvent, which allows it to hold important molecules in solutions.

3.2 Systems in Environmental Science

Key Concepts

- An output of one of Earth's systems is often also an input to that or another system.
- Earth's geosphere, biosphere, atmosphere, and hydrosphere are defined according to their functions in Earth's systems.

SKILL BUILDER Vocabulary Preview

Define each vocabulary term in your own words. Then, write yourself a quick note on how you will remember each. One term has been done for you.

Term	Definition	How I Remember
Feedback loop		
Erosion		
Geosphere		
Lithosphere		
Biosphere		
Atmosphere		
Hydrosphere	All the water on and below Earth's surface and in the atmosphere	*Hydrosphere* reminds me of a water *hydrant.*

SKILL BUILDER Reading Strategy

As you read the lesson, complete each statement by writing in the correct word or words.

1. A _____ is a network of parts, elements, or components that interact with and influence one another.

2. Systems receive and process _____ of energy, matter, or information, and produce _____ of energy, matter, or information.

3. Systems do not have well-defined _____, which makes it difficult to decide where one system ends and another begins.

4. Systems may exchange energy, _____, and/or information with other systems.

5. Inputs into Earth's systems can include both _____ energy and geothermal energy.

6. An event that is both a cause and an effect is a cyclical process known as a _____, and can be either positive or negative.

7. A predator-prey relationship in which the two populations rise and fall in response to each other is an example of a _____ feedback loop.

8. _____ feedback loops enhance stability by canceling an action once it reaches an extreme.

9. Erosion is an example of a _____ feedback loop.

10. Positive feedback loops are relatively _____ in nature but _____ in environmental systems that people have changed.

11. Scientists divide Earth into spheres, which are often described by their _____ rather than by their location.

12. Earth's geosphere is made up of all the _____ at and below the surface of Earth.

13. The sphere of the Earth that consists of all the planet's living or once-living things and the nonliving parts of the environment with which they interact is the _____.

14. The outermost layer of Earth and the geosphere is known as the _____.

15. The hydrosphere includes all water on Earth, including all forms of liquid, solid, and _____.

16. Earth's spheres both overlap and _____.

17. An earthworm tunneling through the soil is an example of the biosphere interacting with the _____.

Interacting Systems

18. Use the concept of a computer system to explain why it is difficult to determine clear distinct boundaries to a system. Include sample descriptions in your answer.

_____

_____

_____

_____

_____

_____

19. Give an example of each type of input into Earth's systems.

_____

_____

20. Explain how a negative feedback loop works. Use a thermostat as an example.

_____

_____

21. Describe the effects of a positive feedback loop.

_____

_____

22. Contrast the two different types of feedback loops in terms of how they affect the stability of a system.

_____

_____

_____

23. **Think Visually** Write in the boxes to complete the following on how the human body relies on a negative feedback loop to respond to heat and cold.

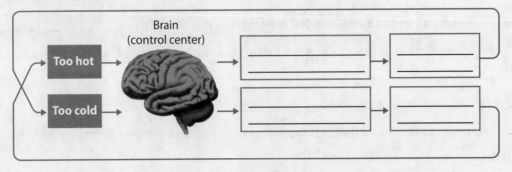

Earth's "Spheres"

For Questions 24–26, write True *if the statement is true. If the statement is false, replace the underlined word to make the statement true. Write your changes on the line.*

_____**24.** The lithosphere is part of the <u>geosphere</u>.

_____**25.** A human being is part of Earth's <u>lithosphere</u>.

_____**26.** The hydrosphere includes water in Earth's <u>atmosphere</u>.

27. How are Earth's spheres defined?

_____

28. What are the components of Earth's geosphere?

_____

29. What materials make up Earth's biosphere?

_____

30. Give an example of how two of Earth's spheres overlap or interact.

_____

_____

3.2 ◉ SELF-CHECK

Answer the questions to test your knowledge of lesson concepts. You can check your work using the answers on the bottom of the page.

31. Compare negative feedback and positive feedback loops. _____

_____

_____

32. Give examples of each of Earth's spheres from the environment in which you live.

_____

_____

_____

31. Both are cyclical processes in which an event is both input and output. In a negative feedback loop, output moving in one direction acts as input that causes the system to move in the other direction, the one canceling the other and so stabilizing the system. In a positive feedback loop, the input and output do not cancel each other out and stabilize the system; instead they drive it to an extreme. **32.** Sample answer: The lake in my neighborhood is part of the hydrosphere; the soil and rock that my school is built on are part of the geosphere; the plants, animals, and people who live in my neighborhood are part of the biosphere; the air I breathe is part of the atmosphere.

3.3 Earth's Spheres

Key Concepts

- Earth's geosphere consists of the crust, the mantle, and the core.
- Earth's biosphere and atmosphere are the living Earth and the ocean of gases that supports and protects it.
- Water cycles through the lithosphere, biosphere, and atmosphere endlessly.

 SKILL BUILDER Vocabulary Preview

Define each vocabulary term in your own words. Then, write yourself a quick note on how you will remember each. One term has been done for you.

Term	Definition	How I Remember
Crust		
Mantle		
Core		
Tectonic plate	A large section of lithosphere that moves over Earth's surface	I picture a dinner plate being moved on a tabletop.
Landform		
Deposition		
Evaporation		
Transpiration		

Term	Definition	How I Remember
Precipitation		
Condensation		
Aquifer		
Groundwater		

The Geosphere

1. Complete the following paragraph with terms from the word bank.

asthenosphere	core	crust	geosphere	mantle	tectonic plates

The _____ is made up of all the rocks and minerals on or below Earth's surface. The outer part of the geosphere is called the _____, which forms the land we live on as well as the ocean bottom. The hot rock beneath this layer is known as the _____ and includes the uppermost lithosphere as well as the softer _____. As this layer moves, it drags large sections of lithosphere, called _____, across Earth's surface. Earth's center is called the _____ and is made up of molten and solid metals.

2. How does plate tectonics influence the characteristics of Earth's surface?

_____

_____

_____

_____

3. Define the three different types of plate boundaries.

_____

_____

_____

_____

The Biosphere and Atmosphere

4. Why is Earth's biosphere called "the living Earth"?

_____

_____

5. Define ozone and explain its purpose.

_____

_____

6. How do the greenhouse gases in Earth's atmosphere affect our environment?

_____

_____

The Hydrosphere

For Questions 7–12, match each term with the statement that best describes it.

_____ **7.** evaporation

_____ **8.** transpiration

_____ **9.** precipitation

_____ **10.** condensation

_____ **11.** aquifer

_____ **12.** water table

a. the process by which water in a lake becomes water vapor

b. the upper limit of fresh water stored underground

c. the process by which water vapor in the air becomes dew

d. the process by which blades of grass release water vapor

e. rain or snow

f. the place where fresh water collects underground

13. On the lines below, write a paragraph that describes the distribution of salt water and fresh water on Earth.

_____

_____

_____

14. Describe two human activities that can affect the water cycle.

_____

_____

_____

SKILL BUILDER Organize Information

15. Complete the chart by filling in at least two characteristics about each sphere.

Sphere	Characteristics
Geosphere	
Atmosphere	
Biosphere	
Hydrosphere	

3.3 SELF-CHECK

Answer the questions to test your knowledge of lesson concepts. You can check your work using the answers on the bottom of the page.

16. Describe how organisms in the biosphere affect the atmosphere and vice versa.

_____

_____

_____

17. Give an example of how water moves through the water cycle in liquid, gaseous, and solid

forms._____

_____

_____

16. Organisms in the biosphere affect the atmosphere by taking in and expelling gases; and the gases in the atmosphere protect and support organisms in the biosphere. **17.** Sample answer: Liquid form: plants take up liquid water from soil; gaseous form: plants release water vapor through their leaves (transpiration); solid form: frozen water falls to Earth as precipitation (snow).

3.4 Biogeochemical Cycles

Key Concepts

 Nutrients cycle through the environment endlessly.

Producers play vital roles in the cycling of carbon through the environment.

The phosphorus cycle keeps phosphorus availability naturally low.

The nitrogen cycle relies on bacteria that make nitrogen useful to organisms and bacteria that can return it to the atmosphere.

SKILL BUILDER Vocabulary Preview

Define each vocabulary term in your own words. Then, write yourself a quick note on how you will remember each. One term has been done for you.

Term	Definition	How I Remember
Law of conservation of matter		
Nutrient		
Biogeochemical cycle		
Primary producer	An organism that produces its own food	Primary producer starts with *P*. So does plants, and plants are primary producers.
Photosynthesis		
Consumer		
Decomposer		
Cellular respiration		

Term	Definition	How I Remember
Eutrophication		
Nitrogen fixation		

Nutrient Cycling

1. What is the law of conservation of matter?

_____

_____

2. Which four nutrients cycle through all of Earth's spheres and organisms?

_____

The Carbon Cycle

For Questions 3–5, write True *if the statement is true. If the statement is false, replace the underlined word or words to make the statement true. Write your changes on the line.*

_____ **3.** Only a <u>producer</u> can use the sun's energy or chemical energy to make food.

_____ **4.** The products of photosynthesis are oxygen and <u>carbon dioxide</u>.

_____ **5.** Bacteria, fungi, and other organisms that break down waste are called <u>consumers</u>.

6. Why is cellular respiration important for life on Earth?

_____

_____

7. What impact do humans have on the carbon cycle?

_____

_____

_____

8. Why do scientists think there is an undiscovered carbon sink somewhere?

_____

_____

The Phosphorus Cycle

9. Why is phosphorus important to living things?

_____

_____

10. Where is phosphorus stored?

_____

_____

11. How do people obtain phosphorus?

_____

_____

12. How does the release of large amounts of phosphorus by humans cause problems?

_____

_____

The Nitrogen Cycle

For Questions 13–15, circle the letter of the correct answer.

13. Most of the nitrogen on Earth is located in the
  A. biosphere.   **C.** atmosphere.
  B. geosphere.   **D.** hydrosphere.

14. Which of the following crops increases the amount of usable nitrogen in soil?
  A. corn   **C.** legumes
  B. wheat   **D.** tomatoes

15. The Haber-Bosch process enabled people to
  A. fix nitrogen artificially.   **C.** clean up nitrogen pollution.
  B. create natural nitrogen.   **D.** acquire nitrogen from plants.

16. Name two ways nitrogen can be fixed naturally for plant use.

_____

_____

17. What happens to nitrogen during the process of denitrification?

_____

_____

SKILL BUILDER Organize Information

18. Fill in the compare/contrast table with information about the different biogeochemical cycles.

	Carbon Cycle	Phosphorus Cycle	Nitrogen Cycle
Role as Nutrient			
Events of Cycle			

EXTENSION Explain how water plays a role in each of these biogeochemical cycles.

3.4 ⦿ SELF-CHECK

Answer the questions to test your knowledge of lesson concepts. You can check your work using the answers on the bottom of the page.

19. Describe how photosynthesis and cellular respiration help drive the carbon cycle.

_____

_____

20. Explain how the hydrosphere and geosphere participate in the phosphorus cycle.

_____

_____

19. In photosynthesis, organisms take sunlight, water, and carbon dioxide from the air and transform it into oxygen and carbohydrates. Cellular respiration puts carbon back into the air as carbon dioxide waste. The two processes keep carbon moving through the cycle. **20.** Most phosphorus is locked up in rocks in the upper layer of the geosphere (lithosphere). Phosphorus is released when water in the hydrosphere wears away rock. The phosphorus is then available for plants and animals to use until it returns to rock as sediment, again becoming part of the lithosphere.

Chapter Vocabulary Review

Match each term with its definition.

_____ **1.** tectonic plate

_____ **2.** macromolecule

_____ **3.** aquifer

_____ **4.** primary producer

_____ **5.** feedback loop

_____ **6.** hydrocarbon

_____ **7.** landform

_____ **8.** atom

_____ **9.** nutrient

_____ **10.** eutrophication

_____ **11.** law of conservation of matter

_____ **12.** erosion

_____ **13.** consumer

a. soil removal by water, wind, ice, or gravity

b. an organism that must eat other organisms to obtain nutrients

c. a protein, nucleic acid, carbohydrate, or lipid

d. an overgrowth of producers often caused by the release of phosphorus

e. an organism that can produce its own food

f. an organic compound that contains only hydrogen and carbon

g. a large section of lithosphere that moves across Earth's surface

h. the basic unit of matter

i. a mountain, island, or continent that forms above and below an ocean's surface

j. a cyclical process that can be either positive or negative

k. an underground water reservoir

l. matter needed by an organism to live

m. that matter can be transformed but not created or destroyed

Use each vocabulary term in a sentence.

14. solution _____

_____

15. hydrosphere _____

_____

16. core _____

_____

EXTENSION On index cards, make drawings to represent ten vocabulary words from the chapter. Write the vocabulary term on the back of each card. With a partner, take turns trying to identify the drawings on each other's cards.

Ecological Footprints

Using Lawn Fertilizer

Approximately 60 million lawns are fertilized each year in the United States. About 15 pounds of nitrogen are used to fertilize each lawn. In this activity, you will learn how to calculate the total amount of nitrogen used to fertilize various numbers of lawns.

Calculating Total Amounts of Nitrogen Applied

1. Determine the number of lawns for your classmates, town, and state. Record your results in the second column of the table. (*Hint:* Assume that each household in your town and state has a lawn and that each lawn is one-third acre.)

Fertilizer Application	Number of Lawns	Pounds of Nitrogen
Your 1/3-acre lawn	1	15
The lawns of your classmates		
The lawns in your town		
All the lawns in your state		
All the lawns in the United States	60,000,000	

You can find the total amount of nitrogen applied to lawns by multiplying the number of lawns by the amount of nitrogen applied per lawn, 15 pounds.

▶ The calculation of the total amount of nitrogen used in fertilizing the lawns of a class of 25 students is modeled at the right:

total amount of nitrogen = **number of lawns** × **pounds per lawn**

= **25 lawns** × **15 lb/lawn**

= **375 lb**

The total amount of nitrogen applied to the lawns of students in a class of 25 students is 375 pounds.

2. Use the model above to calculate the total amount of nitrogen applied to lawns by each group in the table. Write your answers in the third column.

The Gulf of Mexico's Dead Zone

The Changing Size of the Dead Zone

The hypoxic zone, or area of low oxygen, in the Gulf of Mexico varies in size from year to year. The National Oceanic and Atmospheric Administration (NOAA) supports research that measures and monitors the size of the dead zone in the Gulf of Mexico annually. The graph below shows the results of such research. This data help scientists determine which factors cause the dead zone to grow or shrink.

Most analyses show that the biggest factor in the size of the dead zone is the amount of nitrogen and other nutrients that reaches the Gulf from the Mississippi River watershed each spring. The U.S. Geological Survey (USGS) measures the amount of nitrogen that reaches the Gulf each year and correlates that amount with the size of the dead zone. Its scientists have found that when the amount of nitrogen increases, the size of the dead zone increases. Currently there are several plans to reduce the size of the dead zone to an acceptable level, indicated by the Action Plan Goal line on the graph.

Although the dead zone is fueled by nitrogen runoff, scientists know that short-term weather patterns can also have an effect on the size of the hypoxic region. For example, when the region experiences periods of extreme weather, the heavy winds and wave activity cause more oxygen to infuse into the waters—counteracting the effects of nitrogen runoff and slowing the growth of the dead zone. Scientists feel it is important to track and account for these short-term effects, in the model they are developing to study the dead zone as well. This way, they will be able to establish a link between fertilizer runoff and size of the dead zone without having the data skewed due to weather effects. Establishing a good model with all the data available can help achieve the goals needed to reach acceptable levels. With the dead zone reduced in size, the Gulf of Mexico can then be restored for fishing and recreation.

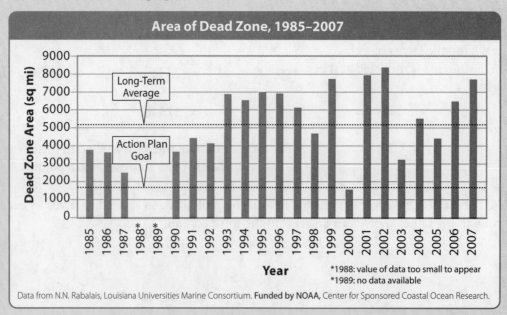

Area of Dead Zone, 1985–2007

Data from N.N. Rabalais, Louisiana Universities Marine Consortium. **Funded by NOAA,** Center for Sponsored Coastal Ocean Research.

Use the information from **The Changing Size of the Dead Zone** to answer the questions below.

1. According to the bar graph, when did scientists begin taking measurements of the dead zone?

   _____

2. What is the largest area that the dead zone has covered? In which year did it occur?

   _____

3. Why is it useful to represent this information in a bar graph?

   _____

4. What is the acceptable size of the dead zone area according to the Action Plan Goal?

   _____

5. What information from the USGS has been used to determine the factors that affect the size of the dead zone? What information was learned?

   _____

   _____

   _____

   _____

21st Century Skills

Find out more about the changing size of the dead zone. Work in small groups and use the Internet and other resources to research plans to reduce the size of the dead zone in the Gulf of Mexico. Think about the plans you investigate and determine which one or ones are most likely to work. Present your findings to the class.

The 21st Century Skills used in this activity include **Critical Thinking and Problem Solving, Communication and Collaboration,** *and* **Information Literacy.**

4 Population Ecology

Before you read the chapter, answer each question with information you know. After you complete the chapter, re-answer the questions using information you learned.

INVESTIGATIVE PHENOMENON **How are changes in environmental conditions related to changes in population size?**

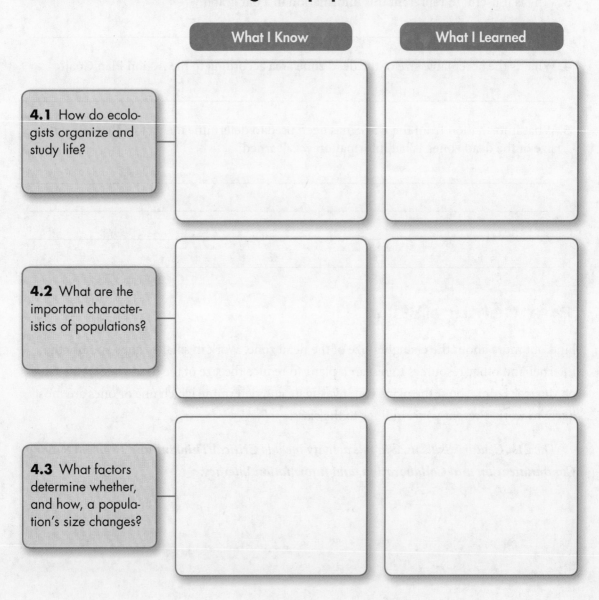

	What I Know	What I Learned
4.1 How do ecologists organize and study life?		
4.2 What are the important characteristics of populations?		
4.3 What factors determine whether, and how, a population's size changes?		

4.1 Studying Ecology

Key Concepts

- Ecologists study life at many levels, from individual organisms to the entire biosphere.
- Ecosystems include both biotic and abiotic factors.
- Organisms depend on resources provided by their habitat for survival.

 SKILL BUILDER **Vocabulary Preview**

Define each vocabulary term in your own words. Then, write yourself a quick note on how you will remember each. One term has been done for you.

Term	Definition	How I Remember
Ecology		
Species		
Population		
Community		
Ecosystem		
Biosphere	All parts of planet Earth that host life, with all of its organisms and environments	I think of *bio*, which means "life" and *sphere*, which is a round object, such as Earth.
Biotic factor		

Term	Definition	How I Remember
Abiotic factor		
Habitat		
Resource		

Levels of Ecological Organization

For Questions 1 and 2, circle the letter of the correct answer.

1. The most basic level of ecological organization is a(n)

   A. biosphere.

   B. individual.

   C. ecosystem.

   D. population.

2. The study of living and nonliving components of a system can best be described as a(n)

   A. abiotic factor.

   B. level hierarchy.

   C. ecosystem ecology.

   D. organism interaction.

3. Describe how a species is commonly defined. Explain why the common definition for species may be problematic for some organisms, such as bacteria.

_____

_____

_____

_____

_____

4. What is community ecology? Give examples.

_____

_____

_____

_____

Biotic and Abiotic Factors

5. **Organize Information** Fill in the T-chart with examples of abiotic and biotic factors in an ecosystem.

Abiotic Factors	Biotic Factors

6. Is a fallen, rotting tree considered an abiotic or biotic factor? Explain.

_____

_____

Habitat

For Questions 7 and 8, complete each statement by writing in the correct word.

7. A cloud forest's soil, rocks, leaf litter, humidity, plant life, and seasonal pools of water are all part of a toad's _____.

8. Habitats provide organisms with the _____ they need to live, such as food, shelter, breeding sites, and mates.

9. Compare and contrast an ecosystem and a habitat.

_____

_____

_____

_____

10. Explain the importance of resources and suitable habitats to an organism.

_____

_____

_____

11. Name at least two specific elements of the golden toad's cloud forest habitat.

_____

_____

 **SKILL BUILDER** **Organize Information**

12. Fill in the table to explain how each concept applies to the golden toad.

Concept	The Golden Toad
Population	
Community	
Ecosystem	
Habitat	
Resource	

Extension On a separate sheet of paper, create another table like the one above. Use the same headings for the left column, but choose a different organism. Write the name of the organism at the top of the table and then complete the rest of the table as it applies to the organism you chose.

4.1 SELF-CHECK

Answer the questions to test your knowledge of lesson concepts. You can check your work using the answers on the bottom of the page.

13. Explain why organization is important to the study of ecology.

_____

_____

14. Why are dead or decaying organisms still considered important parts of an ecosystem?

_____

_____

15. What makes up an organism's habitat?

_____

_____

13. Ecologists use levels of organization to study how organisms interact with each other and their environment. **14.** They are taken in and used as essential materials for living organisms. **15.** The specific environment, including biotic and abiotic elements, around an organism makes up its habitat.

4.2 Describing Populations

Key Concepts

 The overall health of a population can often be monitored by tracking how its size changes.

 A population's density is a measure of how crowded it is.

 Populations can be distributed randomly, uniformly, or in clumps.

 Age structure diagrams show the number of males and females in different age groups within a population.

SKILL BUILDER Vocabulary Preview

Define each vocabulary term in your own words. Then, write yourself a quick note on how you will remember each. One term has been done for you.

Term	Definition	How I Remember
Population size		
Population density		
Population distribution		
Age structure		
Age structure diagram		
Sex ratio	A population's proportion of males to females	I recall that a *ratio* is a proportion between two things and that an organism's *sex* refers to whether it is male or female.

Population Size

For Questions 1–3, complete each statement by writing in the correct word.

1. When a population size _____ or remains steady, this is often a sign of a healthy population.

2. If a population size begins to _____ rapidly, this can be a signal that extinction is coming.

3. Instead of counting each organism individually, ecologists use _____ methods to estimate population sizes.

4. Explain why the passenger pigeon, which was once the most abundant bird in North America, disappeared completely.

_____

_____

_____

_____

5. Describe how you could determine the population size of a specific type of plant in a large forest without counting all of the plants.

_____

_____

Population Density

For Questions 6 and 7, circle the letter of the correct answer.

6. A population's density describes how
   A. old the population is.
   B. crowded the population is.
   C. big the population is.
   D. fast the population is declining.

7. Which piece of information is used along with population size to calculate population density?
   A. area
   B. weight
   C. age
   D. location

8. How can high population density be helpful to a population?

_____

_____

9. How can high population density be harmful to a population?

_____

_____

Population Distribution

10. **Organize Information** Fill in the cluster diagram with short descriptions or drawings of the different types of population distribution.

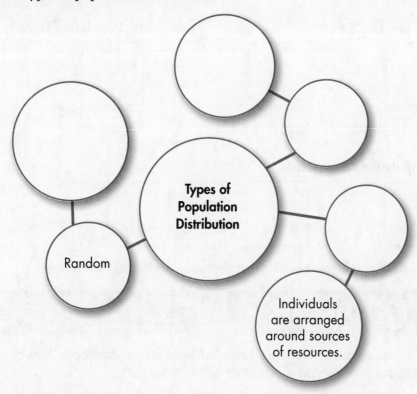

Types of Population Distribution

Random

Individuals are arranged around sources of resources.

11. Which type of population distribution is found most often in nature?

_____

Age Structure and Sex Ratios

12. Describe how to use an age-structure diagram to determine how many males and females are in a population.

_____

_____

_____

13. What will happen to a population made up mostly of individuals that are past reproductive age? _____

_____

14. What can you predict about a population with an age-structure diagram shaped like a pyramid? _____

_____

 **SKILL BUILDER** Think Visually

15. Use dots to represent individuals in populations as you contrast the population
characteristics in each set below.

A. Population Size

[ ]   [ ]

small population   large population

B. Population Density

[ ]   [ ]

low density   high density

C. Population Distribution

[ ]   [ ]   [ ]

clumped distribution   random distribution   uniform distribution

4.2 ⊙ SELF-CHECK

*Answer the questions to test your knowledge of lesson concepts. You can check your
work using the answers on the bottom of the page.*

16. Which way of describing a population would be more informative in terms of available
resources—population size or population density? Explain. _____

_____

_____

17. Describe how you might use population distribution to find the sources of food or other
resources used by a species. _____

_____

_____

18. Explain the significance of an age-structure diagram in which the bars are short along one
side and long on the opposite side. _____

_____

_____

16. Population density better indicates the quantity of room and resources available, since it indicates how
many organisms are living in a specific area. 17. Populations often distribute themselves according to location
of resources. In random or uniform distribution, resources may be widely available; however, if a population
is distributed in clumps, these clumps will likely indicate the location of available resources. 18. This indicates
that the population consists mostly of either males or females. It may also indicate that the population will not
be as successful in reproducing.

4.3 Population Growth

Key Concepts

 A population's growth rate is determined by births, deaths, immigration, and emigration.

 Populations can grow exponentially or logistically.

 Limiting factors and biotic potential regulate a population's growth.

SKILL BUILDER Vocabulary Preview

Define each vocabulary term in your own words. Then, write yourself a quick note on how you will remember each. One term has been done for you.

Term	Definition	How I Remember
Survivorship curve		
Immigration	The arrival of individuals from outside a given area	The prefix *im–* reminds me of "in." That helps me remember that immigration is individuals coming into an area.
Emigration		
Migration		
Exponential growth		
Limiting factor		

Term	Definition	How I Remember
Carrying capacity		
Logistic growth		
Density-dependent factor		
Density-independent factor		
Biotic potential		

SKILL BUILDER Reading Strategy

As you read the lesson, complete the main ideas and details chart.

Main Ideas	Details
Important factors determine population growth.	
Populations grow exponentially or logistically.	
A population's growth is regulated by limiting factors and biotic potential.	

Factors That Determine Population Growth

For Questions 1 and 2, complete each statement by writing in the correct word.

1. Populations _____ when more individuals enter the population than leave it.

2. Populations _____ when more individuals leave the population than enter it.

3. Explain how a population would be affected when the birthrate is significantly higher than the death rate and there are no changes due to immigration or emigration.

_____

4. Describe how emigration and immigration affect the size of a population.

_____

_____

_____

5. Explain how migration causes population size to change cyclically over time.

_____

_____

_____

How Populations Grow

6. Describe the shape of a graph curve indicating exponential growth and a graph indicating logistic growth.

_____

7. Explain how the availability of resources in the environment is linked to exponential growth of a species.

_____

_____

8. Describe how you can recognize where the carrying capacity for a population occurs on a logistic growth curve.

_____

9. Compare and contrast exponential growth and logistic growth.

_____

_____

_____

10. Explain how the carrying capacity for a population can change over time.

_____

_____

_____

_____

Limiting Factors and Biotic Potential

11. Circle the factors below that are density-dependent.

climate change   disease   flood   predation

12. Explain why a forest fire is considered to be a density-independent limiting factor.

_____

_____

13. Give two examples of organisms that differ greatly in their biotic potential.

_____

_____

_____

_____

4.3 ⚪ SELF-CHECK

Answer the questions to test your knowledge of lesson concepts. You can check your work using the answers on the bottom of the page.

14. List two factors that increase the growth rate of a population and two factors that decrease the growth rate of a population.

_____

_____

15. Describe the effects that limiting factors and biotic potential have on a population's growth.

_____

_____

_____

14. Increase: high birthrates, immigration; decrease: high death rates, emigration 15. Limiting factors slow population growth and determine the maximum amount of growth possible in a population. Biotic potential determines the maximum ability to produce offspring under ideal conditions.

Real Data

Turkey Vultures

The graph at the right shows the average number of turkey vultures that were counted on protected lands at the Hawk Mountain Sanctuary in Pennsylvannia. In this activity, you will interpret the graph by describing the trends that it shows and drawing conclusions about the annual migration cycle of turkey vultures.

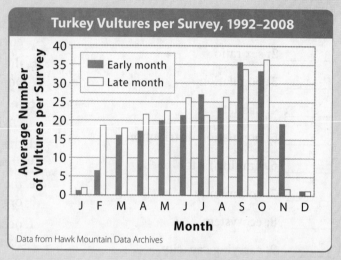

Turkey Vultures per Survey, 1992–2008

Average Number of Vultures per Survey

■ Early month
□ Late month

Month

Data from Hawk Mountain Data Archives

Interpreting the Graph

To understand the information in a graph, the first step is to figure out the information that it shows. Study the axes and note the trend shown by the graph.

1. What do the *x* and *y*-axes show? _____

_____

2. What do the two bars for each month represent? _____

_____

3. To describe the annual trend in the graph, look at the overall changes in the bar height over the entire year. Describe what you see. _____

_____

_____

Inferring From the Graph

Turkey vultures migrate from the north onto the sanctuary lands and reside there for a while before migrating south. You know that when the vultures migrate through the sanctuary, they will increase the population size. Answer the questions below to help you identify when the vultures migrated through the sanctuary.

4. In which two months is the turkey vulture population significantly greater than in the other months? _____

5. When would you conclude that the vultures migrating from the north arrive at the sanctuary? _____

6. When would you conclude that the vultures leave the sanctuary and begin to migrate south? _____

Chapter Vocabulary Review

Match each term with its definition.

_____ 1. immigration

_____ 2. sex ratio

_____ 3. population

_____ 4. habitat

_____ 5. population distribution

_____ 6. limiting factor

_____ 7. community

_____ 8. ecosystem

_____ 9. carrying capacity

_____ 10. exponential growth

_____ 11. population density

_____ 12. species

a. all the living things and their physical environments within a particular area

b. the number of individuals within a population per unit area

c. the largest population size that an environment can sustainably support

d. the arrival of individuals from outside an area

e. the specific environment in which an organism lives

f. occurs when a population increases by a fixed percentage each year

g. the proportion of males to females in a population

h. characteristic of the environment that restricts population growth

i. all the populations in a particular area

j. a group of individuals that interbreed and produce fertile offspring

k. members of a species that live in the same area

l. how organisms are arranged within an area

Use each vocabulary term in a sentence.

13. abiotic factor _____

_____

14. age structure _____

_____

15. density-dependent factor _____

_____

EXTENSION On a separate sheet of paper, create a simple illustration of an ecosystem. Choose five or more vocabulary terms from the chapter to include as labels in your illustration.

Finding Gold in a Costa Rican Cloud Forest

The Disappearance of the Golden Toad

What can cause a thriving population of animals to disappear in the span of one or two years? In the case of the golden toad of Monteverde in Costa Rica, thousands of toads were initially observed during the mating season each year. Then one year, there were only a few toads. Two years later, only a single toad was observed, and then the toads disappeared completely.

Environmental Changes

How the golden toads could disappear so quickly is puzzling, but the case is even more mysterious because the habitat of the golden toad was within a large nature preserve. Often, animal populations are devastated as humans or natural disasters destroy their habitats. But this was not the case in the protected Monteverde Cloud Forest Reserve.

Although the toad's environment was not being visibly destroyed, it was changing in subtle ways. For instance, when scientists gathered data on the toad's environment, they noticed a significant increase in the number of "dry days." A "dry day" is designated as a run of five or more days without measurable rain. These dry days resulted in a decrease of available moisture.

Because toads and other amphibians reproduce and live parts of their lives in water, the amount of moisture in the environment affects them to a greater degree than it affects many other species. Of the 50 species of frogs and toads in the study area, 20—including the golden toad—disappeared during the same time frame.

The Lifting Cloud Base Hypothesis has been proposed to explain this widespread amphibian loss in the cloud forest. According to the hypothesis, as the number of "dry days" increased, the base of the clouds that hung over an area rose in altitude. This caused a decrease in the moisture provided by mist in the forests. As this misty cloud atmosphere rose and was lost, the environment suffered—as plants and animals died off due to the drier climate. This series of events can occur repeatedly.

Many scientists link such series of events to global warming. Others state that the rising cloud base could be caused by deforestation and other human activities. New information also points to another possible scenario that may have killed off the toad. The years following 1986–1987 were exceptionally dry, due to changes in atmospheric and oceanic patterns related to a phenomenon known as El Niño. The exceptional climate conditions during that period could have contributed to the growth and spread of a deadly pathogen— the chytrid fungus—to which the toad was susceptible. The chytrid fungus grows rapidly in warm, dry climates. The fungus has caused declines in amphibians throughout Costa Rica and may have wiped out the golden toad as the weather in the region became warmer and drier. Scientists warn that although amphibians in this ecosystem are the first organisms to disappear when environmental conditions change, other species of organisms and plants may follow.

Use the information in **The Disappearance of the Golden Toad** to answer the questions below.

1. How many golden toads could be observed during mating season when the toad's population was thriving? _____

2. Based on the golden toad population's habitat, why was extinction of the golden toad puzzling? _____

_____

3. Explain why it was significant that large numbers of other frogs and toads became extinct at the same time the golden toads disappeared.

_____

_____

4. Explain what happens to cloud mist as the number of "dry days" increases.

_____

5. Assuming the Lifting Cloud Base Hypothesis to be correct, which part of the Monteverde cloud forest would likely be the least affected by the decrease in moisture? Explain.

_____

_____

6. REVISIT **INVESTIGATIVE** PHENOMENON Relate this case to the **Investigative Phenomenon:** "How are changes in environmental conditions related to changes in population size?" Describe the sequence of events that could have led to the extinction of the golden toad, according to the Lifting Cloud Base Hypothesis.

_____

_____

_____

_____

21st Century Skills

Find out more about other extinctions that occurred in the Monteverde region during this time period. Work in small groups to use the Internet and other resources to learn more about what caused the extinctions you have been studying. Each group should create a poster or presentation to share with the class.

*The 21st Century Skills used in this activity include **Communication and Collaboration, Information Literacy,** and **Productivity and Accountability.***

5 Evolution and Community Ecology

Before you read the chapter, answer each question with information you know. After you complete the chapter, re-answer the questions using information you learned.

INVESTIGATIVE PHENOMENON **How do organisms affect the abiotic and biotic conditions in an environment?**

	What I Know	**What I Learned**
5.1 What role does the environment play in an organism's survival and reproduction?		
5.2 How do species interact in nature?		
5.3 How do energy and nutrients move through communities?		
5.4 How do communities respond to a disturbance?		

5.1 Evolution

Key Concepts

- Biological evolution can occur through mutation, migration, genetic drift, and natural selection.
- Two processes, speciation and extinction, combine to produce the diversity of life on Earth.

SKILL BUILDER Vocabulary Preview

Define each vocabulary term in your own words. Then, write yourself a quick note on how you will remember each. One term has been done for you.

Term	Definition	How I Remember
Evolution		
Gene		
Mutation	An accidental change in DNA	I think of a character's *mutation* in a science fiction movie I saw.
Genetic drift		
Natural selection		
Fitness		
Adaptation		
Artificial selection		
Speciation		
Extinction		

Evolution and Natural Selection

1. Complete the following paragraphs with terms from the word bank.

characteristics	DNA	gene pool	generation	genetic drift
migration	offspring	population	reproduction	survival of the fittest

A change in a population's _____ over time is called biological evolution. There are four primary mechanisms of biological evolution. Mutations are accidental changes in an organism's _____. _____ occurs when individuals immigrate into or emigrate out of a(n) _____. Biological evolution that happens by chance is called _____. Natural selection is the process by which traits that improve an organism's chances for survival and _____ are passed on more frequently to a future _____ than those that do not.

Natural selection follows three conditions: organisms produce more _____ than can survive; individuals of a species vary in their _____; and lastly, individuals vary in their fitness. Natural selection is also known as _____.

2. Explain how a *gene pool* and *biological evolution* are related.

_____

_____

_____

3. How could a natural disaster result in genetic drift?

_____

_____

_____

4. Explain what *survival of the fittest* means.

_____

_____

_____

5. How does artificial selection provide evidence for evolution by natural selection?

_____

_____

_____

_____

Speciation and Extinction

6. **Organize Information** Model the process of speciation by filling in the flowchart with terms from the word bank.

geographical isolation	mutations	two species

Single population		→		→		→	

7. What are some ways allopatric speciation can occur?

_____

_____

_____

8. What must be true for allopatric speciation to occur, regardless of the mechanism of separation?

_____

_____

9. How would a reversal of the process that had isolated populations—for example, geographic separation—affect a species?

_____

_____

10. If populations remain geographically isolated for thousands of generations, what would happen?

_____

11. What are mass extinctions?

_____

12. In general, when does extinction occur?

_____

_____

13. What is the average length of time a species spends on Earth? How have paleontologists calculated this figure?

_____

_____

SKILL BUILDER Organize Information

14. Fill in the cluster diagram with terms from the word bank.

| extinction | genetic drift | migration | mutation | natural selection | speciation |

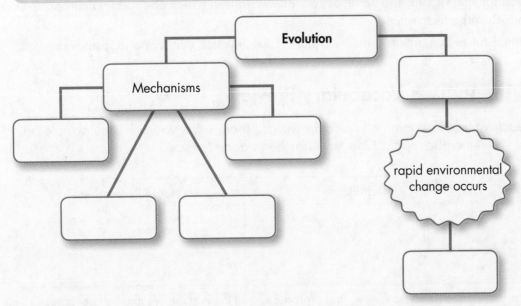

EXTENSION Add to the cluster diagram to show the conditions of natural selection.

5.1 SELF-CHECK

Answer the questions to test your knowledge of lesson concepts. You can check your work using the answers on the bottom of the page.

15. Compare and contrast artificial selection with natural selection.

_____

_____

16. What is an adaptation?

_____

_____

17. What has happened to almost all species that have ever lived on Earth?

_____

15. Both affect the gene pool of a species. Artificial selection is conducted under human direction, while natural selection occurs in nature. 16. An adaptation is a heritable trait that increases an organism's fitness for its environment. 17. Almost all species that have ever lived on Earth are extinct.

5.2 Species Interactions

Key Concepts

 An organism's niche is affected by both its tolerance and competitive interactions.

 Predation, parasitism, and herbivory are interactions in which one species benefits, while the other is harmed.

 Mutualism and commensalism are relationships in which neither participant is harmed.

SKILL BUILDER Vocabulary Preview

Define each vocabulary term in your own words. Then, write yourself a quick note on how you will remember each. One term has been done for you.

Term	Definition	How I Remember
Niche		
Tolerance	The ability to survive and reproduce under changing environmental conditions	I think of the weather temperatures I can *tolerate* in the summer when I play outdoors.
Resource partitioning		
Predation		
Coevolution		
Parasitism		

Term	Definition	How I Remember
Symbiosis		
Herbivory		
Mutualism		
Commensalism		

The Niche and Competition

For Questions 1–5, write True *if the statement is true. If the statement is false, replace the underlined word or words to make the statement true. Write your changes on the line.*

_____ 1. Organisms with wide tolerance ranges, able to use a wide array of habitats or resources, are called <u>specialists</u>.

_____ 2. Zebra mussels have demonstrated <u>competitive exclusion</u> by out-competing all the native mussels in Lake St. Clair.

_____ 3. In a <u>realized</u> niche, a species fulfills all its roles and uses all the resources it can.

_____ 4. Competition among members of the same species is called <u>interspecific</u> competition.

_____ 5. As a result of character displacement, birds that specialize in eating smaller seeds may evolve <u>smaller</u> bills.

6. What is resource partitioning and how is it an adaptation to competition? Provide an example.

_____

_____

_____

_____

Predation, Parasitism, and Herbivory

7. How does predation affect population cycles?

_____

_____

_____

8. Provide an example of a prey defense, and explain how the defense helps the animal survive.

_____

_____

9. Compare and contrast predation and parasitism.

_____

_____

_____

Mutualism and Commensalism

10. **Organize Information** Fill in the chart with the correct information.

Relationship	Number of Species That Benefits	Example of the Relationship
Mutualism		
Commensalism		

11. How do both organisms benefit in a symbiotic association between plant roots and some fungi?

_____

_____

12. Explain why pollination is considered to be one of the most important mutualisms.

_____

_____

_____

SKILL BUILDER Think Visually

13. Redraw the diagram to show the potential effect on the realized niches of Species 1, 2, and 3 if a predator of Species 3 is introduced into the habitat.

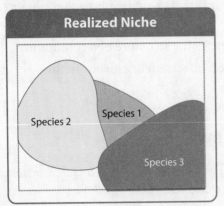

14. Explain the reasoning you used to create your diagram.

_____

_____

_____

EXTENSION Use the Internet to research an example of predation. On a separate sheet of paper, write a paragraph to explain how a niche could be affected if the predator–prey relationship were disrupted in some way.

5.2 ◎ SELF-CHECK

Answer the questions to test your knowledge of lesson concepts. You can check your work using the answers on the bottom of the page.

15. What is the difference between an organism's habitat and its niche?

_____

_____

_____

16. Why might some examples of coevolution be described as *evolutionary arms races*?

_____

_____

_____

15. An organism's habitat is the general place in which an organism lives, while its niche describes how it uses the resources of its habitat and how it interacts with its habitat. 16. Sample answer: When predators and their prey develop stronger and stronger "weapons" (such as a prey species developing a toxin and its predator evolving immunity to it) it can be considered an evolutionary arms race.

5.3 Ecological Communities

Key Concepts

 Organisms are classified as either producers or consumers based on how they obtain energy and nutrients.

 Inefficient energy transfer between organisms shapes the structure of a community.

 Feeding relationships have both direct and indirect effects on organisms in the community.

SKILL BUILDER Vocabulary Preview

Define each vocabulary term in your own words. Then, write yourself a quick note on how you will remember each. One term has been done for you.

Term	Definition	How I Remember
Primary producer		
Photosynthesis		
Chemosynthesis		
Consumer		
Cellular respiration		
Herbivore	An organism that is a primary consumer and eats plants	*Herbs* are plants that are used in cooking.
Carnivore		

Term	Definition	How I Remember
Omnivore		
Detritivore		
Decomposer		
Trophic level		
Biomass		
Food chain		
Food web		
Keystone species		

Producers and Consumers

1. Identify the ultimate source of energy for most of Earth's ecosystems. _____

2. Why are plants considered primary producers?

_____

_____

3. How do the roles of detritivores and decomposers differ in an ecosystem?

_____

_____

_____

Energy and Biomass

For Questions 5 and 6, circle the letter of the correct answer.

4. How many trophic levels are there typically in a community?

_____

_____

5. What is true about energy transfer in communities?

    A. It is 100 percent efficient.

    B. It moves from consumer to producer.

    C. Most of the energy in a trophic level is lost as heat.

    D. Most of the energy in a trophic level transfers to one above it.

6. About how much energy in one trophic level transfers to the trophic level above it?

    A. 5 percent   **C.** 25 percent

    B. 10 percent   **D.** 50 percent

Food Webs and Keystone Species

7. **Organize Information** Fill in the table to organize information about food chains and food webs. Provide at least two characteristics of each.

Food Chain	Food Web

8. What effect would the removal of a keystone species have on an ecological community? Write a short essay that explains this effect in terms of *trophic cascade*. Provide a specific example that illustrates this process.

_____

_____

_____

_____

_____

_____

_____

SKILL BUILDER Think Visually

9. Complete the food chain below. Fill in each circle with one of the organisms in Word Bank A. Next, identify the role of each type of organism in the food chain by writing a label from Word Bank B on the lines below the circles. Then, use the percentages in Word Bank C to show how much energy is transferred to each organism on the lines above the circles.

Word Bank A:	algae	big fish	bird	small fish
Word Bank B:	carnivore	decomposers	herbivore	primary producer
Word Bank C:	0.1%	1%	10%	100%

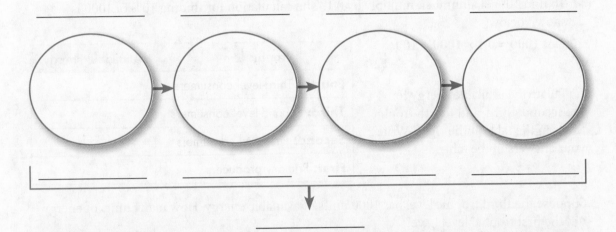

5.3 ○ SELF-CHECK

Answer the questions to test your knowledge of lesson concepts. You can check your work using the answers on the bottom of the page.

10. What is an organism's trophic level?

_____

_____

11. Explain the ten percent rule.

_____

_____

_____

10. An animal's trophic level is its rank in a food chain or food web (feeding hierarchy). 11. The ten percent rule states that only about ten percent of the energy contained in any given trophic level is transferred to the next higher trophic level.

Real Data

Energy Flow in Communities

In this activity, you will determine the relative amounts of available energy at different trophic levels in a community. You will also calculate how many units of energy would be needed at the first trophic level in order to have 1000 units of available energy at other levels.

Finding Energy in Communities

Energy transfer from one trophic level to another in a community is only about 10% efficient. This means that if the primary producers have 1000 units of available energy, then the first-level consumers have 10% of 1000 units of available energy.

▶ To find 10% of a number, multiply by 0.1. The calculation for finding 10% of 1000 is shown below:

10% of 1000 = 0.1 × 1000 = 100.

Calculate the available energy for the second, third, and fourth trophic levels in the table at the right. Write your answers in the table.

Trophic Level	Available Energy
Fourth: Third-level consumers	
Third: Second-level consumers	
Second: First-level consumers	
First: Primary producers	

Finding Initial Energy

Suppose the third trophic level has 1000 units of available energy. How many units of energy did the first trophic level have?

Work Backward

▶ Each increasing trophic level has only 10% of the energy of the trophic level below it. The calculation for finding the energy of the second trophic level, x, if you know that the third trophic level has 1000 units, is shown at the right.

second trophic level ↓		third trophic level ↓
0.1 (x)	=	1000 units
x	=	$\frac{1000}{0.1}$ or 10,000 units

▶ The calculation for finding the energy of the first trophic level, y, if you know that the second trophic level has 10,000 units, is shown at the right.

first trophic level ↓		second trophic level ↓
0.1 (y)	=	10,000 units
y	=	$\frac{10,000}{0.1}$ or 100,000 units

Use the model above to solve each problem.

1. How many units of energy would be needed in the first trophic level to end up with 1000 units of energy in the second trophic level? _____

2. Suppose the fourth trophic level has 1000 units of energy. How many units of energy would the first trophic level have had? _____

5.4 Community Stability

Key Concepts

🔑 Following a disturbance, communities may undergo succession.

🔑 Without limiting factors, species introduced to a new area can become invasive.

SKILL BUILDER **Vocabulary Preview**

Define each vocabulary term in your own words. Then, write yourself a quick note on how you will remember each. One term has been done for you.

Term	Definition	How I Remember
Succession		
Primary succession		
Pioneer species	Species that first colonize newly exposed land	I once heard someone call the first astronaut in space a space *pioneer*.
Secondary succession		
Invasive species		

SKILL BUILDER Reading Strategy

Fill in the table to preview the lesson. Then, in the space that follows the table, write one sentence to explain what you think this lesson will be about.

What is the title of this lesson?	
What are the vocabulary terms for this lesson?	
What are the key concepts for the two main sections of this lesson?	
What do the photos depict?	
What do the diagrams seem to show?	

_____

_____

EXTENSION On a separate sheet of paper, write five questions that come to mind while previewing this lesson. Answer your questions after you have completed the lesson.

Ecological Succession

For Questions 1–3, write True if the statement is true, If the statement is false, replace the underlined word or words to make the statement true. Write your changes on the line.

_____ 1. Secondary succession begins with bare rock.

_____ 2. The first species to colonize newly exposed land are called primary species.

_____ 3. Over the course of ecological succession, species diversity increases over time.

4. Why are lichens successful pioneers?

_____

_____

_____

5. Compare and contrast primary succession and secondary succession.

_____

_____

_____

_____

_____

6. What is the difference between primary and secondary aquatic succession?

_____

_____

_____

7. Summarize the sequence of events that occur when a pond undergoes secondary succession.

_____

_____

_____

_____

Invasive Species

8. When does a species become invasive?

_____

_____

_____

9. Do you think preventing the introduction of invasive species is preferable than trying to control them? Why or why not?

_____

_____

_____

10. **Organize Information** Fill in the chart by answering each question.

Species	Is this invasive species considered harmful?	Explanation
Zebra mussel		
Cane toad		
Honeybee		
Kudzu		

5.4 SELF-CHECK

Answer the questions to test your knowledge of lesson concepts. You can check your work using the answers on the bottom of the page.

11. Why does primary succession usually take longer to occur than secondary succession?

_____

_____

12. Explain what is meant by *climax community*.

_____

_____

13. How might an invasive species disturb an ecological community?

_____

_____

11. Primary succession begins with a bare surface, while secondary succession begins with soil that contains organic matter and sometimes organisms from the prior community. 12. A climax community is a stable community in which succession appears to be complete. 13. An invasive species can upset the ecological balance in a community through unchecked population growth, which results in a reduction or elimination of populations of native species.

Chapter Vocabulary Review

Use the clues to complete the crossword puzzle.

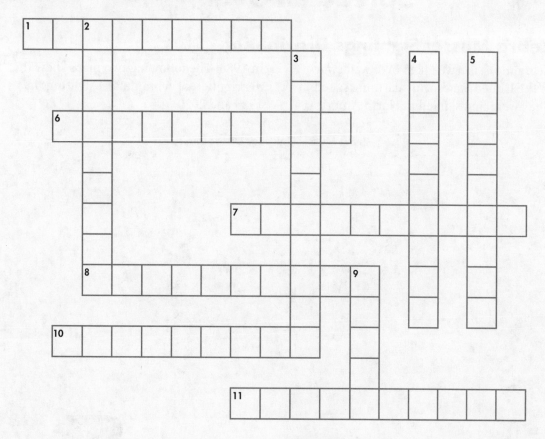

Across

1 a relationship in which two or more species benefit

6 primary consumers

7 a heritable trait that increases individual fitness

8 the disappearance of a species

10 the process by which one species hunts and kills another

11 series of ecological changes over time

Down

2 the ability to survive and reproduce under changing environmental conditions

3 the process by which new species are generated

4 change over time

5 a physically close relationship in which at least one organism benefits

9 an organism's use of resources and functional role in a community

EXTENSION On a separate sheet of paper, write a short story about an imaginary community that uses five or more vocabulary terms from the chapter.

Black and White, and Spread all Over

Zebra Mussel Sightings Distribution

Zebra mussels have taken over waterways in the United States with alarming speed. They were first sighted in North America in 1988. The following two maps show the distribution of zebra mussel sightings in 1989 and 2020.

Zebra Mussel Sightings Distribution

1989

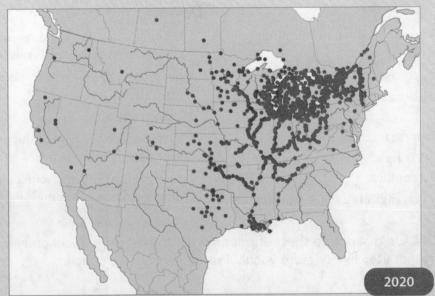

2020

Source: U.S. Geological Survey. [2020]. Nonindigenous Aquatic Species Database. Gainesville, Florida

Use the information in **Zebra Mussel Sightings Distribution** to answer the questions below.

1. Describe the distribution of the mussel one year after it was first sighted.

_____

_____

2. How does the distribution in 2020 compare with that of 1989?

_____

_____

3. Based on the maps, describe the way zebra mussels have spread in the United States.

_____

_____

4. How can you explain the appearance of mussels in the midwestern and western states?

_____

_____

5. REVISIT INVESTIGATIVE PHENOMENON What information can you infer from the maps that relate to the **Investigative Phenomenon:** "How do organisms affect the abiotic and biotic conditions in an environment?"

_____

_____

_____

_____

21st Century Skills

Work as a class to create a compelling multimedia presentation on the invasion of zebra mussels in the United States. Some groups should focus on the year-by-year spread of zebra mussels, which is well documented by the U.S. Geological Survey. Other groups may research the basic biology of the mussels, the extent of the problem, and potential solutions. If possible, suggest your teacher invite environmental officials from the community to participate.

*The 21st Century Skills used in this activity include **Communication and Collaboration, Information, Communication, and Technology (ICT) Literacy,** and **Creativity and Innovation.***

Biomes and Aquatic Ecosystems

Before you read the chapter, answer each question with information you know. After you complete the chapter, re-answer the questions using information you learned.

INVESTIGATIVE PHENOMENON **How do organisms interact with the environment?**

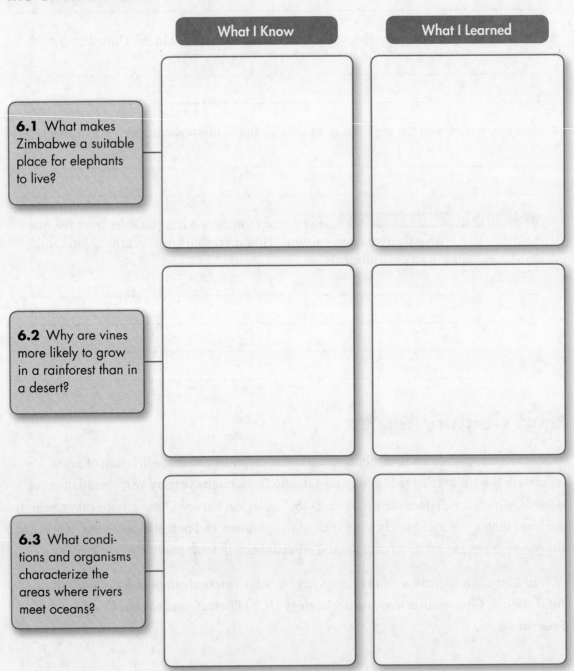

What I Know	What I Learned
6.1 What makes Zimbabwe a suitable place for elephants to live?		
6.2 Why are vines more likely to grow in a rainforest than in a desert?		
6.3 What conditions and organisms characterize the areas where rivers meet oceans?		

6.1 Defining Biomes

Key Concepts

 Biomes are characterized by their climates as well as typical plant and animal life.

 Biomes vary in their rates of net primary production. Warm and wet biomes have the highest net primary production, and cold, dry biomes have the lowest.

SKILL BUILDER Vocabulary Preview

Define each vocabulary term in your own words. Then, write yourself a quick note on how you will remember each. One term has been done for you.

Term	Definition	How I Remember
Biome		
Climate		
Weather	The day-to-day conditions in Earth's atmosphere, such as "hot and humid" or "cold and snowy"	I think of the *daily forecast* when I watch the *weather report* on TV.
Climatograph		
Net primary production		

What Is a Biome?

1. What is similar about the ecosystems that make up a biome?

   _____

2. What biomes are found in southern Africa?

   _____

3. Identify and describe one of the ecosystems in a southern African biome.

   _____

   _____

4. Which abiotic conditions exert the greatest influence on biome classification?

   _____

5. How are climatographs helpful in understanding biomes?

   _____

   _____

6. What is the relationship between latitude and biomes located across Earth?

   _____

   _____

7. Explain how natural selection is important to biomes and organisms.

   _____

   _____

8. Why do different biomes have different characteristic organisms?

   _____

   _____

9. What can cause variation—for example, species composition—among plant and animal communities within biomes?

   _____

   _____

Net Primary Production

10. What does net primary production refer to?

    _____

11. Why are gross primary production and net primary production not the same value?

_____

_____

12. What limits the net primary production in aquatic ecosystems such as lakes and streams?

_____

_____

For Questions 13–15, examine the graph of the net primary productivity of three land biomes, A, B, and C. Circle the letter of the correct answer.

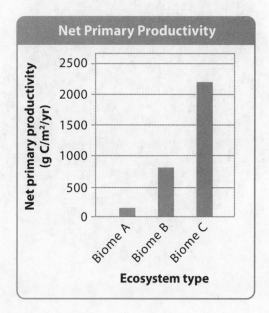

13. Which of the following information does the graph show for the three biomes?

A. the total amount of biomass

B. the mean monthly temperature

C. the rate at which decomposers break down biomass

D. the rate at which primary producers convert energy to biomass

14. Which statement is an inference that can logically be made based on the graph?

A. In Biome A, there are no producer organisms.

B. Biome B has less total biomass than Biome C.

C. Biome A is probably cooler and drier than Biome C.

D. In all three biomes, there are more consumer organisms than producer organisms.

15. Which of the biomes is most likely to be located near the equator?

A. Biome A

B. Biome B

C. Biome C

D. All three biomes are equally likely to be located near the equator.

SKILL BUILDER Think Visually

16. Label the diagram to identify the biomes. On the lines below the diagram, write a sentence to explain how the biomes vary in their net primary productivity. Then, circle the name of the biome that has the highest net primary productivity.

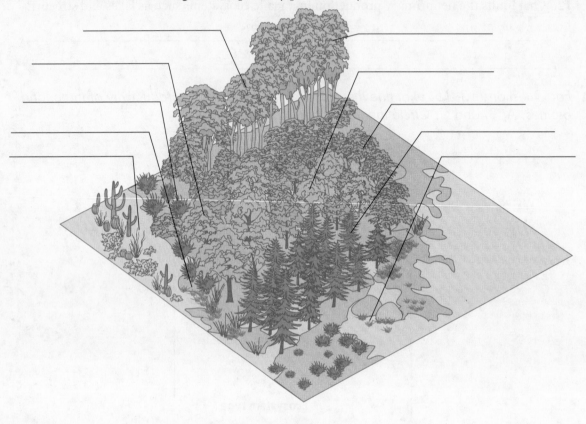

_____

_____

6.1 ○ SELF-CHECK

Answer the questions to test your knowledge of lesson concepts. You can check your work using the answers on the bottom of the page.

17. What primarily determines which biome covers a particular portion of Earth?

_____

18. Which biome would you expect to have the lowest net primary productivity?

_____

17. Climate 18. Desert

6.2 Biomes

 SKILL BUILDER **Vocabulary Preview**

Define each vocabulary term in your own words. Then, write yourself a quick note on how you will remember each. One term has been done for you.

Term	Definition	How I Remember
Canopy		
Emergent layer	Top layer of the rainforest canopy, made up of the tallest trees	*Emerge* is found in *emergent*. I know *emerge* means "to come into view," so the emergent layer must be the one that is seen first.
Understory		
Epiphyte		
Deciduous		
Estivation		

Term	Definition	How I Remember
Coniferous		
Hibernation		
Permafrost		

SKILL BUILDER Reading Strategy

Fill in the chart to preview the lesson. Then, write one sentence to explain what you think this lesson will be about.

What is the title of this lesson?	
What is the guiding question for this lesson?	
How is the lesson organized?	
What do the photos show?	
What do the graphs show?	

_____

_____

EXTENSION On a separate sheet of paper, write five questions that come to mind while previewing this lesson. Answer your questions after you have completed the lesson.

1. **Organize Information** Fill in the chart with information about each biome. To complete the Locations column, you can refer to the map in Lesson 1 as well as the text in this lesson.

Biome	Locations	Climate	Interesting Details
Tropical rain forest			
Tropical dry forest			
Savanna			
Desert			
Temperate rain forest			
Temperate forest			

Biome	Locations	Climate	Interesting Details
Temperate grassland			
Chaparral			
Boreal forest (taiga)			
Tundra			

2. Why does the soil of Antarctica have little organic content?

_____

_____

3. Why are polar ice caps not considered a biome?

_____

_____

_____

4. Identify three adaptations found among animals that live in the polar caps.

_____

_____

5. **Think Visually** Describe the types of plants you might find as you hike up a mountain slope with communities ranging from desert to tundra.

_____

_____

_____

_____

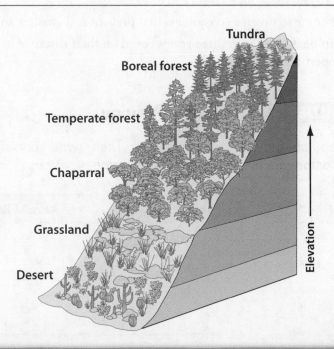

Tundra

Boreal forest

Temperate forest

Chaparral

Grassland

Desert

Elevation

6.2 ● SELF-CHECK

Answer the questions to test your knowledge of lesson concepts. You can check your work using the answers on the bottom of the page.

6. Contrast the precipitation amounts of the biome with the greatest precipitation with those of the biome that has the least precipitation.

_____

_____

7. Write a general statement, one that applies to all biomes, about the type of organisms found within a biome.

_____

_____

6. A tropical rainforest (greatest precipitation) receives about 2 meters of rain each year, while a desert (least precipitation) receives less than 25 centimeters. **7.** Sample answer: Organisms found in each biome have adaptations that allow them to survive in the biome's climate.

6.3 Aquatic Ecosystems

Key Concepts

 Ecologists classify aquatic ecosystems according to criteria such as salinity, depth, and whether the water is flowing or standing.

 Standing freshwater ecosystems include ponds, lakes, inland seas, and wetlands. Flowing freshwater ecosystems include rivers and streams.

 Estuaries are home to diverse ecosystems that prevent soil erosion and flooding.

 The ocean can be divided into three zones based on their distance from shore: intertidal, neritic, and open ocean.

SKILL BUILDER Vocabulary Preview

Define each vocabulary term in your own words. Then, write yourself a quick note on how you will remember each. One term has been done for you.

Term	Definition	How I Remember
Salinity		
Photic zone		
Aphotic zone	The layer below the photic zone where no sunlight penetrates and photosynthesis cannot occur	I know the prefix *a–* can mean "without," so *aphotic* must mean "without light."
Benthic zone		

Term	Definition	How I Remember
Littoral zone		
Limnetic zone		
Wetland		
Flood plain		
Estuary		
Upwelling		

Describing Aquatic Ecosystems

1. Identify three factors that characterize aquatic systems.

_____

_____

2. Explain why a freshwater fish cannot survive in salt water.

_____

_____

_____

3. Give one reason why there tends to be more organisms in the photic zone than in the aphotic zone.

_____

_____

4. **Organize Information** Complete the table below to summarize the general characteristics of flowing and standing water ecosystems.

Type of Ecosystem	Characteristics	Example
Flowing-water ecosystem		
Standing-water ecosystem		

Freshwater Ecosystems

5. **Think Visually** Draw and label a diagram that shows the five aquatic zones in freshwater ecosystems. Add plants and other organisms to your diagram.

6. Provide two reasons to support the following statement: *Wetlands have significant ecological importance.*

_____

_____

7. Why are flood plain soils particularly fertile?

_____

Estuaries

For Questions 8–12, complete each statement by writing the correct word or words.

8. Where fresh and salt water mix in coastal estuaries, they form _____ ecosystems.

9. Freshwater estuaries tend to be diverse ecosystems with a mix of river and

   _____ organisms.

10. Salt marshes stabilize shorelines against _____.

11. In _____ latitudes, mangrove forests are found along gently sloping, silty coasts.

12. The largest _____ in America are in Florida's Everglades region.

13. State the ecological importance of estuaries.

   _____

   _____

The Oceans

14. Explain the effect salinity and temperature have on water density.

   _____

15. Why are upwellings important to ocean ecosystems?

   _____

   _____

16. Identify three major ocean ecosystems.

   _____

17. Compare and contrast kelp forests and coral reefs.

   _____

   _____

   _____

18. Why is microscopic phytoplankton very important as a food source?

   _____

   _____

SKILL BUILDER Think Visually

19. Draw arrows to show the directions of the ocean's warm and cold currents. Use pencils of different colors or some other way to distinguish warm currents from cold currents. Then, add a key to identify how you showed warm and cold currents. Finally, on the lines below the map, explain the relationship between an estuary and the ocean, and how an estuary affects a shoreline.

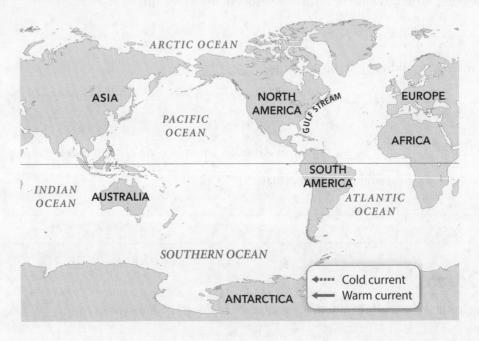

_____

_____

6.3 ⬤ SELF-CHECK

Answer the questions to test your knowledge of lesson concepts. You can check your work using the answers on the bottom of the page.

20. How does ocean depth affect photosynthesis? _____

_____

_____

21. Why is the intertidal zone a challenging environment for organisms that live there?

_____

_____

_____

20. Light does not penetrate below the uppermost zone—the photic zone—so photosynthesis cannot occur below a certain depth. 21. Because the organisms are subject to extremes in temperature, moisture, sun exposure, and salinity, and are exposed to predators at both high and low tide

Chapter Vocabulary Review

Match each term with its definition.

_____ 1. biome

_____ 2. canopy

_____ 3. salinity

_____ 4. littoral zone

_____ 5. estivation

_____ 6. benthic zone

_____ 7. coniferous

_____ 8. aphotic zone

_____ 9. climate

_____ 10. limnetic zone

_____ 11. flood plain

_____ 12. epiphytes

a. tall, dense covering of trees in a tropical rain forest

b. plants that grow on other plants instead of in the soil

c. an aquatic area where no photosynthesis takes place

d. the average temperature and precipitation over long periods

e. the very bottom of a body of water

f. the area some distance from shore where there are no rooted plants

g. a group of ecosystems that share similar abiotic and biotic conditions

h. the area nearest a river's course that is periodically overrun with water

i. a measurement of the amount of salts dissolved in water

j. the shallow near-shore portion of the photic zone

k. a deep, sleeplike period of dormancy during dry conditions

l. producing seed-bearing cones

Use each vocabulary term in a sentence.

13. Weather _____

_____

14. Hibernation _____

_____

15. Estuary _____

_____

16. Understory _____

_____

EXTENSION On a separate sheet of paper, use at least five vocabulary words to write a short paragraph about biomes.

Ecological Footprints

Consumption of Ocean Food

On average, each person in North America consumes about 24.1 kilograms of ocean food per year. The rate of consumption for the world is much lower—about 16.4 kilograms per person per year. In this activity, you will use these consumption rates to calculate the total amounts of ocean food consumed each year by different groups of people.

▶ The calculation of the average amount of ocean food consumed per year by a classroom of 25 students in North America is modeled at the right:

$$\text{ocean food consumed} = \text{number of people} \times \text{annual rate of consumption}$$
$$= 25 \text{ people} \times 24.1 \text{ kg/person}$$
$$= 602.5 \text{ kilograms}$$

1. In 2010, the world population was about 6.8 billion and the U.S. population was 309 million. Use Internet resources to find the population of your state. Then, calculate the amount of ocean food consumed annually by each consumer group in the table using North America's consumption rate. Write your answers in the table.

Consumer Group	Population	Consumption Using North American Rate (24.1 kg per person)	Consumption Using World Rate (16.4 kg per person)
You	1		
Your class			
Your state			
United States	309 million		
World	6.8 billion		

Data from U.N. Food and Agriculture Organization (FAO), Fisheries Department. 2004. *The state of world fisheries and aquaculture: 2008. Data are for 2005, the most recent year for which comparative data are available.*

2. Calculate the amount of ocean food consumed annually by each consumer group using the world's consumption rate. Write your answers in the table.

3. The population of North America equals about 8 percent of the world's population. Use the model shown below to calculate the approximate population of North America. (*Hint:* Use the world population data shown in your table.) _____

North American population = 0.08 × world population

4. Use the population you found in Step 3 to calculate the annual amount of ocean food consumed in North America. (Use the North American rate.) _____

Too Much of a Good Thing?

Addo Elephant National Park

African elephants are larger than Asian elephants, and in fact, are the largest of all land mammals. They have a life span of up to 70 years and can grow to about 6350 kg (14,000 lbs). Their diet consists of roots, grasses, fruit, and bark, and they can consume up to 300 pounds of food each day. They use their tusks for digging for food and water and to strip bark from trees.

For many years elephants were hunted for their ivory. Though an international ban on the ivory trade does exist, illegal hunting continues. Because of these illegal practices and because of loss of habitat, African elephants remain classified as a threatened species. Addo Elephant National Park in South Africa provides a sanctuary to the elephants living there.

Park Expansion

In 2004 the World Bank, South African National Parks (SANParks), and South Africa's government teamed up to infuse the equivalent of $40 million U.S. dollars into the expansion of Addo Elephant National Park. The park is located in the impoverished Eastern Cape province of South Africa.

First established in 1931 on 2000 hectares (4940 acres) of land, the expanded park will stretch across some 236,000 hectares (583,000 acres) and encompass five of the nation's seven land biomes. Once completed, the new Addo Elephant National Park will even include a marine park focused on the protection of marine organisms. Conservation measures will work toward restoration of the park's degraded farmland as impoverished farmers abandon farming for work in the park.

Before expansion, the national park received approximately 120,000 visitors a year, half of which came from foreign nations. After expansion, the park is expected to receive far more visitors, which will greatly boost revenues generated though eco-tourism. The long-term goals of the park's expansion are to protect wildlife, conserve natural resources by reducing reliance on farming, and jumpstart economic growth and employment.

African elephants enjoy savannas and dry woodlands where food and water are plentiful. With the expansion of Addo Elephant National Park, elephants living within its borders will have a vast area to roam. When the park was first established, there were only 11 elephants. Today there are over 450. It remains to be seen, then, what will become of the biodiversity of Addo Elephant National Park as its elephant population expands into new territories. Will Addo face the same fate as Hwange National Park in Zimbabwe, where the overly high elephant density has led to so many environmental and human woes? How best to manage both habitats and the animals that live in those habitats? Will revenues from ecotourism be enough to support a sustainable natural environment, protect wildlife, and maintain the biomes found within the park's borders? These and other questions remain for conservationists, investors, and governments, as the nations in Africa seek answers to very difficult ecological questions.

Use the information in **Addo Elephant National Park** to answer the questions below.

1. Compare the size of the Addo Elephant National Park before and after expansion.

   _____

   _____

2. What long-term goals do the World Bank, SANParks, and the South African government hope the expansion of Addo Elephant National Park will achieve?

   _____

   _____

3. How will expansion of Addo Elephant National Park affect the elephants that live there?

   _____

   _____

4. What effect will expansion of Addo Elephant National Park have on existing biomes?

   _____

   _____

   _____

5. REVISIT INVESTIGATIVE PHENOMENON How does the information in **Addo National Elephant Park** affect your answer to the **Investigative Phenomenon:** "How do organisms interact with the environment?"

   _____

   _____

   _____

21st Century Skills

Work with a partner to find out more about the Addo Elephant National Park, or another national park in Africa. Discover where the park is located, its biomes, and what wildlife is protected there. Learn about the role and influence government and tourism have on the park's management. Create an informational poster on your chosen national park.

The 21st Century Skills used in this activity include Information Literacy, Collaboration, and Critical Thinking and Problem Solving

7 Biodiversity and Conservation

Before you read the chapter, answer each question with information you know. After you complete the chapter, re-answer the questions using information you learned.

INVESTIGATIVE PHENOMENON **Why is it important to measure and protect biodiversity?**

What I Know	What I Learned

7.1 Why is maintaining biodiversity important?

7.2 Why is global biodiversity decreasing?

7.3 How can we protect and preserve biodiversity?

7.1 Our Planet of Life

Key Concepts

- Species diversity, genetic diversity, and ecosystem diversity are all parts of an area's overall biodiversity.
- Biodiversity varies among taxonomic groups and geographic regions.
- Biodiverse ecosystems provide economically valuable services and products.

SKILL BUILDER Vocabulary Preview

Define each vocabulary term in your own words. Then, write yourself a quick note on how you will remember each. One term has been done for you.

Term	Definition	How I Remember
Biodiversity		
Species diversity	The number or variety of species in a particular region	I remember that *species* are *specific* types of organisms and diversity refers to all different kinds.
Genetic diversity		
Ecosystem diversity		

Biodiversity

1. **Think Visually** Fill in the diagram with terms from the word bank to show how these three levels of biodiversity are related. Then, write a caption for the diagram on the lines below.

> **ecosystem diversity**   **genetic diversity**   **species diversity**

Overall Biodiversity

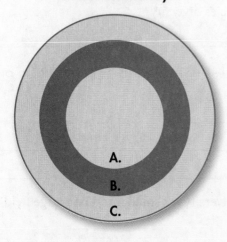

A. _____

B. _____

C. _____

_____

_____

_____

_____

_____

_____

2. Place the following taxonomic groups in order, from largest to smallest: class, domain, family, genus, kingdom, order, phylum, species, subspecies.

_____

_____

3. How does genetic diversity affect a population's chances of survival?

_____

_____

_____

_____

4. Provide one example of an area with high ecosystem diversity and one example of an area with low ecosystem diversity.

_____

_____

Biodiversity Distribution

5. Why is estimating the number of species on Earth so difficult and why do these estimates vary so greatly?

_____

_____

_____

6. Which group of animal has the greatest known species diversity?

_____

7. Would you expect to find greater biodiversity near Earth's poles or near the equator? Explain your answer.

_____

_____

_____

8. Which type of habitat would have greater species diversity—a small forest or a large field of corn? Why?

_____

_____

_____

_____

Benefits of Biodiversity

For Questions 9–12, complete each statement by writing in the correct word or words.

9. A stable ecosystem is both _____ and _____.

10. Genetic _____ is important for agriculture because wild plant strains may have useful traits that can be passed on to their crop plant relatives.

11. Biodiversity is important to the field of _____ because many treatments, including some for cancer and heart disease, come from plant compounds.

12. Environmentally responsible travel to protected areas for the purpose of appreciating nature, promoting conservation, and providing benefits to local peoples is known as _____.

13. What are ecosystem services? List two examples.

_____

_____

SKILL BUILDER Organize Information

14. Draw a cluster diagram to show how Lesson 1 concepts are related. The main idea is already written in the middle. The lines branching off the main idea connect to circles that contain related concepts. A few concepts have been added for you. Continue adding circles and writing in facts and details.

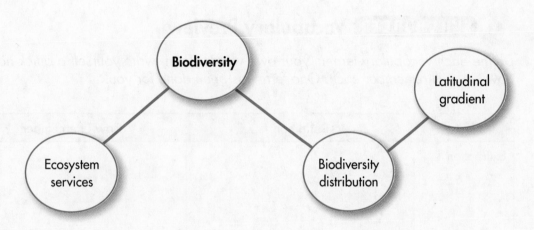

7.1 SELF-CHECK

Answer the questions to test your knowledge of lesson concepts. You can check your work using the answers on the bottom of the page.

15. What are three types of diversity that contribute to a region's overall biodiversity?

_____

16. Describe how species diversity and habitat diversity are related.

_____

_____

17. List three examples of ecosystem services.

_____

15. Genetic diversity, species, and ecosystem diversity 16. The greater the habitat diversity of an area, the greater the species diversity tends to be. 17. Purification of air and water, control of pests and diseases, decomposition of wastes

7.2 Extinction and Biodiversity Loss

Key Concepts

🔑 Scientists monitor biodiversity closely and have noticed significantly higher than normal extinction rates in recent decades.

🔑 Habitat change and loss, invasive species, pollution, overharvesting, and climate change are the major causes of biodiversity loss.

SKILL BUILDER Vocabulary Preview

Define each vocabulary term in your own words. Then, write yourself a quick note on how you will remember each. One term has been done for you.

Term	Definition	How I Remember
Extirpation		
Endangered species	A species that has a high risk of extinction	An *endangered* species is *in danger* of going extinct.
Threatened species		
Habitat fragmentation		
Poaching		

SKILL BUILDER **Reading Strategy**

Fill in the table to preview the lesson. Then, in the space that follows the table, write one sentence to explain what you think this lesson will be about.

What is the title of this lesson?	
What are the vocabulary terms for this lesson?	
What are the key concepts for the two main sections of this lesson?	
What do the photos depict?	
What do the diagrams show?	

_____

_____

EXTENSION Use the Internet to research threatened and endangered species in your state. On a separate sheet of paper, name and describe at least one plant and one animal that is threatened or endangered.

Biodiversity at Risk

1. Is extinction a natural process? Explain.

_____

_____

2. Compare and contrast extinction with extirpation.

_____

_____

_____

3. How does the background rate of extinction differ from mass extinctions?

_____

_____

_____

4. Which type of species is more likely to become extinct, an endangered species or a threatened species? Explain.

_____

_____

Causes of Biodiversity Loss

5. **Organize Information** Fill in the cause-and-effect diagram with a short description that explains how each process leads to loss of biodiversity.

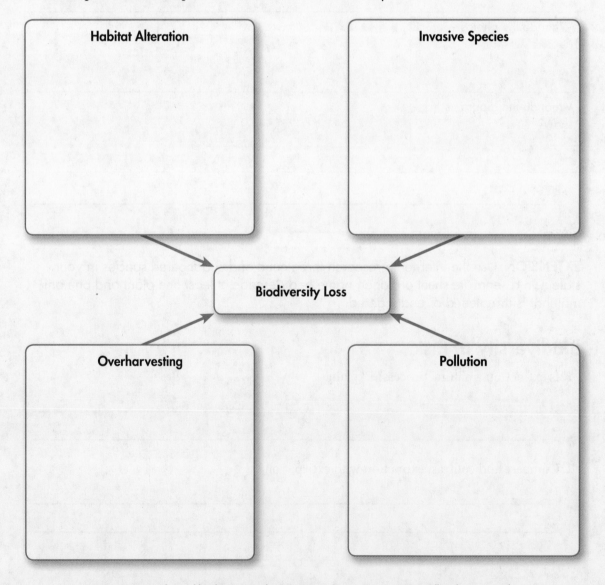

Habitat Alteration

Invasive Species

Biodiversity Loss

Overharvesting

Pollution

6. How do the effects of climate change differ from the effects of habitat alteration, invasive species, overharvesting, and pollution?

_____

_____

_____

7. A conservation plan could proceed with a single 20-square kilometer habitat preserve or with two habitat preserves, measuring a total of 20 square kilometers combined. Which preserve format would support more species? Explain.

_____

_____

_____

_____

8. What human activities lead to habitat loss?

_____

9. What are "habitat islands," and how do they occur?

_____

_____

_____

10. How did studies of oceanic islands help scientists understand the effect of habitat fragmentation on species diversity?

_____

_____

_____

11. What is the greatest cause of biodiversity loss today?

_____

12. What factors determine whether nonnative species are considered invasive?

_____

_____

13. List two nonnative species—one that is invasive, and another that is not invasive.

_____

_____

14. Many protected animals are lost to poaching. What is a main motivation behind poaching?

_____

_____

_____

15. How do warming temperatures affect animals that live in cold climates?

_____

_____

_____

7.2　　SELF-CHECK

Answer the questions to test your knowledge of lesson concepts. You can check your work using the answers on the bottom of the page.

16. What evidence suggests that we could be experiencing a sixth mass extinction?

_____

_____

17. What information is represented by the Living Planet Index?

_____

_____

18. List five causes of biodiversity loss.

_____

_____

_____

19. What is the greatest cause of biodiversity loss today? Explain.

_____

_____

_____

_____

16. The current global extinction rate is much higher than the usual background extinction rate. **17.** Population trends for a group of organisms that are closely tracked **18.** Habitat change and loss, invasive species, pollution, overharvesting, and climate change **19.** Habitat fragmentation is the greatest cause of biodiversity loss. Ongoing development destroys resources organisms need to survive and results in smaller islands of habitat that can support fewer species.

Name _____ Class _____ Date _____

7.3 Protecting Biodiversity

Key Concepts

- Nations can pass laws and sign international treaties that protect biodiversity.
- Species Survival Plans manage, protect, and reintroduce threatened and endangered species.
- Strategies that manage whole ecosystems and habitats, such as the hotspot approach, conservation concessions, and wildlife corridors, protect many species at once.

SKILL BUILDER Vocabulary Preview

Define each vocabulary term in your own words. Then, write yourself a quick note on how you will remember each. One term has been done for you.

Term	Definition	How I Remember
Endangered Species Act (ESA)		
Captive breeding		
Species Survival Plan (SSP)		
Biodiversity hotspot	An area that both supports an especially high number of endemic species and is rapidly losing biodiversity	I think of a *hotspot* as a place with a lot of activity—some of it critical—so a *biodiversity hotspot* is an active place where a lot of species are concentrated and there is something urgent happening.
Endemic		

Legal Efforts

1. Complete the following paragraph with terms from the word bank.

| biodiversity treaty | CITES | DDT | Endangered Species Act | law | treaties |

In the United States, the main _____ that protects biodiversity is the
_____. In effect since 1973, it has helped with the recovery of a number
of species including the bald eagle and other birds that were at risk of extinction due to
effects of the pesticide _____. Several _____ help to
protect biodiversity on an international level. _____, for example, has
been in effect since 1975 and bans the international transport of endangered species.
The Convention on Biological Diversity, sometimes commonly referred to as the
_____, has the commitment of about 200 nations. Although it has been
signed by the United States, it has not yet been ratified.

2. What are the three main parts of the Endangered Species Act?

_____

_____

_____

_____

3. Do you think the costs outweigh the benefits of treaties that serve to protect biodiversity?
Explain.

_____

_____

_____

_____

Single-Species Approaches

4. How does captive breeding help to protect single species?

_____

_____

_____

5. How would cloning, if successful, save a species from extinction?

_____

_____

_____

For Questions 6 and 7, circle the letter of the correct answer.

6. Which of the following involves inserting DNA from an endangered species into a cultured egg cell that has had its nucleus removed?

   A. cloning

   B. captive breeding

   C. Species Survival Plan

   D. species reintroduction

7. Which of the following is a main goal of a Species Survival Plan?

   A. breeding new species

   B. using DNA to recover extinct species

   C. reintroducing captive-bred organisms into the wild

   D. cloning extremely endangered organisms to increase their population size

Ecosystem and Habitat Approaches

For Questions 8 and 9, write True if the statement is true. If the statement is false, replace the underlined word or words to make the statement true. Write your changes on the line.

_____ **8.** Most laws provide protection for <u>habitats and ecosystems</u>.

_____ **9.** Many conservation efforts attempt to protect the land, wildlife, and economic interests of the <u>local</u> people.

10. What is a biodiversity hotspot?

_____

_____

11. What are the two main outcomes of a debt-for-nature swap?

_____

_____

12. Give one example of a conservation concession.

_____

_____

13. What is the main purpose of a wildlife corridor?

_____

_____

14. What is one benefit and one drawback of mapping hotspots?

_____

_____

SKILL BUILDER Organize Information

15. Use what you learned about legal efforts and single-species approaches to complete the table below. Two entries have been done for you.

Ways to Protect Biodiversity			
Categories	**Examples**	**Benefits**	**Drawbacks**
Legal efforts		Gives a chance for threatened and endangered species in the United States to recover	
Single-species approaches	Captive breeding		

7.3 ⬤ SELF-CHECK

Answer the questions to test your knowledge of lesson concepts. You can check your work using the answers on the bottom of the page.

16. Name three examples of laws or treaties that protect biodiversity.

_____

17. In what types of institutions do captive breeding programs take place?

_____

18. What are two examples of economic approaches to conservation?

_____

16. Endangered Species Act, CITES, Convention on Biological Diversity (biodiversity treaty) 17. Zoos, aquariums, botanical gardens 18. Debt-for-nature swap and conservation concession

Real Data

Golden Lion Tamarin

In this activity, you will determine the percent change in reintroduced golden lion tamarin populations at the National Zoo during 5-year intervals between 1985 and 2005.

Calculating Percent Increase

If a population doubles in size, it increases by 100%. To find the percent increase in a population's size, first subtract the original population size from the final population size. Then, divide the resulting number by the original population size and multiply by 100 to convert the number to a percentage.

▶ The formula for finding percent change is shown below:

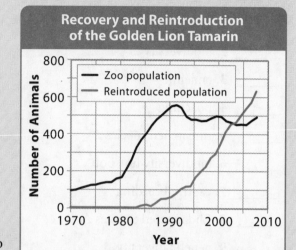

Recovery and Reintroduction of the Golden Lion Tamarin

Source: J. D. Ballou and J. Mickelberg, *International Studbook for Golden Lion Tamarins* (Washington, D.C.: National Zoological Park, Smithsonian Institution, 2007). B. Holst et al., *Lion Tamarin Population and Habitat Viability Assessment Workshop 2005, Final Report* (Apple Valley, MN: IUCN/SSC Conservation Breeding Specialist Group, 2006).

$$\% \text{ increase} = \frac{\text{final population size} - \text{original population size}}{\text{original population size}} \times 100$$

Calculate the percent increase in population sizes of reintroduced golden lion tamarins. Write your answers in the table.

Years	Original Size of Reintroduced Population	Final Size of Reintroduced Population	Percent Increase in Population Size
1985–1990	30	70	133%
1990–1995			
1995–2000			
2000–2005			

Use the information in the table to answer each question.

1. Which 5-year time span saw the greatest percent increase in the size of the reintroduced golden lion tamarin population? _____

2. If the trend shown in the graph continued, by approximately what percent do you think the reintroduced golden lion tamarin population would have increased between 2005 and 2010? _____

Chapter Vocabulary Review

Match each term with its definition.

_____ 1. extirpation

_____ 2. biodiversity

_____ 3. endemic

_____ 4. poaching

_____ 5. threatened species

_____ 6. biodiversity hotspot

_____ 7. captive breeding

_____ 8. Endangered Species Act

_____ 9. genetic diversity

_____ 10. endangered species

a. differences in DNA among individuals within species and populations

b. a U.S. law that protects biodiversity

c. mating and raising animals in zoos and similar controlled conditions

d. a part of the world that harbors particularly high biodiversity

e. found nowhere else in the world

f. regional extinction

g. illegal capturing or killing of an organism

h. the variety of life across all levels of ecological organization

i. a species at risk of extinction

j. a species at risk of becoming endangered

Use each vocabulary term in a sentence.

11. Species diversity _____

_____

12. Habitat fragmentation _____

_____

13. Species Survival Plan _____

_____

14. ecosystem diversity _____

_____

EXTENSION Sort the ten chapter vocabulary words above into three groups. Compare your groupings with a classmate's. Discuss the basis on which you sorted the terms.

Saving the Siberian Tiger

Siberian Tiger Monitoring Sites

The following map shows the distribution of Siberian tiger monitoring sites in the Russian Far East. These 16 sites were set up as part of the Siberian Tiger Monitoring Program, a collaborative effort between the Wildlife Conservation Society and several Russian governmental and non-governmental organizations.

Categorized as protected or unprotected, the monitoring sites are scattered across Siberian tiger habitat in the Sikhote-Alin Mountains. The tables below the map indicate the estimated number of tigers at each of the 16 sites in 2009, based on expert assessments of tiger track data.

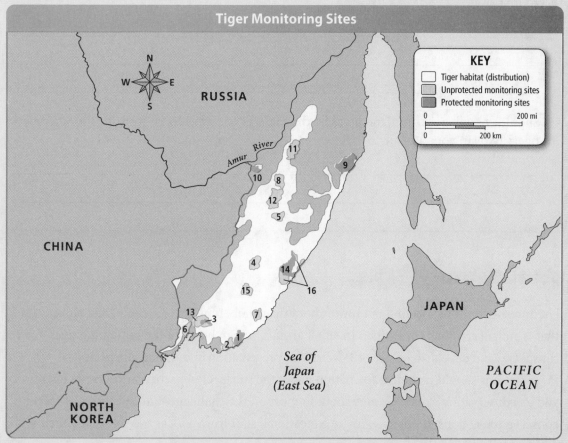

Based on research by the Wildlife Conservation Society.

Results of Tiger Survey, 2009

Site	1	2	3	4	5	6	7	8	9	10	11	12	13	14	15	16
Estimated Tiger Population	8	4	5	3	3	2	1	4	1	0	1	3	3	8	5	5

Use the information in **Siberian Tiger Monitoring Sites** to answer the questions below.

1. How many of the monitoring sites are protected areas? How many sites are unprotected?

   _____

2. Which monitoring site is the farthest north? Which site is the farthest south?

   _____

3. Based on the tiger estimates data, which of the protected monitoring sites has the smallest tiger population?

   _____

4. If a conservation organization were interested in constructing a wildlife corridor within the Siberian tiger range, where would you suggest the corridor be constructed? Explain your answer.

   _____

   _____

   _____

5. Should coastal areas or inland areas be the focus of conservation efforts for the Siberian tiger? Explain your answer.

   _____

   _____

   _____

21st Century Skills

Use Internet resources to find out more about tigers. Siberian tigers are one tiger subspecies that is endangered but not extinct. In small groups, research one of the remaining tiger subspecies and develop a poster or PowerPoint presentation about that subspecies. Presentations should include information about the subspecies' particular traits, its range, and its conservation status. Groups should report on the challenges and successes of recent conservation actions. If possible, invite educational staff from a local zoo to discuss their work with tigers.

*The 21st Century Skills used in this activity include **Critical Thinking and Problem Solving, Information, Communication, and Technology (ICT) Literacy, Creativity and Innovation, and Communication and Collaboration.***

8 Human Population

Before you read the chapter, answer each question with information you know. After you complete the chapter, re-answer the questions using information you learned.

INVESTIGATIVE PHENOMENON **How does the human population affect the environment?**

	What I Know	What I Learned
8.1 What social and environmental factors affect human population size?		
8.2 How do human population growth trends differ between developed nations and developing nations?		
8.3 How does a country's wealth relate to its consumption of resources?		

8.1 Trends in Human Population Growth

Key Concepts

 Technological advances, especially in agriculture and industry, changed the ways people lived and triggered remarkable increases in population size.

 In recent years the human population growth rate has decreased, but the population still continues to grow.

 Demographers study the size, density, and distribution of human populations.

SKILL BUILDER Vocabulary Preview

Define each vocabulary term in your own words. Then, write yourself a quick note on how you will remember each. One term has been done for you.

Term	Definition	How I Remember
Industrial Revolution		
Infant mortality		
Life expectancy	The average number of years a person is expected to live	*Life* expectancy tells how long a person is *expected* to live.
Growth rate		
Demography		

SKILL BUILDER Reading Strategy

As you read the lesson, complete the main ideas and details chart.

Main Ideas	Details
History of human population growth	
Recent trends in human population growth	
Describing the human population	

History of Human Population Growth

For Questions 1–3, complete each statement by writing the correct word or words.

1. During the Industrial Revolution, many people moved from rural areas to

_____.

2. Around the time of the Industrial Revolution, scientists came to understand that many

diseases are caused by _____.

3. Medical advances during the Industrial Revolution included the development of

_____, which treat bacterial infections and _____, which can help to prevent or reduce severity of illnesses caused by both viruses and bacteria.

4. Name three changes in agriculture that occurred during the Industrial Revolution.

_____

_____

Recent Trends in Human Population Growth

For Questions 5–9, write True *if the statement is true. If the statement is false, replace the underlined word to make the statement true. Write your changes on the line.*

_____ **5.** Developments during the Industrial Revolution resulted in <u>increases</u> in infant mortality.

_____ **6.** Developments during the Industrial Revolution resulted in <u>increases</u> in life expectancy.

_____ **7.** For much of the twentieth century, the human population growth rate <u>rose</u> from year to year.

_____ **8.** Population growth rates <u>differ</u> greatly among different regions of the world.

_____ **9.** When the human population reaches carrying capacity, its growth rate will be <u>negative</u>.

10. Name three environmental factors that limit human population growth.

_____

Describing the Human Population

11. What types of predictions can be made using demographic data?

_____

_____

12. Name three nations that have some of the highest levels of human population density.

_____

13. Why do regions with extreme climates, such as tundra and deserts, have low levels of human population density?

_____

_____

Name _____ Class _____ Date _____

14. **Organize Information** Fill in the spider map with information about demography. The diagonal lines have been labeled with main topics related to demography. Add details about the main topics on the horizontal lines.

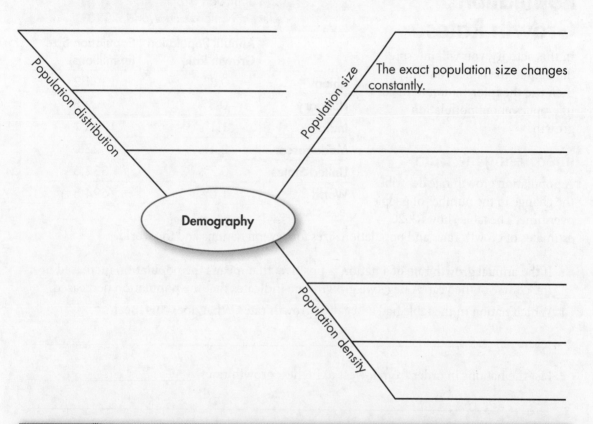

Population distribution

Population size
The exact population size changes constantly.

Demography

Population density

8.1 ⊙ SELF-CHECK

Answer the questions to test your knowledge of lesson concepts. You can check your work using the answers on the bottom of the page.

15. Identify three developments that occurred during the Industrial Revolution that

    contributed to a rapid increase in human population growth. _____

    _____

16. What will happen to the population growth rate when the human population reaches

    carrying capacity? _____

17. What does a demographer study? _____

    _____

and distribution of human populations.

15. Improvements in sanitation, improvements in medical technology, changes in agricultural practices 16. The growth rate will be zero. 17. A demographer studies human population statistics—including the size, density,

Real Data

Population Growth Rates

In this activity, you will interpret the data in the table. You will then use the information to make inferences about population growth.

Interpreting the Data

A population growth rate describes the change in the number of people over time. The table shows 2020 estimates of growth rates and population sizes for several nations and the world.

Population Growth Rate of Selected Nations and World, 2020		
	Annual Population Growth Rate	**Population Size (in millions)**
China	0.3%	1394.2
Hungary	−0.3%	9.8
India	1.1%	1326.1
Madagascar	2.4%	27.0
United States	0.7%	332.6
World	1.0%	7694.3

Data: CIA

▶ If the annual growth rate of a nation is positive, that means the population increased over the course of the year. A negative growth rate indicates that the population decreased.

1. Which nation in the table had a negative growth rate? What does this mean?

_____

2. List the nations in order from lowest to highest growth rates. _____

_____

Making Inferences

▶ To estimate the increase in a nation's population over the following year, multiply its current population size by its annual population growth rate. The calculation for China is modeled below:

increase in population	= **1394.2 million × 0.3%**	**Use the data from the table.**
	= **1394.2 × 0.003**	**Write the percent as a decimal.**
	= **4.18 million**	**Multiply.**

So, in one year, China will add about 4.18 million people to its population.

3. About how many people will India, Madagascar, and the United States each add to their

populations over the course of a year? Round to the nearest hundredth. _____

_____

4. Which of the nations listed in the table will likely add the most people to the world over

the course of a year? _____

8.2 Predicting Population Growth

Key Concepts

 Fertility rate helps demographers predict the rates at which populations will grow in the future.

Age structure and sex ratios define a population's potential for growth.

The demographic transition may explain the reason that some industrialized nations have experienced a large drop in birthrates and death rates.

Social factors, such as wealth and education, affect a nation's population growth and its resource use.

SKILL BUILDER Vocabulary Preview

Define each vocabulary term in your own words. Then, write yourself a quick note on how you will remember each. One term has been done for you.

Term	Definition	How I Remember
Total fertility rate		
Replacement fertility	The total fertility rate for a nation that would keep its population size stable	I think of *replacement* fertility as the rate at which the number of people born would *replace* the number of people who died.
Demographic transition		

SKILL BUILDER Reading Strategy

Before you read the lesson, fill in the first column of the KWL chart below with what you already know about predicting human population growth. Fill in the second column with what you want to know about this topic. After you have read the lesson, fill in the third column with what you have learned.

I Know	I Want to Know	I Learned

EXTENSION Use the Internet to research population growth rates in your state over the last 30 years. Create a poster with information about your state's recent trends in population growth.

Fertility Rate

For Questions 1 and 2, circle the letter of the correct answer.

1. Fertility rates have started to decrease in many nations. How has this affected the size of the human population throughout the world?

   A. The population size is steady.

   B. The population size is decreasing.

   C. The population size is still increasing.

   D. Fertility rates are not related to population size.

2. What type of fertility rate would keep a nation's population stable?

   A. total fertility

   B. natural fertility

   C. doubling fertility

   D. replacement fertility

3. How do fertility rates compare to overall population rates of the world?

_____

Age Structure and Sex Ratios

4. How is information on age structure and sex ratios useful to demographers?

_____

5. Most people in population *A* are pre-reproductive age. In population *B*, most people are post-reproductive age. Which population will likely experience a greater population growth rate over the next few decades? Explain.

_____

_____

_____

6. How might human activities skew sex ratios?

_____

_____

_____

_____

The Demographic Transition

7. **Organize Information** Fill in the flowchart with the names and brief descriptions of what happens to population growth in each stage of the demographic transition.

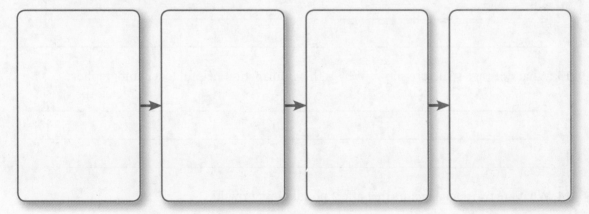

8. During which stage of the demographic transition do population growth rates increase?

_____

9. In which stage of the demographic transition is the United States today?

_____

Social Factors

10. Complete the following paragraph with terms from the word bank.

| decline | growing | higher | lower |

The fertility rates, infant mortality rates, and death rates of developing nations

are _____ than those of developed nations, while life expectancy is

_____. Still, developing nations tend to have _____

populations, while the populations of developed nations stay relatively constant. Fertility rates

are strongly connected to education. When women have educational opportunities and are

able to decide whether and when to have children, fertility rates often _____.

11. Provide at least three examples of national policies that can influence population size.

_____

_____

_____

8.2 SELF-CHECK

Answer the questions to test your knowledge of lesson concepts. You can check your work using the answers on the bottom of the page.

12. Name at least three reasons that, historically, total fertility rates were once higher

worldwide. _____

_____

_____

13. What does age structure show? Why is this information helpful to a demographer?

_____

_____

_____

14. What are two social factors that affect population growth? _____

_____

12. Historically, people tended to have more children to ensure that at least some would survive childhood. On farms, people had more children so they could help with farm work. And, as parents got older, they could rely on their children to support them. **13.** Age structure shows the proportion of individuals in a population currently of reproductive age, as well as those who will be reproducing in the future. This information helps a demographer predict how a population will change over time. **14.** Sample answer: Wealth and education

8.3 People and Their Environments

Key Concepts

- Humans have an enormous impact on their environment.
- Technology can have both negative and positive impacts on the environment.

 SKILL BUILDER Vocabulary Preview

Define the vocabulary term in your own words. Then, write yourself a quick note on how you will remember it.

Term	Definition	How I Remember
Wealth gap		

Impacts of Population

For Questions 1–5, write True if the statement is true. If the statement is false, replace the underlined word or words to make the statement true. Write your changes on the line.

_____ 1. When people have more money, then tend to produce <u>less</u> waste.

_____ 2. Population growth rate is usually lower in <u>poor</u> societies.

_____ 3. People in developed nations tend to have <u>larger</u> ecological footprints.

_____ 4. Due to land overuse, the once-productive Sahel region turned into <u>desert</u>.

_____ 5. The wealth gap between developed and developing nations is <u>small</u>.

6. How does the ecological footprint of the United States compare with the world average ecological footprint?

_____

_____

7. Describe the relationship between affluence and ecological footprint.

_____

_____

8. What can happen in poorer nations where population growth outpaces economic growth?

_____

_____

9. Write a brief paragraph about the negative effects of land clearing.

_____

_____

_____

_____

_____

_____

10. What are two ways that international organizations are helping people in developing nations earn a living while reducing negative effects to their local environment?

_____

_____

_____

11. What percent of global resources—energy, food, water, and other essentials—are available for four fifths of the world's people?

_____

12. What types of environmental challenges does a developing nation encounter as it develops?

_____

_____

_____

_____

_____

13. How does the size of the human population relate to quality of life?

_____

_____

_____

_____

_____

_____

Impacts of Technology

14. **Organize Information** Fill in the T-chart with information about the positive and negative impacts of technology on the environment. Provide at least two examples of each.

Positive Impacts of Technology	Negative Impacts of Technology

15. If the technology that brought about modern life never existed, how would human population growth have been affected?

_____

_____

_____

16. Technology has allowed for the construction of skyscrapers and other high-rise buildings. How could these buildings be viewed as having a positive and a negative environmental effect?

_____

_____

_____

_____

17. Provide one example of a technology used in most urban areas that has a negative effect on the environment. Explain the negative effect.

_____

_____

18. Provide one example of a technology often used in urban areas that has a positive effect on the environment.

_____

_____

19. How can technology help reduce the environmental effect of a growing population?

_____

_____

SKILL BUILDER Organize Information

20. Fill in the table comparing the environmental effects of population and technology use in affluent and poor societies.

	Impacts of Population	Use of Technology
Affluent societies		
Poor societies		

8.3 SELF-CHECK

Answer the questions to test your knowledge of lesson concepts. You can check your work using the answers on the bottom of the page.

21. How is global wealth distributed among nations? _____

_____

_____

22. How does technology negatively affect the environment? _____

_____

21. Global wealth is unevenly distributed across the global population. Developed nations generally have a much larger share of wealth than developing nations have. 22. Technology can lead to the exploitation of resources, cause pollution, and result in the loss of biodiversity.

Chapter Vocabulary Review

Complete each statement by writing in the correct word or words.

| demographer | demographic transition | growth rate | Industrial Revolution |
| infant mortality | replacement fertility | total fertility rate | wealth gap |

1. During the _____, the human population's _____ began to rise exponentially, but recently it has started to decline.

2. Changes in the human population can be tracked using data gathered by a _____.

3. One important statistic that demographers examine is the average number of children that a female member of a population has in her lifetime, or a population's

_____.

4. In today's world, there is a striking _____ between the populations of different regions.

5. Advances during the Industrial Revolution led to decreased _____.

6. As nations move through the _____, demographic trends change.

7. If a population's total fertility rate maintains a stable population, it is at

_____.

Define each vocabulary term below.

8. wealth gap _____

_____

9. demographic transition _____

_____

_____

_____

10. Industrial Revolution _____

_____

EXTENSION On a separate piece of paper, organize the sentences from Questions 1–7 above into two paragraphs. Add additional sentences to connect ideas and fill in missing details.

China's Changing Population Needs

Breaking the Rules

China's one-child policy didn't apply to all Chinese citizens. There are exceptions for rural families, ethnic minorities, and urban couples in which both parents are from single-child families. But what about the approximately 36 percent of the Chinese population bound by this policy? Are there ways around the rules?

More Than One

A survey conducted by the National Population and Family Planning Commission of China found that almost 80 percent of the citizens polled, who can only have one-child families, would like to have a two-child family. Although most of the population might like to have two children, social stigma, fines, and other penalties prevent many couples bound by the one-child policy from having more than one child.

Some couples have found ways around the rules. Couples leaving China for work or study may have children while they are living abroad. If these families return to China, their children—regardless of how many they have—are welcomed, too. Some Chinese couples with the resources to live abroad may take advantage of this loophole in the one-child policy in order to have more than one child. Of course, not all couples that have children abroad do so to escape the one-child policy. Some couples may intend to move abroad permanently. When unforeseen circumstances result in these couples returning to China, they may return with more than one child.

Another way the one-child policy can be rendered ineffective is through the birth of twins, triplets, or other multiple births. There are no penalties for having more than one child if the children all come from one pregnancy. A multiple pregnancy is a matter of chance, but a woman's age and family history are also factors. Women of older reproductive age have a higher incidence of multiple pregnancies because their ovaries are more likely to release multiple eggs at once. Women who have twins in their family have a higher than average chance to have twins themselves. But there are ways through which any couple can improve the likelihood of a multiple pregnancy.

One way people try to have twins is by taking fertility drugs. The use of fertility drugs is known to increase the chances for a multiple pregnancy. By some reports, the rate of multiple births may be twice as high in China as it was before this trend. Although the sale of fertility drugs is regulated, in reality, the drugs can be rather easily purchased.

Use the information in **Breaking the Rules** to answer the questions below.

1. Approximately what percent of China's population is bound to the one-child rule?

_____

2. What are three reasons a couple might be exempt from the one-child rule?

_____

_____

3. What medical technology have some Chinese chosen to pursue in order to increase the possibility of multiple children in a single pregnancy?

_____

4. Do you think that more countries should adopt China's one-child policy? Explain your answer.

_____

_____

_____

5. Why might wealthy families be able to avoid the one-child policy more easily than poor families?

_____

6. What is one loophole to the one-child policy?

_____

_____

21st Century Skills

China's population policy undergoes revisions at intervals. How do you think the policy should be revised in its next review? With your group members, develop a plan for revisions to the policy. Your plan should include three main revision points. Present your plan to the class. After all plans have been presented, discuss the strengths of each plan—and formulate a strong single plan resulting from the work of each group.

*The 21st Century Skills used in this activity include **Critical Thinking and Problem Solving, Communication and Collaboration, Flexibility and Adaptability,** and **Social and Cross-Cultural Skills.***

Environmental Health

Before you read the chapter, answer each question with information you know. After you complete the chapter, re-answer the questions using information you learned.

INVESTIGATIVE PHENOMENON **How do we balance the relationship between our own health and the health of the environment?**

	What I Know	What I Learned
9.1 What is environmental health?		
9.2 How do biological and social factors in the environment affect human health?		
9.3 How do chemicals in our environment affect our health?		
9.4 How can physical events in the environment affect our health?		

9.1 An Overview of Environmental Health

Key Concepts

- Environmental health hazards can be biological, social, chemical, or physical.
- Epidemiology is the study of disease in human populations, while toxicology is the study of how poisonous substances affect organisms' health.
- People respond differently to environmental hazards due to individual differences such as age, sex, weight, health issues, and genetic makeup.
- Risk assessment is the process of measuring the chance that an environmental hazard will cause harm.

 SKILL BUILDER **Vocabulary Preview**

Define each vocabulary term in your own words. Then, write yourself a quick note on how you will remember each. One term has been done for you.

Term	Definition	How I Remember
Environmental health		
Hazard		
Pathogen		
Epidemiology		
Toxicology	The study of how poisonous substances affect an organism's health	I know that *toxic* means "poisonous" and *–ology* indicates the study of a subject.
Toxicity		
Dose		

Term	Definition	How I Remember
Response		
Dose-response relationship		
Risk		
Risk assessment		

SKILL BUILDER Reading Strategy

As you read the lesson, complete the main ideas and details chart.

Main Ideas	Details
Types of hazards	
Epidemiology and toxicology	

Main Ideas	Details
The role of the individual	
Risk assessment	

Types of Hazards

For Questions 1–3, circle the letter of the correct answer.

1. An earthquake is an example of a

    A. social hazard.   **C.** chemical hazard.

    B. physical hazard.   **D.** biological hazard.

2. Which of the following is not considered to be a biological hazard?

    A. flu virus   **C.** cigarette smoke

    B. pet dander   **D.** bacterium that causes strep throat

3. Environmental health is the study of how environmental factors affect human health and

    A. length of life.   **C.** population size.

    B. quality of life.   **D.** population growth.

4. Explain the difference between social hazards such as smoking cigarettes and living near a factory that releases harmful chemicals into the water.

_____

_____

_____

5. List three examples of physical hazards.

_____

_____

_____

Epidemiology and Toxicology

For Questions 6–11, match each term with the statement that best describes it.

_____ **6.** dose

_____ **7.** epidemiology

_____ **8.** response

_____ **9.** threshold dose

_____ **10.** toxicity

_____ **11.** toxicology

a. how harmful a substance is

b. the amount of a substance an organism is exposed to

c. the effect as a result of exposure to a substance

d. the study of how poisonous substances affect health

e. the study of disease in human populations

f. the amount of a substance needed to cause a response

12. What is a dose-response relationship?

_____

_____

_____

13. Which two factors does toxicity depend on?

_____

_____

_____

The Role of the Individual

For Questions 14–16, write True *if the statement is true. If the statement is false, replace the underlined word or words to make the statement true. Write your changes on the line.*

_____ **14.** People respond <u>differently</u> to the same environmental hazards.

_____ **15.** People with compromised immune systems are often <u>less</u> sensitive to biological and chemical hazards than healthy people.

_____ **16.** Many diseases have <u>either</u> genetic <u>or</u> environmental factors.

17. Explain why someone who eats healthy food and does not smoke may still develop a disease such as cancer.

_____

_____

_____

18. Explain why alcohol use may cause damage to a developing fetus even though it may not harm the health of the mother.

_____

_____

_____

Risk Assessment

19. What is the process of risk assessment used to determine?

_____

20. Describe the steps that a scientist takes when doing a risk assessment for a chemical hazard. _____

_____

_____

_____

21. How are risk assessments of environmental hazards useful to policymakers?

_____

_____

9.1 ◯ SELF-CHECK

Answer the questions to test your knowledge of lesson concepts. You can check your work using the answers on the bottom of the page.

22. What are three examples of pathogens?

_____

23. What are epidemiology and toxicology?

_____

_____

24. Why do people respond differently to environmental hazards?

_____

_____

22. Sample answer: Viruses, bacteria, pet dander 23. Epidemiology is the study of diseases in human populations. Toxicology is the study of how poisonous substances affect organisms. 24. Because they have different genetics and sensitivities, and they live in different environments

9.2 Biological and Social Hazards

Key Concepts

 Infectious diseases are spread by direct human contact, through contaminated food and water, and by animals.

Since new diseases are continually emerging, it is important to know how, where, and to what extent they are spreading.

Some social hazards result from lifestyle choices a person makes, while other social hazards cannot be controlled.

SKILL BUILDER Vocabulary Preview

Define the vocabulary term in your own words. Then, write yourself a quick note on how you will remember it. One term has been done for you.

Term	Definition	How I Remember
Infectious disease		
Emerging disease	A disease that has appeared in the human population for the first time or has existed for a while but is increasing or spreading rapidly	Think of an animal *emerging* from a jungle.

Infectious Disease

For Questions 1–7, complete each statement by writing in the correct word or words.

1. Infectious diseases are caused by pathogens, which are _____ hazards.

2. Pathogens spread through the human population by humans, water or food, or by _____.

3. Globally, infectious diseases are the _____ cause of deaths annually.

4. Organisms such as ticks and mosquitoes serve as _____ for infectious diseases by carrying pathogens.

5. People who are infected with tuberculosis release bacteria-laden droplets into the _____ when they cough, sneeze, speak, and spit.

6. Developed nations greatly reduce the risk of infectious diseases through the use of _____ treatment facilities that treat sewage to reduce the incidences of diseases such as cholera.

7. The bacterium that causes cholera is a _____ pathogen.

8. **Organize Information** Fill in the table with details on how each infectious disease is spread.

Infectious Disease	Mode of Transmission
AIDS	
Tuberculosis	
Cholera	
Malaria	

Emerging Diseases

For Questions 9–14, write True *if the statement is true. If the statement is false, replace the underlined word to make the statement true. Write your changes on the line.*

_____ 9. An emerging disease is a disease that appears for the first time or has existed for a while and is increasing <u>slowly</u> around the world.

_____ 10. A <u>pandemic</u> is an outbreak of a disease that becomes widespread and affects a whole region or even the entire world.

_____ 11. The <u>Zika virus</u> is an example of an emerging disease.

_____ 12. Some diseases, such as tuberculosis, are becoming resistant to <u>pathogens</u> due to natural selection.

_____ 13. In the United States, the <u>WHO</u> is the primary national center for responding to emerging diseases.

_____ 14. If global temperatures <u>fall</u>, tropical diseases will expand into new, formerly cool areas.

15. Why are emerging diseases a cause for concern?

_____

_____

16. Explain how climate change may encourage an increase in the spread of disease.

_____

_____

17. Why is it important that international and local government agencies work together to control the spread of emerging diseases?

_____

_____

18. Describe ways that the CDC has helped contain the spread of the Zika virus.

_____

_____

_____

Social Hazards

19. Name three examples of social hazards.

_____

_____

20. Explain how cigarette smoke can be a hazard to someone even if he or she does not smoke.

_____

_____

_____

21. Describe how the choices you make concerning what you eat can increase or reduce the social hazards you face.

_____

_____

_____

_____

SKILL BUILDER Organize Information

22. Fill in the concept map with terms from the word bank.

| organisms | antibiotic resistance | CDC | changing environment |
| international | national | humans | WHO |

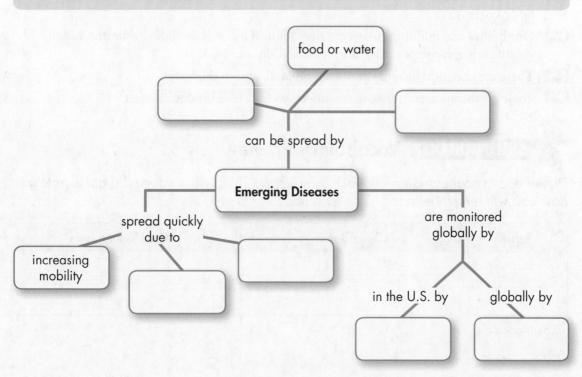

food or water

can be spread by

Emerging Diseases

spread quickly
due to

increasing
mobility

are monitored
globally by

in the U.S. by   globally by

Extension Extend the concept map by adding an example to each of the boxes of the "can be spread by" and "spread quickly due to" branches.

9.2 SELF-CHECK

Answer the questions to test your knowledge of lesson concepts. You can check your work using the answers on the bottom of the page.

23. What are three ways pathogens can spread? _____

_____

24. How do governments and organizations respond to emerging diseases?

_____

_____

_____

23. From one person to another, from drinking contaminated water, through a tick or mosquito bite **24.** Monitor world health events, identify emerging diseases, post the information on the World Wide Web, develop and apply disease prevention and control measures, develop vaccines

9.3 Toxic Substances in the Environment

Key Concepts

- All chemicals can be hazardous in large enough quantities.
- Chemical hazards can cause cancer, birth defects, and improper functioning of human body systems.
- Our homes and buildings may contain chemical hazards including asbestos, radon, volatile organic compounds, carbon monoxide, and lead.
- There are chemical hazards in the air, on land, and in the water.
- Toxic chemicals accumulate in organisms as they feed on one another.

 SKILL BUILDER Vocabulary Preview

Define each vocabulary term in your own words. Then, write yourself a quick note on how you will remember each. One term has been done for you.

Term	Definition	How I Remember
Pollution		
Carcinogen		
Teratogen		
Neurotoxin	A chemical that harms the nervous system	*Neuro* refers to the *nervous* system. A *toxin* is something harmful.
Asbestos		
Radon		
Bioaccumulation		
Biomagnification		

Chemical Hazards

1. Define "chemical hazard."

_____

2. What is pollution?

_____

_____

3. Are chemical hazards and pollutants the same thing? Why or why not? Explain.

_____

_____

_____

Types of Chemical Hazards

4. Complete the following paragraph with terms from the word bank.

carcinogens	neurotoxins	teratogen

Chemical hazards affect human health in different ways. Some heavy metals act as _____ that can cause slurred speech or loss of muscle control. Chemicals that cause cancer are known as _____ . Some chemicals that do not harm adults are still hazards if they affect the development of human embryos. This type of chemical hazard is known as a _____ .

5. Why are carcinogens difficult for toxicologists to identify?

_____

_____

6. Explain what a mutagen is and describe possible effects.

_____

_____

_____

7. Describe some common allergens and explain how they harm people.

_____

_____

_____

8. What is an endocrine disruptor?

_____

_____

_____

Indoor Chemical Hazards

For Questions 9–13, match each term with the statement that best describes it.

_____ **9.** asbestos

_____ **10.** carbon monoxide

_____ **11.** lead

_____ **12.** radon

_____ **13.** VOCs

a. a gas that can cause headaches, dizziness, fatigue, and eventually death

b. can be in air, water, soil, paint, or dust and damages organs of the body

c. used for insulation, can cause cancer

d. contain carbon and are released into the air by products such as plastics

e. a colorless, odorless radioactive gas that is released from soil and can cause cancer

14. Explain why you should not tear down asbestos and simply throw it away if you find it in your home.

_____

_____

15. List three types of tests you could do at your house to protect against chemical hazards.

_____

_____

Outdoor Chemical Hazards

16. Explain why citizens of one town might need to be concerned with the chemical hazards in the air of a town many miles away.

_____

_____

17. Describe how chemical hazards can get into soil and some of the ways that they can cause harm to humans.

_____

_____

_____

18. The fish in a stream running by a small town are dying in large numbers. Why might chemical hazards be suspected?

_____

_____

Biomagnification

19. **Think Visually** In each arrow, write one way that a chemical such as DDT can get into waterways. In each block, add dots to represent levels of chemical concentrations and how they change due to biomagnification.

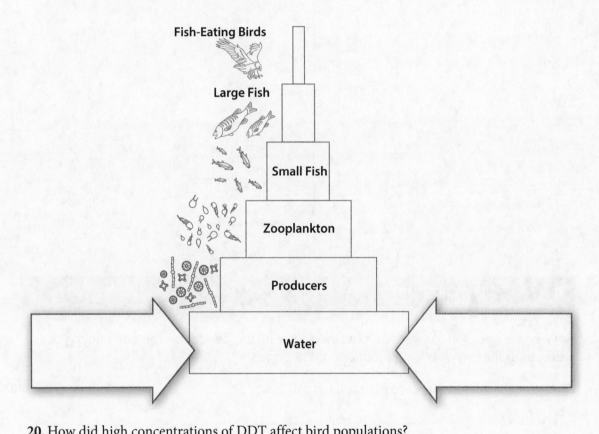

20. How did high concentrations of DDT affect bird populations?

_____

_____

_____

21. Explain why a persistent organic pollutant (POP) is a problem that is often handled by international agreements or treaties.

_____

_____

_____

SKILL BUILDER Organize Information

22. Complete the T-chart by writing in details and examples of indoor chemical hazards and outdoor chemical hazards.

Indoor Chemical Hazards	Outdoor Chemical Hazards

9.3 ◯ SELF-CHECK

Answer the questions to test your knowledge of lesson concepts. You can check your work using the answers on the bottom of the page.

23. Define the different types of chemical hazards. _____

_____

_____

_____

24. What is biomagnification? _____

_____

_____

23. Carcinogens cause cancer; chemical mutagens cause genetic changes; teratogens harm embryos and fetuses; neurotoxins affect the nervous system; allergens cause an immune response; endocrine disruptors interfere with the hormone system. **24.** Biomagnification occurs as organisms feed on other organisms and toxic chemicals accumulate in their bodies. As the levels progress up the food chain, the concentrations of toxic chemicals increase.

9.4 Natural Disasters

Key Concepts

 The shaking that occurs during an earthquake can destroy natural landforms as well as human-made structures.

 The molten rock, gas, ash, and cinders released during a volcanic eruption can cause significant damage and loss of life in nearby cities and towns.

 Tornadoes, hurricanes, and thunderstorms are powerful weather events that can damage property and threaten human lives.

 An avalanche is a mass of sliding snow that can bury people and places in its path.

SKILL BUILDER Vocabulary Preview

Define each vocabulary term in your own words. Then, write yourself a quick note on how you will remember each. One term has been done for you.

Term	Definition	How I Remember
Earthquake		
Landslide		
Tsunami		
Volcano		
Tornado	A funnel of rotating air that drops down from a storm cloud	The word *twister* is another word for *tornado* and describes its action.
Hurricane		
Thunderstorm		
Avalanche		

Earthquakes

For Questions 1–5, complete each statement by writing the correct word or words.

1. Earthquakes are created when large sections of Earth's crust, called _____, move and energy is released.

2. Earthquakes can be strong enough to cause the ground to sink and soil to _____.

3. Earthquakes can trigger a(n) _____, causing rock and soil to slide down a slope.

4. When an earthquake occurs at the bottom of the ocean, it can create a(n) _____ that can cause massive damage and loss of life if it hits coastal areas.

5. Scientists cannot predict when earthquakes will occur, but in the United States, they occur most often in the states of _____ and _____.

6. Describe the series of events in Earth's crust that lead up to an earthquake.

   _____

   _____

   _____

Volcanoes

For Questions 7–9, write True *if the statement is true. If the statement is false, replace the underlined word or words to make the statement true. Write your changes on the line.*

_____ 7. Volcanoes are often located <u>near the edges</u> of tectonic plates.

_____ 8. A volcano can spew clouds of gas, ash, and cinders into the atmosphere, causing global temperatures to <u>rise</u>.

_____ 9. A volcanic eruption can also cause damage by triggering <u>landslides and mudflows</u>.

10. Describe how a volcanic eruption actually creates new rock layers on Earth's surface.

    _____

    _____

11. How can scientists help people prepare for a volcanic eruption?

    _____

    _____

    _____

Storms

For Questions 12–15, match each type of storm with the statement that best describes it.

_____**12.** storm surge

_____**13.** hurricane

_____**14.** thunderstorm

_____**15.** tornado

a. brings with it high winds, heavy rain, and a storm surge

b. a dome of water that crashes along the coast

c. can include lightning, heavy rain, and sometimes hail

d. takes the form of a funnel of rotating air

16. Describe the dangers of a tornado and explain what actions people should do to stay safe if a tornado is predicted.

_____

_____

_____

_____

17. Why was the damage to parts of Texas from Hurricane Harvey (2017) so extensive?

_____

_____

18. What are some ways to prepare for a hurricane?

_____

_____

Avalanches

19. Describe the conditions that cause an avalanche.

_____

_____

_____

_____

20. Describe some actions that a skier could take if he or she is caught in an avalanche.

_____

_____

_____

SKILL BUILDER Organize Information

21. Fill in the compare and contrast table with information concerning the characteristics of the different types of natural disasters.

	Earthquakes	Volcanoes	Storms	Avalanches
How they start				
Damage they cause				
Safety measures				

9.4 SELF-CHECK

Answer the questions to test your knowledge of lesson concepts. You can check your work using the answers on the bottom of the page.

22. How do earthquakes and volcanoes affect humans and Earth's surface? _____

_____

_____

_____

23. Describe the different types of storms that can damage property and threaten human lives.

_____

_____

_____

22. Earthquakes can cause the earth to shake, the ground to sink, and soil to liquefy. They can also trigger landslides and tsunamis that can destroy structures and kill people. Volcanoes erupt molten lava, ash, gas, and cinders that can cover large areas of land where people lived and farmed. Eruptions also set off dangerous mudflows and fill valleys with thick deposits of ash. They also add layers of rock to Earth's surface. 23. Tornadoes are windstorms in the form of funnels of rotating air. Hurricanes are powerful storms that form over the ocean and can come ashore with very high winds and storm surges. Thunderstorms produce lightning and thunder and sometimes hail.

Chapter Vocabulary Review

Complete the crossword puzzle using the correct vocabulary terms.

Across

1. Disease-causing agent
6. The process of magnifying the concentrations of toxins, with each step up the food chain
8. Amount of substance an organism is exposed to
9. Odorless gas that causes cancer
10. Factor that threatens human health
11. Disease appearing for the first time

Down

2. Forms over tropical oceans
3. How harmful a substance is
4. When Earth shakes due to movement of tectonic plates
5. Describes diseases caused by a pathogen
7. Substance that harms a fetus

EXTENSION On a separate sheet of paper, write a paragraph that correctly uses five or more vocabulary terms from the chapter.

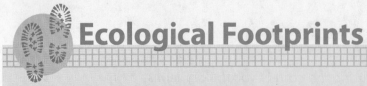

Annual Pesticide Use

In this activity, you will apply population and pesticide usage data to make inferences about the average pesticide use per person.

Organizing Data in a Table

First, read the information below and organize the data in a table.

> In 2001, the population of the United States was about 285 million (0.285 billion). The world's population was about 6.1 billion. At the same time, annual pesticide use in the United States was around 1.20 billion pounds. World pesticide use was around 5.05 billion pounds.

1. What two categories of data are being described?

_____

2. In 2001, what was the U.S. population and the world population (in billions of people)? What were the amounts of annual pesticide use in each? Write your answers in the table.

Region	Population (billions of people)	Annual Pesticide Use (billions of pounds)
United States		
World		

Finding Pesticide Use Per Person

▶ The calculation for finding the annual pesticide use per person in the United States is modeled below:

$$\text{pesticide use per person in the United States} = \frac{\text{annual pesticide use in United States}}{\text{population of United States}}$$

$$= \frac{1.20 \text{ billion pounds}}{0.285 \text{ billion people}}$$

$$\approx 4.21 \text{ pounds/person}$$

A person in the United States uses about 4 pounds of pesticide per year.

3. Follow the model above to calculate the world's average annual pesticide use in pounds per person.

_____

The Rise and Fall of DDT

Malaria and Climate in Africa

The map on the left shows the general climate of the nations within Africa. Using the information below the maps, color in the nations on the map on the right according to the level of malaria found there. Use one color for nations where malaria is currently a problem. Use a second color for nations that have had problems in the past. Use a third color for nations that are malaria-free. Be sure to make a key identifying which category each color represents.

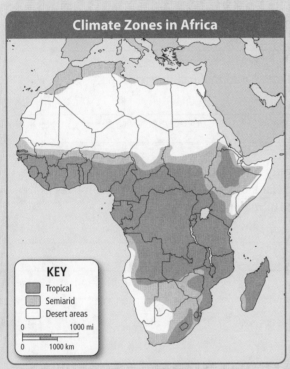

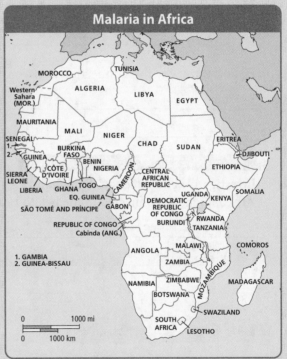

Adapted from World Wildlife Fund, Terrestrial Ecoregions

Malaria Status	Nations
Active malaria transmission	Angola, Benin, Burkina Faso, Cameroon, Chad (south), Congo, Central African Republic, Democratic Republic of Congo, Equatorial Guinea, Eritrea, Ethiopia, Gabon, Gambia, Ghana, Guinea, Guinea Bissau, Ivory Coast, Liberia, Madagascar, Malawi, Mozambique, Nigeria, Rwanda Burundi, Senegal, Sierra Leone, Somalia, Sudan (south), Tanzania, Togo, Uganda, Zambia, Zimbabwe
Past malaria problems have been eliminated	Botswana, Namibia
Malaria-free	Algeria, Chad (north), Egypt, Libya, Mali, Mauritania, Morocco, Niger, South Africa, Sudan (north), Tunisia, Western Sahara

Use the information from **Malaria and Climate in Africa** to answer the questions below.

1. Can you identify any pattern in the map you created of malaria incidence level?

   _____

   _____

2. Compare your map to the map of different climates. What difference or similarities do you see?

   _____

3. Infer what influence climate has on the presence or absence of malaria in a particular nation.

   _____

   _____

   _____

4. Hypothesize why this connection between climate and malaria may exist.

   _____

   _____

5. **REVISIT** **INVESTIGATIVE** PHENOMENON Apply the information about climate to the **Investigative Phenomenon.** Explain how a social factor such as where a person lives in Africa might be connected to the health risks of malaria.

   _____

   _____

   _____

21st Century Skills

Find out more about the debate on using DDT to combat malaria. Work in small groups to research the opinions presented by organizations such as the World Health Organization (WHO) and the Malaria Foundation International. Then, research opinions by the Pesticide Action Network North America (PANNA). How are the different sides of this issue expressed by these organizations? Write a paragraph explaining which opinions you agree and disagree with, as well as the course of action you support.

*The 21st Century Skills used in this activity include **Critical Thinking and Problem Solving, Information Literacy, Media Literacy, Social and Cross-Cultural Skills,** and **Leadership and Responsibility.***

10 Urbanization

Before you read the chapter, answer each question with information you know. After you complete the chapter, re-answer the questions using information you learned.

INVESTIGATIVE PHENOMENON **How can we balance the ways we use land with the needs of the environment?**

	What I Know	What I Learned
10.1 How do we use the land we live on?		
10.2 How can the effects of urbanization lead to sprawl?		
10.3 What are the characteristics of a sustainable city?		

10.1 Land Use and Urbanization

Key Concepts

- Land cover influences land use, and humans change both when they build urban areas.
- Urbanization occurs when people move out of rural areas toward areas with more or better jobs.
- Cities have both negative and positive impacts on the environment.

SKILL BUILDER Vocabulary Preview

Define each vocabulary term in your own words. Then, write yourself a quick note on how you will remember each. One term has been done for you.

Term	Definition	How I Remember
Land cover		
Land use		
Urban area		
Rural area		
Urbanization		
Infrastructure	The facilities, services, and installations necessary for the functioning of a community	*Structures,* such as schools, bridges, and water towers, are an important part of *infrastructure.*
Heat island		

Land Cover and Land Use

For Questions 1–4, circle the letter of the correct answer.

1. The vast grasslands that once covered the middle of North America have mainly been replaced by
   A. forest land.
   B. urban areas.
   C. parks and preserves.
   D. rangeland and cropland.

2. In which of the following categories of land cover would you most likely expect to find the highest human population?
   A. cropland
   B. rangeland
   C. urban areas
   D. rural areas

3. Cities and suburbs are examples of
   A. cropland.
   B. rangeland.
   C. rural areas.
   D. urban areas.

4. Which of the following statements is true about land cover?
   A. Land cover refers to human activities that take place on the land.
   B. Land cover is independent of land use.
   C. Land cover changes as people settle into an area.
   D. Land cover remains the same as people settle into an area.

5. Name at least three examples of land cover types that the U.S. Geological Survey researches.

   _____

   _____

6. Explain how land cover is related to land use.

   _____

   _____

7. How do scientists assess changes in land cover and land use?

   _____

   _____

   _____

   _____

Urbanization

8. Describe how the Industrial Revolution affected urbanization.

_____

_____

_____

_____

9. What are some factors that would promote the growth of a town into a large city?

_____

_____

Urban Environmental Impacts

For Questions 10–14, write True *if the statement is true. If the statement is false, replace the underlined word or words to make the statement true. Write your changes on the line.*

_____ **10.** <u>Light pollution</u> describes the way that city lights brighten the night sky, obscuring the stars and planets.

_____ **11.** The environmental and health impacts of pollution are shared <u>evenly</u> among urban residents.

_____ **12.** The poor typically live <u>upstream</u> from polluting facilities.

_____ **13.** Cities must <u>export</u> almost all of the resources used by their residents.

_____ **14.** The ecological footprints of cities are <u>smaller</u> than their actual land areas.

15. Explain why a city's residents might not realize how much garbage their city produces.

_____

_____

_____

_____

16. Explain how a city's infrastructure can lead to the formation of a heat island.

_____

_____

_____

_____

SKILL BUILDER Organize Information

17. Fill in the spider map to describe urbanization and how it impacts the environment.

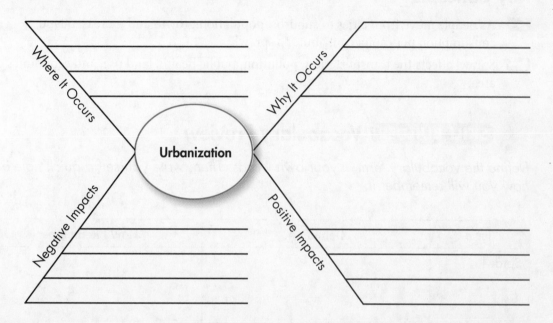

10.1 ⊙ SELF-CHECK

Answer the questions to test your knowledge of lesson concepts. You can check your work using the answers on the bottom of the page.

18. Contrast urban areas and rural areas by describing how people use each.

_____

_____

19. Is the U.S. population is becoming more or less urbanized over time? Explain.

_____

_____

20. Relate the high population density of cities to the efficiency with which resources can be distributed within the city.

_____

_____

18. Sample answer: More people live and work in urban areas. Rural areas are used for farming, recreation, and preservation of natural areas. **19.** Sample answer: The U.S. population is becoming more urbanized over time because currently 80 percent of the population is urban, compared to 65 percent in 1950. **20.** Less fossil fuel is needed to deliver resources and goods to people living close together than to sparsely populated areas.

10.2 Sprawl

Key Concepts

 As people move from cities to suburbs, population growth and increased land consumption per capita contribute to sprawl.

As people move from cities to suburbs, population growth and increased land
consumption per capita contribute to sprawl.

Sprawl affects the transportation, pollution, public health, land use, and economics of an area.

SKILL BUILDER **Vocabulary Preview**

Define the vocabulary term in your own words. Then, write yourself a quick note on how you will remember it.

Term	Definition	How I Remember
Sprawl		

 SKILL BUILDER **Reading Strategy**

Before you read the lesson, fill in the first column of the KWL chart below with what you already know about sprawl, how it occurs, and its impacts. Fill in the second column with what you want to know about these topics. After you have read the lesson, fill in the third column with what you have learned.

I Know	I Want to Know	I Learned

How Sprawl Occurs

1. **Organize Information** Fill in the table with a description of each pattern of sprawl.

Pattern of Sprawl	Description
Uncentered commercial (strip) development	
Low-density single-use residential development	
Scattered (leapfrog) development	
Sparse street network	

2. Describe one negative and one positive viewpoint of sprawl.

_____

_____

_____

3. What are the two major contributors to sprawl?

_____

_____

4. How is the degree of sprawl determined?

_____

_____

5. What is meant by *per capita land consumption*?

_____

_____

6. Why has per capita land consumption increased?

_____

_____

_____

Impacts of Sprawl

7. Why does sprawl tend to result in greater use of fossil fuels?

_____

_____

_____

8. How does sprawl affect public health?

_____

_____

_____

_____

9. How does the spread of low-density development affect agricultural land and forests?

_____

_____

_____

_____

10. Explain how city centers are affected economically when people move out into the sprawling communities.

_____

_____

_____

_____

_____

11. Complete the following paragraph with terms from the word bank.

carbon dioxide	climate change	ecosystems	fossil fuel	transportation

The impacts of sprawl on _____ and pollution are related. Because people in sprawling communities drive more due to limited public transportation options, they use more _____. _____ emissions from vehicles increase, contributing to air pollution and global _____. Transportation-related pollution also includes motor oil and road salt runoff from roads and parking lots. This runoff contaminates waterways, which poses risks to _____ and human health.

10.2 SELF-CHECK

Answer the questions to test your knowledge of lesson concepts. You can check your work using the answers on the bottom of the page.

12. Identify two factors that encouraged the growth of the suburbs in the mid-1900s.

_____

_____

13. What are three reasons why per capita land consumption has increased?

_____

_____

_____

14. Some people think all growth is good growth. Others believe growth is a problem because it leads to the problems of sprawl. Use what you have read in this lesson to develop a well-supported opinion of sprawl. Support your opinion with at least one fact from the lesson that supports your opinion.

_____

_____

_____

_____

12. Sample answer: Cars became more affordable and highways were improved. **13.** Sample answer: Most people like having more space and privacy; highways and the Internet have freed businesses from dependence on a centralized infrastructure; and workers have greater flexibility to live farther from their jobs due to telecommuting and highways. **14.** Accept all well-supported opinions. Sample answer: Sprawl is a problem because it results in increased use of automobiles. This in turn leads to increased pollution and poor health.

Real Data

Population Density and Carbon Emissions

The graph at the right shows the population densities and carbon emissions from transportation for seven cities.

In this activity, you will describe the relationship between the two sets of data. You will then apply this relationship to predict how a change in sprawl would affect carbon emissions from transportation.

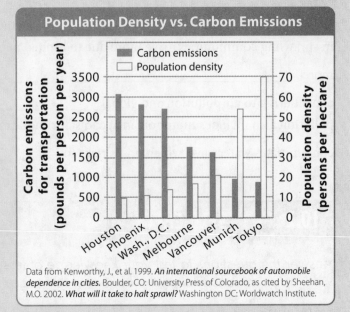

Population Density vs. Carbon Emissions

Data from Kenworthy, J., et al. 1999. *An international sourcebook of automobile dependence in cities.* Boulder, CO: University Press of Colorado, as cited by Sheehan, M.O. 2002. *What will it take to halt sprawl?* Washington DC: Worldwatch Institute.

Interpreting the Graph

To make predictions using the graph, first interpret the graph and describe the relationship that exists between the two sets of data.

1. Explain why the graph has two vertical axes. What do the axes represent?

_____

_____

_____

2. Which city has the lowest population density (i.e., the most sprawl)? Which city has the highest amount of carbon emissions for transportation? _____

3. In general, how is carbon emissions per person affected as population density increases?

_____

Making Predictions

4. As people move from the city to the suburbs, sprawl increases. Suppose Houston passes laws limiting sprawl causing the city's population density to double. Use the relationship shown in the graph to predict how carbon emissions per person would change for Houston. Explain your reasoning.

_____

_____

_____

10.3 Sustainable Cities

Key Concepts

- City planners use many tools in the attempt to make urban areas more livable.
- Transportation options are vital to livable cities.
- Parks and open space are key elements of livable cities.
- The goal of a green building is to save energy and other resources without sacrificing people's comfort.
- There has been promising progress toward urban sustainability.

 SKILL BUILDER **Vocabulary Preview**

Define each vocabulary term in your own words. Then, write yourself a quick note on how you will remember each. One term has been done for you.

Term	Definition	How I Remember
City planning		
Geographic information system (GIS)		
Zoning		
Urban growth boundary (UGB)		
Smart growth	A philosophy of urban growth that focuses on economic and environmental approaches that lead to sustainable growth and the avoidance of sprawl	*Smart growth* starts with an *S,* which makes me think of *sustainable,* which also starts with an *S.*

Term	Definition	How I Remember
Ecological restoration		
Greenway		

City Planning

1. Complete the following paragraph with terms from the word bank.

> **city planning**   **geographic information system (GIS)**
> **smart growth**   **urban growth boundary (UGB)**   **zoning**

The process of designing urban areas to make them livable is called _____.

_____, a philosophy used to manage the spread of urban areas, guides this

process. This philosophy can lead to the establishment of a _____, which limits

the spread of urban areas. City planners use many tools, for example _____,

that allow data to be manipulated on computers. Decisions made about land use must be put

into practice to be effective. City planners use _____ to put decisions into use.

2. Describe the type of zoning typically seen in urban environments.

_____

_____

3. What do all urban growth boundaries have in common? Explain.

_____

_____

4. What philosophy of urban growth requires building up, not out?

_____

5. Describe *new urbanism*.

_____

_____

_____

Transportation Options

6. List three examples of mass transit options in livable cities.

_____

7. Describe at least two examples of advantages of mass transit over automobile use.

_____

_____

8. What are some ways city governments encourage the use of mass transit?

_____

_____

_____

Open Space

9. Identify two ecological processes that are positively affected by the presence of parks and open space in urban areas.

_____

10. **Organize Information** Fill in the cluster diagram with examples of open space in a city.

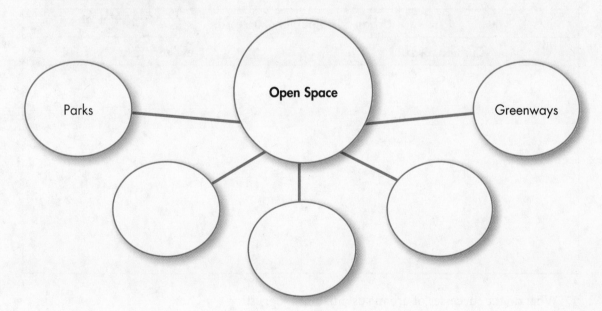

11. Describe how greenways are valuable to humans and to wildlife.

_____

_____

Green Building Design

12. What is a another term for *green building design*?

_____

13. What is the goal of green building design?

_____

_____

14. In what types of buildings has green building design been successful?

_____

_____

15. List three features that might be included in a green building.

_____

_____

Urban Sustainability Successes

16. **Organize Information** Fill in the chart with short descriptions of how each location has made progress toward urban sustainability.

Urban Sustainability Successes	
Curitiba, Brazil	**New York City**

17. What do the successes of urban sustainability suggest?

_____

_____

_____

_____

SKILL BUILDER Organize Information

18. Fill in the concept map with terms from the word bank.

city planning	ecological restoration	geographic information system (GIS)
mass transit	open spaces	urban growth boundary (UGB)	zoning

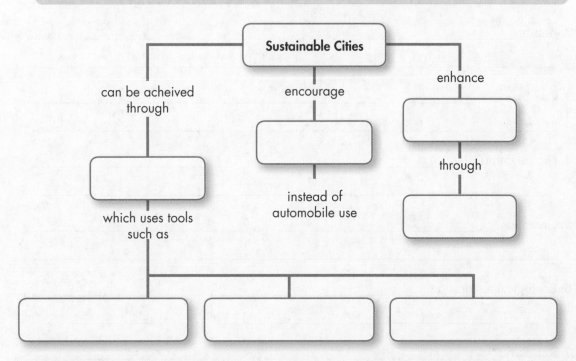

Sustainable Cities

can be acheived through

encourage

enhance

instead of automobile use

through

which uses tools such as

EXTENSION Redraw this concept map on a separate sheet of paper. Show how the terms *smart growth* and *green building design* could logically be added to the concept map. Include boxes, arrows, and linking words as needed to add the new terms.

10.3 ⊙ SELF-CHECK

Answer the questions to test your knowledge of lesson concepts. You can check your work using the answers on the bottom of the page.

19. Describe the philosophy of smart growth. _____

_____

20. Identify one positive and one negative impact of zoning. _____

_____

_____

19. Sample answer: A philosophy of urban growth that focuses on economic and environmental approaches that leads to sustainable growth and avoidance of sprawl. 20. Sample answer: One positive impact of zoning is that it gives homeowners security in knowing what types of development can occur near their homes. One negative impact of zoning is its limitation on personal property rights when government restricts land use.

Chapter Vocabulary Review

Write a definition for each of the following terms.

1. Sprawl _____

_____

2. Zoning _____

_____

3. City planning _____

_____

4. Urbanization _____

_____

5. Greenway _____

_____

6. Ecological restoration _____

_____

7. Rural area _____

_____

Write a sentence that shows the relationship between the two terms.

8. Heat island, infrastructure _____

_____

_____

9. Land cover, land use _____

_____

10. Urban growth boundaries, smart growth _____

_____

EXTENSION On a separate sheet of paper, write a short paragraph describing the benefits of sustainable cities. Your paragraph should include at least one vocabulary term from each of the three lessons in the chapter. Underline each of the lesson vocabulary terms you use.

Growing Pains in Portland, Oregon

Portland's Urban Growth Boundary

Urban growth boundaries (UGB) are one tool used by city planners to help minimize sprawl and encourage sustainable cities. These boundaries are used to protect farmlands, forests, and natural ecosystems outside the boundaries by preventing growth in these areas. They also encourage strong cities by allowing transportation needs to be anticipated, encouraging shorter commute times, and preventing development from moving away from the downtown area.

Like all cities in Oregon, Portland has a UGB, which separates urban land from rural land. Portland's regional government, Metro (formerly known as the Metropolitan Service District), is responsible for managing the UGB. The Metro Council is required by the state legislature to have a 20-year supply of land available for future residential development within the boundary. It is also required by law to review the land supply every five years, and to expand the boundary if necessary to meet changing needs.

Portland's UGB includes more than just the city of Portland. The map below shows the areas included in the Portland UGB, as of May 2006. As you can see on the map, many smaller cities are encompassed in the UGB. In fact, more than 250,000 acres of land in three counties are included within the Portland UGB.

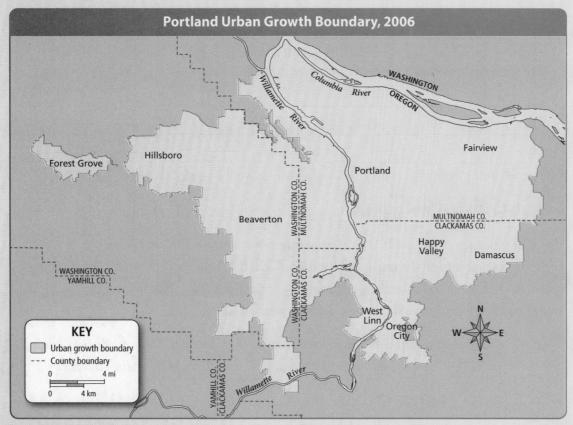

Portland Urban Growth Boundary, 2006

KEY
- Urban growth boundary
- County boundary

0 ___ 4 mi
0 ___ 4 km

© 2010 Metro Regional Government. All Rights Reserved.

Use the information in **Portland's Urban Growth Boundary** to answer the questions below.

1. Portland's urban growth boundary (UGB) currently includes land located in three counties. Name two cities in the Washington County portion of the urban growth boundary.

   _____

2. Identify the river that flows through the center of Portland's UGB.

   _____

3. Portland's UGB was first established in 1979, and has been adjusted in the years following. In 2002, its lines were redrawn to include a large parcel of land south of the Multnomah–Clackamas county line, which included the cities of Damascus and Happy Valley. Place an X on the map to indicate where the 2002 addition to the UGB occurred.

4. If the population living within Portland's UGB grows more rapidly than the UGB around Portland expands, how would the per capita land consumption need to change to accommodate the new residents? Explain.

   _____

   _____

   _____

5. **REVISIT INVESTIGATIVE** PHENOMENON Use the information shown in the map and provided in the activity to explain how UGBs can help people balance their needs for housing and jobs with the needs of the environment.

   _____

   _____

   _____

21st Century Skills

Find out more about Portland's UGB. Using Internet resources, find articles expressing a variety of viewpoints on the impacts of Portland's UGB. Working with a small group, choose two articles to evaluate. Determine whether or not the opinions expressed in the articles are well supported with factual information. Share your group's findings with the class.

*The 21st Century Skills used in this activity include **Information, Communication, and Technology (ICT) Literacy, Communication and Collaboration,** and **Media Literacy.***

11 Forestry and Resource Management

Before you read the chapter, answer each question with information you know. After you complete the chapter, re-answer the questions using information you learned.

INVESTIGATIVE PHENOMENON **Why is it important to manage Earth's resources sustainably?**

What I Know	What I Learned

11.1 How can we manage renewable resources for sustainable use?

11.2 Is there a balance between the ecological and economic values of forest resources?

11.3 What challenges does sustainable forestry face?

11.1 Resource Management

Key Concepts

 People need to manage the harvesting of renewable resources in order to ensure their availability.

 Maximum sustainable yield, ecosystem-based management, and adaptive management are three approaches to resource management.

SKILL BUILDER Vocabulary Preview

Define each vocabulary term in your own words. Then, write yourself a quick note on how you will remember each. One term has been done for you.

Term	Definition	How I Remember
Resource management		
Maximum sustainable yield (MSY)	The largest amount of a resource that can be used without long-term damage to the resource	I remember that this practice is meant to *maximize* harvest and *minimize* damage.
Ecosystem-based management		
Adaptive management		

Renewable Resource Management

1. What are four examples of renewable resources?

_____

2. Why must renewable resources be managed?

_____

_____

_____

3. How do resource managers base their decisions on resource management? Explain.

_____

_____

_____

_____

4. Explain the importance of maintaining healthy topsoil.

_____

_____

_____

5. How are soil and fresh water resources dependent on each other?

_____

_____

_____

6. What is the difference between game and nongame species?

_____

7. What types of wildlife are targeted by poachers?

_____

_____

8. Why is timber so important to people?

_____

_____

Management Approaches

9. **Organize Information** Fill in the table with information about three common approaches to types of renewable resource management.

Maximum Sustainable Yield	Ecosystem-Based Management	Adaptive Management

10. Explain how managing a population using the maximum sustainable yield approach can change the whole ecosystem?

_____

_____

_____

11. What is the focus of ecosystem-based management?

_____

_____

12. What is one drawback to ecosystem-based management?

_____

13. Which management approach can be considered a cyclical process in which practices are constantly being adjusted based on new information?

_____

14. Why is adaptive management considered a union between science and management?

_____

_____

_____

SKILL BUILDER **Organize Information**

15. Fill in the cluster diagram on resource management.

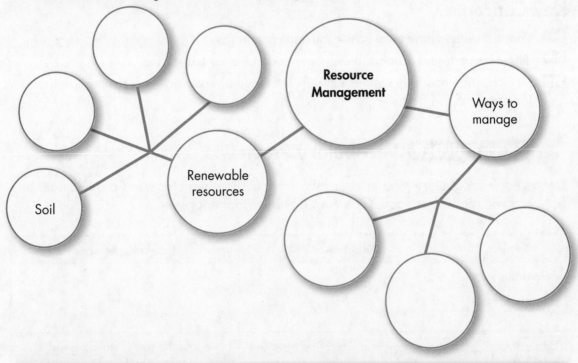

11.1 ⬤ SELF-CHECK

Answer the questions to test your knowledge of lesson concepts. You can check your work using the answers on the bottom of the page.

16. In addition to scientific research, name at least two factors that influence resource

management decisions. _____

17. Why might a resource manager choose to focus on an entire ecosystem and not just on a

particular resource? _____

_____

18. What are three main resource management approaches? _____

_____

19. What is one benefit and one drawback of adaptive management?

_____

_____

16. Sample answer: Politics, economics, social issues **17.** Managing an entire ecosystem can help maintain the ecological processes of which the resource is a part, promoting long-term protection of the resource **18.** Maximum sustainable yield, ecosystem-based management, adaptive management **19.** Benefit: It is informed by scientific research; drawback: It is time-consuming and complicated.

11.2 Forests and Their Resources

Key Concepts

- Forest resources have great ecological and economic value.
- There are costs and benefits to every method of timber harvesting.
- Deforestation may help nations develop, but it can be ecologically destructive in the long run.

 SKILL BUILDER Vocabulary Preview

Define each vocabulary term in your own words. Then, write yourself a quick note on how you will remember each. One term has been done for you.

Term	Definition	How I Remember
Even-aged		
Uneven-aged	Forest regrowth in which the trees are different ages; occurs after selective logging	I imagine the trees "standing up" unevenly, at all different heights because they are at different ages.
Clear-cutting		
Seed-tree approach		
Shelterwood approach		
Selection system		
Deforestation		
Old-growth forest		

Forest Resources

1. Complete the following paragraph with terms from the word bank.

climate	economic	erosion	habitats

Forests provide many different _____ for plants and animals. Forests provide many ecosystem services, such as slowing runoff, minimizing flooding, and preventing soil _____. Forest plants help to moderate the _____ by storing carbon and releasing oxygen. Forests also have _____ value, providing wood for shelter, fuel, and many products that people use daily.

2. Name at least two products, besides timber and paper, that come from forest resources.

_____

3. Forest *X* has some of the country's oldest trees and has never been logged. Forest *Y* was planted around 30 years ago. In which of the two forests would you expect to find greater biodiversity? Explain.

_____

_____

Timber Harvesting

4. Which type of regrowth harbors greater biodiversity—uneven-aged or even-aged regrowth? Explain.

_____

_____

5. What do most logging methods have in common?

_____

_____

_____

6. Which logging method has the greatest impact on forest ecosystems? Explain.

_____

_____

_____

_____

7. **Organize Information** Fill in the concept map with terms from the word bank.

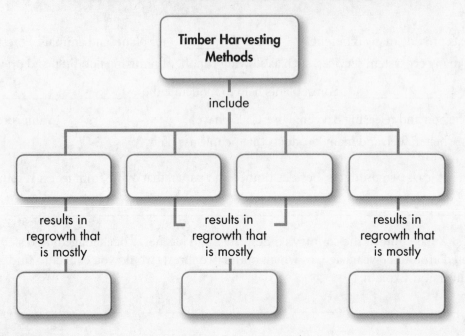

clear-cutting   even-aged   seed-tree approach

selection system   shelterwood approach   uneven-aged

Timber Harvesting Methods

include

results in regrowth that is mostly

results in regrowth that is mostly

results in regrowth that is mostly

Deforestation

8. What are the costs and benefits of deforestation?

_____

_____

_____

9. How does deforestation add carbon dioxide to the atmosphere?

_____

_____

_____

10. How has deforestation shaped the landscape of the United States?

_____

_____

_____

11. What has allowed developing nations today to exploit their resources faster than the

United States did? _____

SKILL BUILDER Organize Information

12. Complete the Venn diagram below comparing timber harvesting and deforestation. Write details about each in the circles. Where the circles overlap, write characteristics that the concepts share.

Timber Harvesting   **Deforestation**

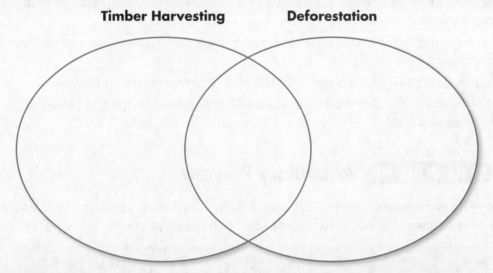

EXTENSION Choose a third concept to add to the Venn diagram. Add a third circle and label it with the name of the concept. Then, fill in the characteristics of the new concept and the characteristics that the new concept shares with one or both of the other concepts.

11.2 ⦿ SELF-CHECK

Answer the questions to test your knowledge of lesson concepts. You can check your work using the answers on the bottom of the page.

13. Name at least one way that forests are economically valuable and one way that they are ecologically valuable. _____

_____

_____

14. Describe the costs and benefits of clear-cutting. _____

_____

_____

15. Why is there so little old-growth forest in the United States today? _____

_____

_____

13. Economically valuable: timber, fuel, paper, medicine, food; **ecologically valuable:** provide habitat for many organisms, prevent soil erosion, help regulate the water cycle, moderate climate **14.** Clear-cutting is extremely disruptive to ecosystems, but it is cost-efficient for timber removal. **15.** Most old-growth forest in the United States was cut down for timber, farmland, and to fuel the Industrial Revolution.

11.3 Forest Management

Key Concepts

- Logging in national forests is managed by the Forest Service, but profits go to timber companies.
- Most logging in the United States today takes place on tree plantations owned by timber companies.
- Suppression of all wildfires can endanger ecosystems, property, and people.
- The response of timber companies to consumer demand is helping to promote sustainable forestry.

 SKILL BUILDER **Vocabulary Preview**

Define each vocabulary term in your own words. Then, write yourself a quick note on how you will remember each. One term has been done for you.

Term	Definition	How I Remember
Multiple use		
Monoculture	A large planting of just one kind of crop	The prefix *mono–* means "one," so a *monoculture* is a planting of just one type of crop.
Prescribed burn		
Salvage logging		
Sustainable forestry certification		

SKILL BUILDER Reading Strategy

As you read the lesson, take notes on key terms and concepts covered under the headings. Make an outline and summarize lesson concepts in the chart below.

Key Words	Outline

Summary

U.S. National Forests

1. What is the role of the Forest Service? What controversy surrounds its practices?

_____

_____

_____

_____

_____

2. Describe the policy of multiple use that guides national forest management.

_____

_____

3. Describe the effect the passage of the National Forest Management Act in 1976 had on the trend in logging between the 1980s and early 2000s.

_____

_____

_____

Private Land

4. Where are monocultures in the United States typically located?

_____

5. Why do most ecologists and foresters consider tree plantations to be more like cropland than forestland?

_____

_____

6. How can plantations be managed so that they are more similar to natural forests?

_____

Fire Policies

7. **Organize Information** Fill in the cause-and-effect diagram with information about the effects of prescribed burns.

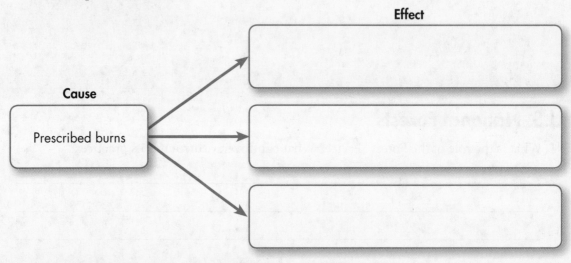

8. What results from the suppression of small, natural fires?

_____

_____

9. Describe how the Kirtland's warbler depends on fire for survival.

_____

_____

10. Do prescribed burns threaten property? Explain.

_____

_____

Sustainable Forestry Products

11. How can consumers be assured of a timber company's sustainable practices?

_____

_____

12. **Organize Information** Fill in the cluster diagram about sustainable forest products. Continue adding circles and writing in facts and details.

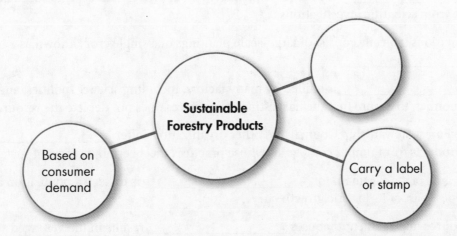

11.3 ● SELF-CHECK

Answer the questions to test your knowledge of lesson concepts. You can check your work using the answers on the bottom of the page.

13. What were the main requirements of the National Forest Management Act?

_____

_____

14. Where does most logging in the United States occur? _____

_____

15. How does fire suppression affect ecosystems? _____

_____

_____

13. The development of plans for management of renewable resources within national forests 14. On private land owned by timber companies 15. Suppression of natural wildfires harms ecosystems that depend on fire and leads to a buildup of fuel.

Chapter Vocabulary Review

Complete each statement by writing the correct word or words.

1. The practice of _____ was promoted by the 2003 Healthy Forests Restoration Act.

2. The seed-tree approach and the _____ are less harmful to forest communities than clear-cutting, but still result in mostly even-aged regrowth.

3. _____ is a resource management approach that is customized based on data from scientific investigations.

4. Plantations typically consist of large-scale plantings of a single crop, known as _____.

5. _____ is guided by many factors, including science, politics, and economics, to ensure that the harvesting of resources does not deplete the resources.

6. The Forest Stewardship Council and other organizations offer _____ to products from timber companies whose practices meet certain criteria of sustainability.

7. The goal of management for _____ is to keep a population at the steepest part of its logistic growth curve.

8. Resource management that uses _____ results in uneven-aged stands of regrown trees.

9. _____ stands result from the regrowth of trees that were harvested by clear-cutting.

10. Due to _____ in the late 1800s and early 1900s, very little old-growth forest remains in the United States.

Use each vocabulary term in a sentence.

11. clear-cutting _____

_____

12. prescribed burn _____

_____

13. sustainable foresty certification _____

_____

EXTENSION On a separate sheet of paper, write a paragraph about timber harvesting in the United States. Your paragraph should include at least one vocabulary term from each of the three lessons in the chapter. Underline each of the lesson vocabulary terms you use.

Ecological Footprints

Global Paper Consumption

In this activity, you will use the graph at right to estimate paper consumption in different regions of the world. You will then use this information to determine the amount of paper consumed per person in each region.

Estimating Paper Consumption

The x-axis of the graph shows six different regions of the world. For each region, shaded bars show paper consumption at four different time points. The last bar of each set represents the year 2000.

▶ To estimate paper consumption in 2000, draw an imaginary line from the top of the last bar in each set over to the y-axis. Estimate the number where this line intersects the y-axis.

▶ The estimation of paper consumption for Asia in the year 2000 is shown on the graph.

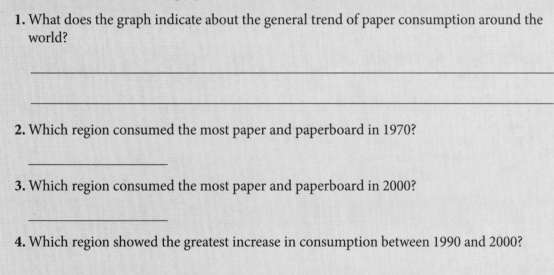

Global Consumption of Paper and Paperboard 1970–2000

Millions of tons of paper and paperboard consumed

Continent

Data from the Food and Agriculture Organization of the United Nations

Use the information in the graph to answer each question.

1. What does the graph indicate about the general trend of paper consumption around the world?

   _____

   _____

2. Which region consumed the most paper and paperboard in 1970?

   _____

3. Which region consumed the most paper and paperboard in 2000?

   _____

4. Which region showed the greatest increase in consumption between 1990 and 2000?

   _____

5. Fill in your estimates for Asia, Europe, and Latin America in the table on the next page. Check your estimates by summing the totals for paper consumed in the six regions, which should equal the world consumption, 351 million tons.

Region	Population In 2000 (millions)	Total Paper Consumed In 2000 (millions of tons)	Paper Consumed Per Person In 2000 (pounds)
Africa	840	6	14
Asia	3766		
Europe	728		
Latin America	531		
North America	319	108	658
Oceania	32	5	
World	6216	351	113

Source: Population Reference Bureau

Calculating Paper Consumed Per Person

To calculate the amount of paper consumer per person, convert the units for total paper consumed from millions of tons to pounds (lb). Then, divide this number by the population.

1 ton = 2000 lb

1 million = 1,000,000

▶ To calculate the pounds of paper consumed per person in Africa in the year 2000, use the steps shown below:

Step 1	Convert the amount of paper from millions of tons to tons.	**6 million tons = 6,000,000 tons**
Step 2	Convert the result from tons to pounds.	$6{,}000{,}000 \text{ tons} \times \dfrac{2000 \text{ lb}}{\text{ton}} = 12{,}000{,}000{,}000 \text{ lbs}$
Step 3	Write out the number of people.	**840 million people = 840,000,000 people**
Step 4	Divide the number of pounds by the number of people. Round to the nearest tenth.	$\dfrac{12{,}000{,}000{,}000 \text{ lb}}{840{,}000{,}000 \text{ people}} = \dfrac{14.3 \text{ lb}}{\text{person}}$

6. Follow this process to calculate the amount of paper consumed per person for Asia, Europe, Latin America, and Oceania for the year 2000. Write your answers in the table.

Battling Over Clayoquot's Big Trees

UNESCO Biosphere Reserves

United Nations Educational, Scientific, and Cultural Organization (UNESCO) Biosphere Reserves are intended to promote the sustainable harvest of resources while protecting ecosystem integrity. Biosphere Reserves are divided into three zones: core protected, buffer, and transition. Resources cannot be harvested in the core protected areas of the reserve. Resources can be harvested in limited amounts in buffer zones. More active resource use and human activity are allowed in the transition zones.

Clayoquot Sound became a UNESCO Biosphere Reserve in 2000. The Reserve covers nearly 350,000 hectares of Vancouver Island, British Columbia. Approximately 51 percent of the Reserve is designated as transition zone. Around 31 percent of the Reserve is core protected zone and just under 18 percent is buffer zone. In addition to old-growth temperate rain forest, the Reserve includes a diversity of ecosystems in the area's wetlands, lakes, rivers, shorelines, near-shore ocean, and mountaintops. The map below shows the various zones of Clayoquot Sound and the villages within the Reserve.

©UNESCO

Use the information from **UNESCO Biosphere Reserves** to answer the questions below.

1. Locate the village of Esowista. In which type of zone is it located? _____

2. Identify the village that is not part of the biosphere. _____

3. Identify the part of Clayoquot Sound that contains the largest continuous transition area.

_____

4. Describe the types of activities you think might take place in transition areas.

_____

_____

5. Imagine you are a scientist providing advice on a possible expansion of the Clayoquot Sound Biosphere Reserve core area. Where would you suggest this expansion occur? Explain your answer.

_____

_____

_____

_____

6. **REVISIT** **INVESTIGATIVE** PHENOMENON How does the Clayoquot Sound UNESCO Biosphere Reserve help address the **Investigative Phenomenon:** "Why is it important to manage Earth's resources sustainably?"

_____

_____

_____

21st Century Skills

In small groups, use the Internet to learn more about UNESCO Biosphere Reserve sites. Then, select a natural area in your region that you think should be protected by a similar reserve. Make a map of your proposed core, buffer, and transition zones. On a separate sheet of paper, write a one-page explanation of your proposal.

*The 21st Century Skills used in this activity include **Creativity and Innovation, Critical Thinking and Problem Solving, Communication and Collaboration, Social and Cross-Cultural Skills,** and **Productivity and Accountability.***

12 Soil and Agriculture

Before you read the chapter, answer each question with information you know. After you complete the chapter, re-answer the questions using information you learned.

INVESTIGATIVE PHENOMENON **How can we balance our growing demand for food with our need to protect the environment?**

	What I Know	What I Learned
12.1 Why does it take so long for soil to form?		
12.2 How can erosion be both helpful and harmful to soil formation?		
12.3 What are the benefits and environmental consequences of industrial farming?		
12.4 How can we increase food production sustainably?		

12.1 Soil

Key Concepts

 Soil is a complex substance that forms through weathering, deposition, and decomposition.

 A soil profile consists of layers known as horizons.

 Soils can be classified by their color, texture, structure, and pH.

SKILL BUILDER Vocabulary Preview

Define each vocabulary term in your own words. Then, write yourself a quick note on how you will remember each. One term has been done for you.

Term	Definition	How I Remember
Soil		
Parent material	The base geological material in a particular location	Soil comes from parent material, like children come from *parents*.
Bedrock		
Weathering		
Soil horizon		
Soil profile		

Term	Definition	How I Remember
Clay		
Silt		
Sand		
Loam		

Soil Formation

1. Mineral matter and organic matter together make up about 50 percent of soil. What two substances make up the other 50 percent?

_____

_____

For Questions 2–4, write True *if the statement is true. If the statement is false, replace the underlined word or words to make the statement true. Write your changes on the line.*

_____ 2. <u>Parent material</u> is the base geological material from which soil is formed.

_____ 3. Weathering is often the <u>last</u> process in soil formation.

_____ 4. <u>Deposition</u> of formerly living things allows nutrients to be incorporated into soil.

Soil Horizons

5. Why is topsoil crucial for agriculture?

_____

_____

6. **Think Visually** Label the diagram with the name and a description of each soil horizon. The first one has been done for you.

O Horizon: Litter layer
Consists mostly of organic matter

A Horizon: _____
_____
_____

E Horizon: _____
_____
_____

B Horizon: _____
_____
_____

C Horizon: _____
_____
_____

R Horizon: _____
_____
_____

Soil Characteristics

For Questions 7 and 8, circle the letter of the correct answer.

7. Soil texture is based on
   A. fertility.
   B. particle size.
   C. acidity or alkalinity.
   D. the arrangement of soil particles.

8. The type of soil with the smallest average particle size is
   A. silt.
   B. clay.
   C. sand.
   D. loam.

9. Explain how the size of pores between particles in soil affect plant growth.

_____

_____

SKILL BUILDER **Organize Information**

10. Fill in the table by identifying the three main processes involved in soil formation and the four main characteristics used in soil classification.

Soil	
Is Formed By	**Is Classified By**

EXTENSION On a separate sheet of paper, redraw this table. Add a third column labeled "Is Influenced By." Then, fill in three factors that influence the formation of soil.

12.1 ○ SELF-CHECK

Answer the questions to test your knowledge of lesson concepts. You can check your work using the answers on the bottom of the page.

11. Explain the roles of physical and chemical weathering in soil formation.

_____

_____

12. Identify two common characteristics of soil as you move downward through the lower horizons.

_____

_____

13. What does the color of soil indicate about its fertility?

_____

_____

11. Sample answer: Physical weathering causes rocks to break down into smaller particles; chemical weathering changes parent material into other materials. **12.** As you move downward through a soil profile, particle size increases and the concentration of organic material decreases. **13.** Sample answer: Darker soil has a higher concentration of humus and nutrients than pale soil; therefore, it is more fertile.

12.2 Soil Degradation and Conservation

Key Concepts

- Certain farming, ranching, and forestry practices can erode soil, but other practices can protect it.
- Desertification reduces productivity of arid lands.
- U.S. and international agricultural organizations promote soil conservation.
- Irrigation and pesticide use can improve soil productivity in the short term, but they can pollute soil in the long term.

 SKILL BUILDER Vocabulary Preview

Define each vocabulary term in your own words. Then, write yourself a quick note on how you will remember each. One term has been done for you.

Term	Definition	How I Remember
Soil degradation		
Intercropping		
Crop rotation		
Cover crop	A crop planted to reduce erosion after a field has been harvested and before the next planting	A *cover* crop *covers* the soil, reducing its exposure to wind and rain.
Shelterbelt		
Tilling		
Terracing		

Term	Definition	How I Remember
Contour farming		
Overgrazing		
Desertification		
Irrigation		
Salinization		
Pesticide		

SKILL BUILDER **Reading Strategy**

As you read the lesson, take notes on key words covered under the heading. Make an outline and summarize lesson concepts in the chart below.

Key Words	Outline

Summary

Erosion

1. 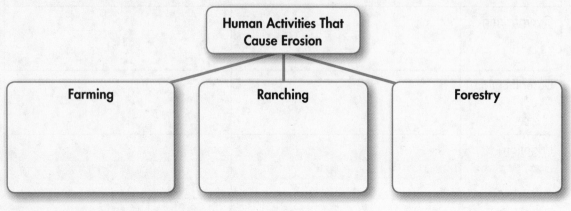 Organize Information Fill in the cluster diagram with short descriptions of the ways that specific human activities can cause erosion.

2. Describe two farming practices that can reduce erosion.

_____

_____

_____

_____

3. Describe a positive feedback cycle produced by overgrazing.

_____

_____

_____

Desertification

4. List eight factors that contribute to desertification.

_____

_____

5. Why is desertification a global problem?

_____

_____

Soil Conservation Policies

6. What environmental event in the 1930s led the U.S. government to formalize its soil conservation policies?

_____

7. Write a brief paragraph that describes one policy or organization that promotes soil conservation.

_____

_____

_____

_____

Soil Pollution

8. Compare and contrast pollution caused by irrigation and by pesticides.

_____

_____

_____

_____

For Questions 9 and 10, complete each statement by writing in the correct word.

9. The best way to prevent salinization in _____ areas is to plant crops that do not need a lot of water.

10. Drip irrigation is efficient because it gets water directly to a plant's _____.

12.2 ◉ SELF-CHECK

Answer the questions to test your knowledge of lesson concepts. You can check your work using the answers on the bottom of the page.

11. Write a sentence that shows the relationship between the terms *erosion* and *desertification*.

_____

12. Identify one thing shelterbelts and terracing have in common. _____

_____

13. Explain the role of farming and ranching in the formation of the Dust Bowl. _____

_____

_____

11. Sample answer: Erosion is one cause of desertification. 12. Sample answer: Both are farming methods that reduce erosion. 13. Sample answer: Farming and ranching removed native grasses, which left the soil exposed. During a drought, strong winds carried away the exposed topsoil.

12.3 Agriculture

Key Concepts

 Agriculture began about 10,000 years ago, when a warmer climate enabled humans to plant seeds and raise livestock.

 Industrial agriculture and the green revolution have saved millions of people from starvation.

 Chemical pesticides, biological pest control, and integrated pest management can all effectively protect crops from pests.

 Insects and other animals are essential to the reproduction of many crops.

SKILL BUILDER **Vocabulary Preview**

Define each vocabulary term in your own words. Then, write yourself a quick note on how you will remember each. One term has been done for you.

Term	Definition	How I Remember
Traditional agriculture		
Yield		
Industrial agriculture		
Green revolution	A movement in which agricultural scientists from developed nations introduced new technology, crop varieties, and farming practices to the developing world	The green revolution increased the number of green plants that could grow in developing nations.
Biological pest control		

Term	Definition	How I Remember
Integrated pest management (IPM)		
Pollinator		

SKILL BUILDER Reading Strategy

Before you read the lesson, fill in the first column of the KWL chart below with what you already know about how agriculture has changed over time. Fill in the second column with what you want to know about this topic. After you have read the lesson, fill in the third column with what you have learned.

I Know	I Want to Know	I Learned

Development of Agriculture

1. What environmental change occurred on Earth 10,000 years ago that allowed humans to plant seeds and raise livestock?

_____

2. Describe selective breeding.

_____

3. Complete the following paragraph by writing the correct words.

Agriculture probably began when _____ brought wild fruits, grains, and nuts back to their camps. Some of the _____ fell to the ground and grew into plants that produced good fruit. The plants that grew from these seeds likely produced fruits _____ and _____ than most. As these plants _____ with others nearby that shared those characteristics, they produced new generations of plants with large and tasty fruits.

Industrial Agriculture

For Questions 4 and 5, circle the letter of the correct answer.

4. The introduction of synthetic fertilizers and chemical pesticides to farming date back to the

    A. late 1800s.
    C. green revolution.
    B. mid-1900s.
    D. Industrial Revolution.

5. Industrial agriculture is both

    A. low yield and low input.
    C. high yield and low input.
    B. low yield and high input.
    D. high yield and high input.

6. Identify three positive impacts of the green revolution.

_____

_____

_____

7. Identify three negative impacts of the green revolution.

_____

_____

_____

Pests

8. Does monoculture make a crop more or less vulnerable to pests? Explain your answer.

_____

_____

_____

9. Describe the "evolutionary arms race" between pest and pesticide.

_____

_____

_____

10. **Organize Information** Fill in the table with a description of each type of pest management.

Type of Pest Management	Description
Chemical pesticides	
Biological pest control	
Integrated pest management (IPM)	

Pollinators

11. Describe the role pollinators play in agriculture.

_____

_____

12. Identify two factors that have reduced the populations of pollinators.

_____

12.3 ◯ SELF-CHECK

Answer the questions to test your knowledge of lesson concepts. You can check your work using the answers on the bottom of the page.

13. Compare the yields of traditional agriculture and industrial agriculture.

_____

_____

14. Identify one way that the Industrial Revolution changed agriculture.

_____

_____

13. Industrial agriculture typically produces greater yields than traditional agriculture. 14. Sample answer: The Industrial Revolution introduced fossil-fuel engines to agriculture, which gave farmers more efficient ways to harvest, process, and transport crops.

12.4 Food Production

Key Concepts

 Because hunger continues and the population is growing, we need to find a way to increase food production sustainably.

 Genetically modified food is a promising way to increase food production, but there needs to be more research into potential risks.

 Feedlots, aquaculture, and other methods of industrial food production are efficient, but they have disadvantages.

 Sustainable alternatives to industrial agriculture include organic agriculture and locally supported agriculture.

SKILL BUILDER Vocabulary Preview

Define each vocabulary term in your own words. Then, write yourself a quick note on how you will remember each. One term has been done for you.

Term	Definition	How I Remember
Arable land		
Food security		
Malnutrition	A shortage of nutrients the body needs	The prefix *mal–* means "bad," so *malnutrition* means "bad or poor nutrition."
Genetic engineering		
Genetically modified (GM) organism		

Term	Definition	How I Remember
Biotechnology		
Feedlot		
Aquaculture		
Seed bank		
Sustainable agriculture		
Organic agriculture		

Food Security

1. Identify three things that are required to make the food supply secure.

_____

_____

2. Describe the disease that results when people eat too little protein.

_____

_____

Genetically Modified Organisms

3. Identify one potential risk of GM crops.

_____

4. Identify two potential benefits of GM crops.

_____

5. Crops with GM traits that could benefit farmers in developing nations—increased nutrients, drought tolerance, and salinity tolerance—are not widely available. Why do you think this is so?

_____

_____

Industrial Food Production

6. [Organize Information] Fill in the table by identifying one advantage and one disadvantage for each method of industrial food production.

Method of Food Production	Advantage	Disadvantage
Feedlots		
Aquaculture		

7. Why is plant diversity important to the world's food supply?

_____

_____

Sustainable Agriculture

For Questions 8–10, write True *if the statement is true. If the statement is false, replace the underlined word or words to make the statement true. Write your changes on the line.*

_____ **8.** Sustainable agriculture <u>does not</u> deplete soil faster than it forms.

_____ **9.** In recent years, the market for organic produce has <u>decreased</u> sharply.

_____ **10.** A partnership between consumers and local farms is known as <u>community-supported</u> agriculture.

11. Is the demand for organic foods in the United States increasing or decreasing over time? Explain your answer.

_____

_____

_____

SKILL BUILDER Organize Information

12. Fill in the concept map with terms from the word bank.

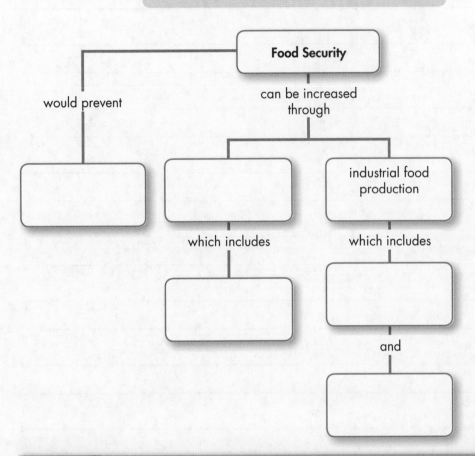

aquaculture   biotechnology   feedlots
genetic engineering   malnutrition

Food Security

would prevent

can be increased through

[ ]

[ ]   industrial food production

which includes

[ ]

which includes

[ ]

and

[ ]

12.4 SELF-CHECK

Answer the questions to test your knowledge of lesson concepts. You can check your work using the answers on the bottom of the page.

13. How is the availability of arable land related to the need for increased agricultural

production? _____

_____

14. What are two benefits of buying locally grown food? _____

_____

13. Sample answer: There is not much more arable land available, so production on currently used land must increase to meet the increasing need for food. 14. Sample answer: Locally grown food is typically fresher than food that has traveled long distances. Also, buying locally grown food boosts local economies.

Chapter Vocabulary Review

Write a definition for each of the following terms.

1. Sustainable agriculture _____

_____

2. Weathering _____

_____

3. Irrigation _____

_____

4. Yield _____

_____

5. Soil profile _____

_____

6. Bedrock _____

_____

7. Aquaculture _____

_____

8. Terracing _____

_____

Write a sentence that shows the relationship between the terms.

9. Biological pest control, integrated pest management _____

_____

10. Traditional agriculture, industrial agriculture, yield _____

_____

EXTENSION On a separate sheet of paper, write a letter that will convince a friend to buy locally produced food. Your letter should include at least four vocabulary terms from the chapter. Underline each of the vocabulary terms you use.

Ecological Footprints

Food Transportation Costs

In this activity, you will calculate the daily and annual food transportation costs for different groups of people.

Calculating Daily Costs

The price you pay for food includes the transportation costs of getting the food from the fields to your table. The daily cost of food transportation for one person equals about $1.50.

To find the daily food transportation cost for a group of people, multiply the daily cost for one person, $1.50, by the number of people.

▶ The calculation of the daily food transportation cost for people living in the United States in 2010 (about 309 million) is modeled at the right:

$$\text{daily cost} = \frac{\text{number of}}{\text{people}} \times \frac{\text{daily cost}}{\text{for 1 person}}$$

$$= 309 \text{ million} \times \$1.50$$

$$= \$463.5 \text{ million}$$

1. Record the number of people in your class, your town, and your state. Then, calculate the daily cost of food transportation for each group. Write your answers in the table.

	Number of People	Daily Cost	Annual Cost
You	1	$1.50	$547.50
Your class			
Your town			
Your state			
United States	309 million	$463.5 million	

Calculating Annual Costs

To find the annual transportation cost, multiply the daily cost by 365.

▶ The calculation of the annual cost for one person is modeled at the right:

$$\text{annual cost} = \text{daily cost} \times 365$$

$$= \$1.50 \times 365$$

$$= \$547.50$$

2. Calculate the annual cost of food transportation for each group in the table. Write your answers in the table.

Possible Transgenic Maize in Oaxaca, Mexico

Transgenic Crops

Transgenic crops are fast becoming more important to the world's food supply. Nations where transgenic crops are widely grown point to reduced dependence on pesticides and increased yields. But not all nations approve of genetically modified crops.

Some are concerned that inserted genes will become part of the genetic makeup of native wild plants through crossbreeding. The timeline below summarizes information about maize in Oaxaca and the distribution of transgenic corn worldwide.

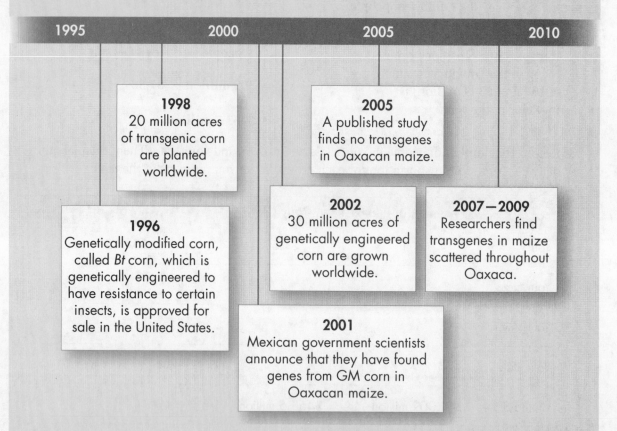

1995 — 2000 — 2005 — 2010

1998
20 million acres of transgenic corn are planted worldwide.

1996
Genetically modified corn, called *Bt* corn, which is genetically engineered to have resistance to certain insects, is approved for sale in the United States.

2005
A published study finds no transgenes in Oaxacan maize.

2002
30 million acres of genetically engineered corn are grown worldwide.

2007–2009
Researchers find transgenes in maize scattered throughout Oaxaca.

2001
Mexican government scientists announce that they have found genes from GM corn in Oaxacan maize.

Corn has a great importance as a food crop in Mexico. It also has tremendous cultural significance. After all, Oaxaca, Mexico, was the site where wild corn was first bred for desirable traits. It is no surprise, then, that the Mexican government has been actively involved in regulating the use of transgenic corn in Mexico. Before 1998, transgenic corn was grown in some experimental plots in Mexico. In 1998, the Mexican government passed legislation that banned the use of transgenic corn in Mexico. For 11 years, experimental cultivation of transgenic corn was not permitted. In 2009, new legislation was passed that now permits the cultivation of transgenic corn on experimental plots. So, the story of transgenic corn in Mexico will continue to unfold in the coming years.

Use the information from **Transgenic Crops** to answer the questions below.

1. Explain how the information in the timeline could lead people to different conclusions about the impact of GM corn on native maize species.

_____

_____

2. Use the information in the timeline to infer whether the risk of contamination of native plants with transgenes is becoming more likely or less likely over time. Explain your answer.

_____

_____

_____

3. Notice that the information about the number of acres of transgenic corn provided in the timeline is for the entire world. Different nations have different regulations about transgenic plants. Give one reason why national regulations on transgenic crops might not prevent transgenes from showing up in another nation's wild plants.

_____

_____

_____

4. REVISIT INVESTIGATIVE PHENOMENON Use the information in the timeline to explain how transgenic corn can help people balance the growing demand for food and the need to protect the environment.

_____

_____

_____

21st Century Skills

Find out more about transgenic food crops and regulations associated with their use. With a small group, discuss what you have learned. Then, decide what regulations you think should be placed on the use or importation of transgenic food crops. Share your opinion with the class.

*The 21st Century Skills used in this activity include **Information, Communication, and Technology (ICT) Literacy; Communication and Collaboration;** and **Media Literacy.***

13 Mineral Resources and Mining

Before you read the chapter, answer each question with information you know. After you complete the chapter, re-answer the questions using information you learned.

INVESTIGATIVE PHENOMENON **Can we make the benefits of mining outweigh the costs?**

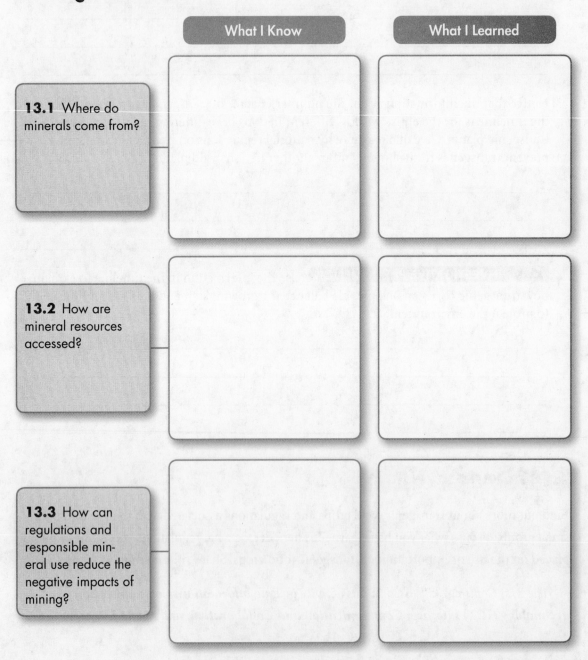

	What I Know	What I Learned
13.1 Where do minerals come from?		
13.2 How are mineral resources accessed?		
13.3 How can regulations and responsible mineral use reduce the negative impacts of mining?		

13.1 Minerals and Rocks

Key Concepts

 A mineral is a naturally occurring, inorganic solid that has an orderly crystalline structure and a definite chemical composition.

 Minerals can form by crystallization from magma or lava, from precipitation related to evaporation or hydrothermal solutions, from exposure to high pressure and temperature, or can be produced by organisms.

 Forces deep inside and at the surface of Earth produce changes in rock that cause the same material to cycle between igneous, sedimentary, and metamorphic rock stages.

SKILL BUILDER Vocabulary Preview

Define each vocabulary term in your own words. Then, write yourself a quick note on how you will remember each. One term has been done for you.

Term	Definition	How I Remember
Mineral		
Precipitation		
Polymorph		
Rock		
Rock cycle	A very slow process in which rocks change between igneous, sedimentary, and metamorphic types of rock	The word *cycle* lets me know that this process includes events that happen repeatedly.

What Are Minerals?

For Questions 1–4, write True *if the statement is true. If the statement is false, replace the underline word or words to make it true. Write your changes on the line.*

_____ 1. Geologists have so far identified about <u>1000</u> minerals.

_____ 2. Minerals are formed from <u>inorganic</u> materials.

_____ 3. Each type of mineral has a unique <u>crystal</u> structure.

_____ 4. Most minerals are compounds composed of <u>one</u> element(s).

5. List the five criteria a material must meet to be considered a mineral.

_____

6. Describe the proportion of elements in minerals that contain more than one element.

_____

_____

7. Name a mineral that is made of only one element.

_____

Mineral Formation

8. (Organize Information) Fill in the table with a description of the ways that minerals can form.

Ways That Minerals Can Form	Description
Crystallization from magma or lava	
Precipitation	
Pressure and temperature	
Produced by organisms	

9. What factor affects the size of the crystals in minerals that form from magma or lava? Explain your answer.

_____

_____

_____

10. What is a vein, and how does it form?

_____

_____

_____

11. Name an example of a mineral formed by an organism.

_____

Rocks

For Questions 12–14, circle the letter of the correct answer.

12. Rock that forms as magma cools slowly and solidifies below Earth's surface is called

    A. intrusive igneous rock.   **C.** clastic sedimentary rock.

    B. extrusive igneous rock.   **D.** chemical sedimentary rock.

13. Which of the following is NOT a factor in the formation of metamorphic rock?

    A. deposition   **C.** recrystallization

    B. high pressure   **D.** high temperature

14. An example of metamorphic rock is

    A. shale.   **C.** marble.

    B. basalt.   **D.** limestone.

15. What causes rocks to move, and how does that movement relate to the rock cycle?

_____

_____

_____

_____

16. Describe how sedimentary rocks are formed.

_____

_____

_____

_____

SKILL BUILDER Organize Information

17. Complete the following diagram to show the various geologic processes involved in the rock cycle. Draw different arrows to represent each process and complete the key below the map. Note that one process can affect more than one type of rock material. On the lines below the key, explain where minerals that make up the rocks in the rock cycle originally come from.

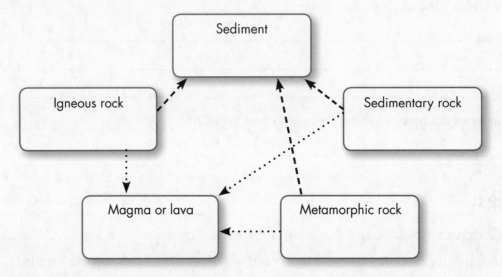

KEY		
Weather and erosion ------►	Melting ··········►	
Sediment settles	Cooling and crystalization	
Heat and pressure		

_____

_____

_____

13.1 ◉ SELF-CHECK

Answer the questions to test your knowledge of lesson concepts. You can check your work using the answers on the bottom of the page.

18. Name two polymorphs of carbon. _____

19. What are the three different types of rock? _____

_____

18. Sample answer: Graphite, diamond 19. Igneous, sedimentary, metamorphic

13.2 Mining

Key Concepts

🔑 Mining companies seek and gather valuable resources such as metals, nonmetallic minerals, and fuel sources.

🔑 Mining companies have developed many techniques to access resources close to the surface of Earth, deep underground, and even underwater.

🔑 After mining, ores and other extracted materials are processed to separate the desired materials, combine them with other materials, or alter their properties.

 SKILL BUILDER Vocabulary Preview

Define the vocabulary term in your own words. Then, write yourself a quick note on how you will remember it.

Term	Definition	How I Remember
Ore		
Strip mining	A method of mining in which layers of surface soil and rock are removed from large areas to expose the resource	When you *strip* something off, you pull away layers, just as *strip mining* pulls away layers of soil and rock.
Subsurface mining		
Open pit mining		
Mountaintop removal		

Term	Definition	How I Remember
Placer mining		
Tailings		
Smelting		

What Is Mined?

For Questions 1–5, complete each statement by writing in the correct word or words.

1. Some minerals are widespread throughout Earth's crust, but occur in such low

_____ that mining is not economically practical.

2. An ore is mined so that _____ can be removed from it.

3. For material to be considered an ore, the _____ of a mineral must be of a certain level.

4. About 100 minerals are considered gemstones, which are _____ minerals.

5. Some substances used for _____ sources, such as coal, are mined.

6. Describe the origins of the metal tantalum, and explain why tantalum is important.

_____

_____

_____

_____

_____

7. What does mining involve?

_____

_____

_____

_____

_____

Mining Methods

8. Complete the following paragraph with terms from the word bank.

> **mountaintop removal**   **open pit mining**   **placer mining**   **solution mining**
>
> **strip mining**   **subsurface mining**   **undersea mining**

_____ involves sifting through material in riverbeds. Companies use

the _____ method when a resource is near Earth's surface in horizontal

deposits. In _____, miners dig a large hole to extract a resource. With

_____, mining companies clear cut forests, remove topsoil, and then blast

away rock to reach a resource. When a resource is found in pockets deep underground,

_____ is used. One way to extract a resource without removing ore from the

ground is _____. The least used method is _____, because

it is so expensive.

9. Describe solution mining.

_____

_____

_____

Processing Minerals and Metals

10. **Organize Information** Fill in the flowchart with the main steps involved in processing minerals.

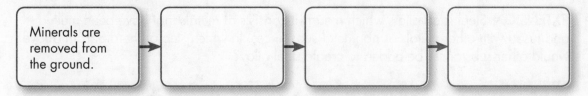

Minerals are removed from the ground. → → →

11. Why are minerals processed?

_____

_____

12. What are tailings, and why are they so controversial?

_____

_____

_____

Name _____ Class _____ Date _____

 SKILL BUILDER Think Visually

13. Label the diagram using sentences from the sentence bank to show how steel is produced and used.

> Areas are explored.
>
> Disposal
>
> Steel is used to make appliances and other products.
>
> Iron ore is removed from the ground.
>
> Iron ore is smelted to further extract iron. Mixed with other metals or chemicals, it is melted and reprocessed into steel rods and sheets.
>
> Iron is separated from the ore.

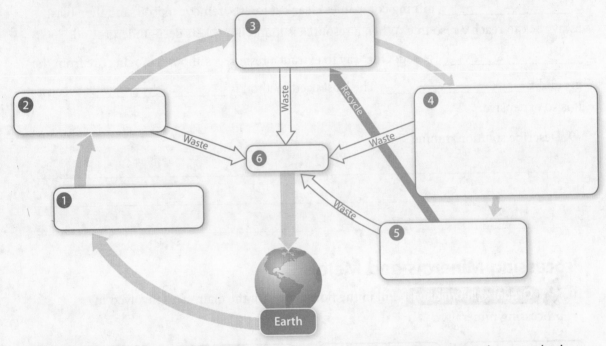

EXTENSION Steel is an alloy, which means it consists of metals that have been melted and fused with other metals or nonmetal substances. In which step of the diagram above would other substances be added to create steel alloy?

13.2 ◯ SELF-CHECK

Answer the questions to test your knowledge of lesson concepts. You can check your work using the answers on the bottom of the page.

14. Name two metallic minerals that are mined.

_____

15. Where does mineral processing usually begin? _____

14. Sample answer: Copper, iron 15. Sample answer: At the mining site

13.3 Mining Impacts and Regulation

Key Concepts

 Environmental impacts of mining include increased erosion, increased sediment and debris, and pollution of water, land, and air. Mining can also have negative impacts on society.

 Regulations that govern mining consider the environmental and safety impacts of mining along with the economic costs to the industry.

 Because minerals are a nonrenewable resource, we need to be concerned about finite supplies and ways to use them more responsibly, such as reusing and recycling.

 SKILL BUILDER **Vocabulary Preview**

Define the vocabulary term in your own words. Then, write yourself a quick note on how you will remember it.

Term	Definition	How I Remember
Acid drainage		

 SKILL BUILDER **Reading Strategy**

As you read the lesson, complete the main ideas and details chart.

Main Ideas	Details
Negative impacts of mining	

Main Ideas	Details
Mining regulation	
Responsible mineral use	

Negative Impacts of Mining

1. Explain the process of acid drainage.

_____

_____

_____

_____

2. In what ways can mining be both economically good and bad for a community?

_____

_____

_____

_____

_____

For Questions 3 and 4, circle the letter of the correct answer.

3. Which of the following mining methods disrupts the sea floor?

   A. strip mining

   B. open pit mining

   C. solution mining

   D. undersea mining

4. Which impact of mining can cause respiratory diseases, such as lung cancer, due to dust and particle exposure?

   A. air pollution

   B. water pollution

   C. increased erosion

   D. excessive sediment and debris

Mining Regulation

5. Organize Information Fill in the table to compare and contrast U.S. mining regulations.

Regulation	Description
General Mining Law of 1872	
Mineral Leasing Act of 1920	
Surface Mining Control and Reclamation Act of 1977	
Federal Mine Safety and Health Act of 1977	
Hardrock Mining and Reclamation Act of 2009	

6. Describe the environmental problems that remain even after a coal mining company has "reclaimed" a former mining site.

_____

_____

_____

_____

Responsible Mineral Use

For Questions 7 and 8, complete each statement by writing the correct word or words.

7. Extracting aluminum from ore takes 20 times more _____ than obtaining it from _____ sources.

8. In many cases, reusing and _____ products that contain minerals decreases energy use and saves consumers and businesses _____.

9. Describe what you can do in your daily life to reduce your use of, reuse, or recycle minerals.

_____

_____

_____

13.3 SELF-CHECK

Answer the questions to test your knowledge of lesson concepts. You can check your work using the answers on the bottom of the page.

10. How can reducing use, reusing, and recycling help extend Earth's supply of minerals?

_____

_____

11. How can reducing use, reusing, and recycling help save energy? How does this help address environmental issues? _____

_____

_____

10. Sample answer: If we reuse and recycle already mined minerals, then we will not have to conduct as much "new" mining. That means we would use less of a limited resource. 11. Sample answer: It takes much less energy to reuse and/or recycle "used" minerals than it does to mine "new" minerals. We would pollute less as well.

Chapter Vocabulary Review

Match each term with its definition.

_____ **1.** mineral

_____ **2.** ore

_____ **3.** precipitation

_____ **4.** tailings

_____ **5.** placer mining

_____ **6.** acid drainage

_____ **7.** smelting

_____ **8.** polymorph

_____ **9.** rock

_____ **10.** open pit mining

a. when the liquid in a solution evaporates and remaining solids form minerals

b. sifting through material in modern or ancient riverbed deposits

c. a naturally occurring solid mass of minerals and mineral-like material

d. heating ore beyond its melting point and combining it with other metals or chemicals

e. minerals that consist of the same element but have different crystal structures

f. a naturally occurring, inorganic solid that has an orderly crystalline structure and a definite chemical composition

g. when sulfuric acid causes metals to leach from rocks, leading to water pollution

h. a waste product generated by mining

i. digging a large hole to remove ore and rock

j. a mineral that is mined so that a metal can be removed from it

Write a sentence that shows the relationship between the terms.

11. Rock cycle, minerals_____

_____

12. Mountaintop removal, tailings_____

_____

_____

13. Subsurface mining, metals_____

_____

EXTENSION On a separate sheet of paper, write a short paragraph describing the benefits and drawbacks of mining. Your paragraph should include at least one vocabulary term from each of the three lessons in the chapter. Underline each of the lesson vocabulary terms you use.

Ecological Footprints

Metal Consumption

The known amounts of seven metals in the world are shown in the table below. Also shown for each metal are the amount that is used per year and the amount that would be used at United States consumption rates, which are much higher than the world averages.

Metal	Known World Reserves (thousand pounds)	Amount Used Per Year (thousand pounds)	Years of supply left	Amount Used Per Year If Everyone Consumed at U.S. Rate (thousand pounds)	Years of Supply Left at U.S. Consumption Rate
Manganese	5,200,000	11,600.0		20,020.0	
Titanium	1,500,000	6100.0		31,900.0	
Nickel	150,000	1660.0		5082.0	
Tin	11,000	300.0		1290.0	
Tungsten	6300	89.6		316.8	
Antimony	4300	135.0		503.8	
Indium	16	0.5		2.1	

Data are for 2007, from 2008 U.S. Geological Survey Mineral Commodity Summaries. World consumption data are assumed to be equal to world production data. World reserves include amounts known to exist, whether or not they are presently economically extractable.

In this activity, you will calculate the years of supply left for each metal and the years of supply that would be left if U.S. consumption rates were applied.

▶ To find the years of supply left, divide the known world reserves by the rate at which the metal is used. The calculation for the years that the tin supply will remain is modeled below.

World Rate

$$\text{years of tin supply left} = \frac{\text{amount in world reserves}}{\text{rate of use}} \quad \longleftarrow \text{ thousand pounds} \\ \longleftarrow \text{ thousand pounds/year}$$

$$= \frac{11,000}{300} \text{ or about 36.7 years}$$

U.S. Rate

$$\text{years of tin supply left} = \frac{11,000}{1290} \text{ or about 8.5 years}$$

1. Use the world rate to calculate the years of supply left for each of the remaining metals in the table. Write your answers in the fourth column of the table.

2. Calculate the years of supply left for each metal if the world were to consume the metals at the U.S. rate. Write your answers in the sixth column of the table.

Mining for...Cell Phones?

Coltan Mining Takes Its Toll

The human impact of coltan mining is high. In the Democratic Republic of the Congo (DRC), millions of civilians were killed in a 1998–2003 civil war over access to natural resources and other issues. Coltan mining, both forced and voluntary, helped fund the war. Although the war is over, the fighting—and the mining of coltan—continues today. Coltan mining and the war that accompanied it have affected not only the lives of many people, but of many animals, too. Take the eastern lowland gorilla, for example.

The Plight of the Eastern Lowland Gorilla

The eastern lowland gorilla lives mainly in the rain forests of the eastern part of the Democratic Republic of the Congo. In 1994, there were 17,000 of these gorillas in the Congo. Today, there are fewer than 5000. The gorillas have fallen prey—sometimes literally—to a perfect storm of attacks on their survival.

First there was the civil war. As battles raged throughout the DRC, human refugees fled onto land that was gorilla habitat. Camps set up there effectively took the land from the gorillas. Some conflicts destroyed gorilla habitat outright.

A seemingly unrelated activity, mining, has drastically affected gorilla population numbers as well. An ore called *coltan* contains the mineral tantalite, which is used to make a metal called tantalum. Tantalum is used in the production of cell phones and other electronics. Since the price of tantalum skyrocketed in the early 2000s, many people have illegally mined coltan from Congolese streams through placer mining. The mining pollutes water and damages gorilla habitat, but that is not the only blow it deals to the eastern lowland gorillas. People who are mining coltan often slaughter the gorillas and other wild animals for food—a practice known as the "bushmeat trade." People living in refugee camps, loggers, and soldiers also eat bushmeat.

In addition, as more people move into gorilla habitats, they pass microorganisms such as the deadly Ebola virus and *E.coli* bacteria to gorillas that threaten both people and primates. This cross-species contamination usually happens via water or soil.

In 2010, the United Nations issued a report predicting that gorillas might vanish from the DRC and surrounding areas within 10 to 15 years if more is not done to protect them. Conservation groups such as Conservation International (based in Washington, D.C.) have pledged several million dollars to help protect gorillas in the DRC, notably in Maiko National Park. The future of the eastern lowland gorilla remains to be seen.

Use the information in **Coltan Mining Takes Its Toll** to answer the questions below.

1. Describe how mining for coltan damages gorilla habitat.

_____

_____

_____

2. How is coltan mining related to the bushmeat trade?

_____

_____

3. Do you think that the eastern lowland gorillas' situation will change in the future?

_____

_____

_____

_____

4. REVISIT INVESTIGATIVE PHENOMENON Use the information provided in the article to further examine the **Investigative Phenomenon:** "Can we make the benefits of mining outweigh the costs?"

_____

_____

_____

_____

_____

21st Century Skills

Find out more about the eastern lowland gorilla's plight in the Congo. Work in small groups to find online, the United Nations Environment Programme's (UNEP) report, *The Last Stand of the Gorilla—Environmental Crime and Conflict in the Congo.* Pick one of the proposals in the report and evaluate whether you think it would work to benefit the gorillas. Present your group's ideas and conclusions about the proposal you focused on.

*The 21st Century Skills used in this activity include **Creativity and Innovation, Critical Thinking and Problem Solving, Communication and Collaboration,** and **Information Literacy.***

14 Water Resources

Before you read the chapter, answer each question with information you know. After you complete the chapter, re-answer the questions using information you learned.

INVESTIGATIVE PHENOMENON ## Why is the level of water in the Colorado River so low?

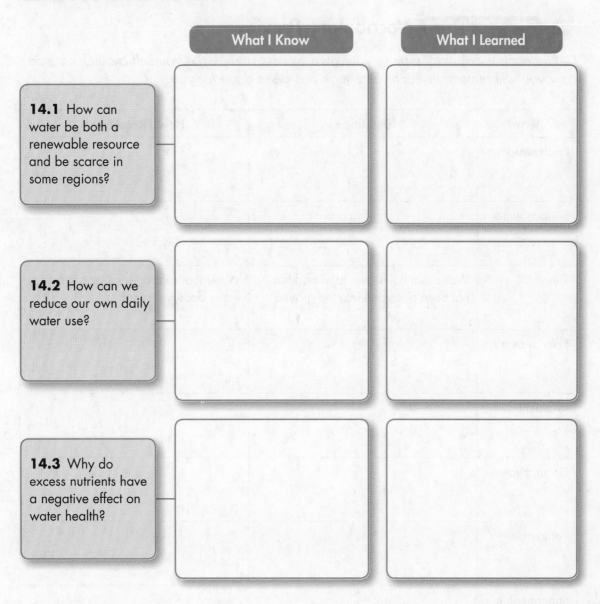

	What I Know	What I Learned
14.1 How can water be both a renewable resource and be scarce in some regions?		
14.2 How can we reduce our own daily water use?		
14.3 Why do excess nutrients have a negative effect on water health?		

14.1 Earth: The Water Planet

Key Concepts

- As a natural resource, freshwater is renewable. However, quantities of fresh water on Earth are limited.
- Surface water is contained within watersheds.
- Groundwater can be accessed by wells.

SKILL BUILDER Vocabulary Preview

Define each vocabulary term in your own words. Then, write yourself a quick note on how you will remember each. One term has been done for you.

Term	Definition	How I Remember
Fresh water		
Surface water		
Runoff	Water that flows over land and has not been absorbed into the ground	Water that *runs off* land and into water bodies is *runoff*.
River system		
Watershed		
Groundwater		
Permeable		
Impermeable		

Term	Definition	How I Remember
Aquifer		
Water table		
Recharge zone		
Well		

Where Is Our Water?

For Questions 1–6, complete each statement by writing the correct word or words.

1. Fresh water is a renewable _____.

2. Another name for the water cycle is the _____.

3. About 97.5% of Earth's water is _____.

4. _____ is water that is relatively pure, with few dissolved salts.

5. More than three quarters of the fresh water on Earth is _____, the rest is liquid.

6. Fresh water is distributed _____ in both time and space.

7. Explain why liquid fresh water is considered a limited resource.

_____

_____

_____

8. Explain why the available amount of water per person differs between countries.

_____

_____

_____

_____

_____

Surface Water

For Questions 9 and 10, circle the letter of the correct answer.

9. Water that flows over land and has not been absorbed into the ground is called
   A. ocean water
   B. runoff
   C. groundwater
   D. a tributary

10. All of the land area that supplies water to a particular river system is called a
    A. glacier
    B. river
    C. watershed
    D. tributary

11. Why does effective watershed management require the cooperation of everyone in the watershed?

    _____

    _____

    _____

Groundwater

12. Complete the following paragraph with terms from the word bank.

aquifer	groundwater	impermeable	permeable

Water trickles down through the soil and rock to become _____. As water is pulled down by gravity, it passes through layers of soil and rock. These

_____ layers have spaces, or pores, for water to pass through. When the

water reaches an _____ layer, it becomes trapped. It cannot move any deeper. The water then begins to fill up the spaces above. This underground layer of rock, sand, or gravel that holds water is called an _____.

13. What is a recharge zone?

    _____

    _____

14. What happens when the water table drops below the depth of a well?

    _____

 **SKILL BUILDER** Think Visually

15. Label the diagram using terms from the word bank.

| aquifer | impermeable layer | river | water table | well |

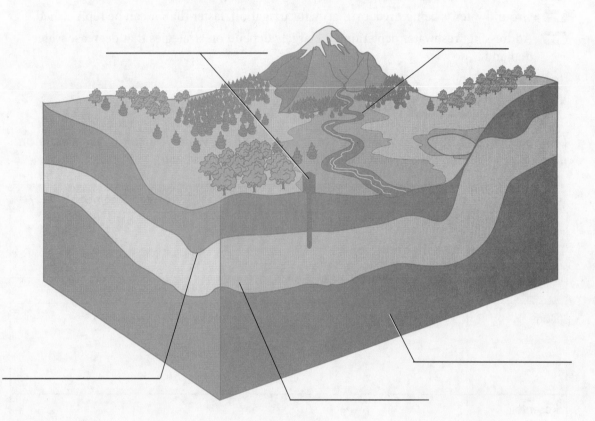

EXTENSION On the diagram, draw a well that is dry, and a tributary to the river.

14.1 ○ SELF-CHECK

Answer the questions to test your knowledge of lesson concepts. You can check your work using the answers on the bottom of the page.

16. What is a watershed? _____

_____

17. What is groundwater? _____

_____

16. All the land area that drains water into a river system 17. Water found below Earth's surface

14.2 Uses of Fresh Water

Key Concepts

- Fresh water is used for agriculture, industrial, and personal activities.
- Because of overuse, surface water resources are being depleted.
- Groundwater is being used, primarily for irrigation, faster than it can be replenished.
- Addressing freshwater depletion will largely depend on strategies that decrease water demand.

 SKILL BUILDER **Vocabulary Preview**

Define each vocabulary term in your own words. Then, write yourself a quick note on how you will remember each. One term has been done for you.

Term	Definition	How I Remember
Water diversion		
Dam		
Reservoir		
Salinization	The buildup of salts in the surface layer of soil	When I see *sal*, I think *salt*. Salinization is to add salt
Desalination		
Xeriscaping		

How We Use Water

1. **Organize Information** Fill in the cluster diagram with short descriptions of the ways we use water.

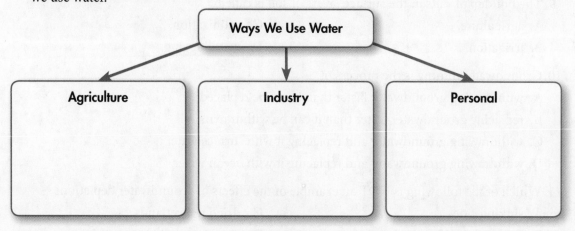

2. Why does it make sense that 40 percent of the water used by the United States is for industrial uses?

_____

_____

Using Surface Water

For Questions 3–6, write True if the statement is true. If the statement is false, replace the underlined word or words to make the statement true. Write your changes on the line.

_____ 3. The process of moving water from its source to places where humans use it is called <u>water diversion</u>.

_____ 4. Dams can help <u>regulate</u> river flow.

_____ 5. Lakes that store water for human use are called <u>dams</u>.

_____ 6. Drought and overuse have caused significant surface water <u>reservoirs</u>.

7. What are some of the benefits and costs of dams?

_____

_____

_____

8. Why is the Colorado River a good example of surface water depletion?

_____

_____

Using Groundwater

For Questions 9–11, circle the letter of the correct answer.

9. The buildup of salts in the surface layers of soil is called
   - A. agriculture.
   - B. irrigation.
   - C. salinization.
   - D. waterlogging.

10. Groundwater mining is the process of
   - A. withdrawing groundwater faster than it can be replaced.
   - B. replacing groundwater faster than it can be withdrawn.
   - C. withdrawing groundwater and replacing it with surface water.
   - D. withdrawing groundwater and replacing it with ocean water.

11. Which of the following is NOT an example of the effects of groundwater depletion?
   - A. sinking cities
   - B. depleted aquifers
   - C. dried up wetlands
   - D. rising water tables

12. What is groundwater mostly used for in the United States?

_____

13. What is waterlogging?

_____

_____

Solutions to Freshwater Depletion

14. **Organize Information** Fill in the table with solutions that increase supply and reduce demand.

Solutions that Increase Supply	Solutions that Reduce Demand

15. Which solutions to freshwater depletion do you think are most sustainable? Explain your thinking.

_____

_____

SKILL BUILDER Think Visually

16. Fill in the cluster concept map with terms from the word bank.

agriculture   decrease demand   groundwater depletion   increase supply   industry

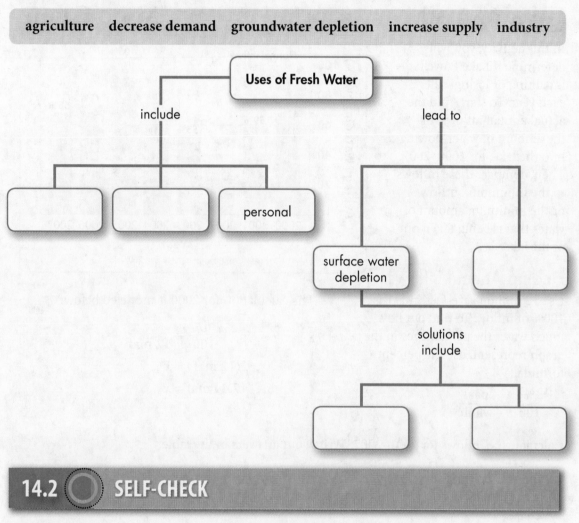

Uses of Fresh Water

include   lead to

personal

surface water
depletion

solutions
include

14.2 ⬤ SELF-CHECK

Answer the questions to test your knowledge of lesson concepts. You can check your work using the answers on the bottom of the page.

17. Why is groundwater mining causing groundwater depletion in some areas?

_____

_____

18. Why is drip irrigation an example of a solution that reduces the demand for water?

_____

_____

17. Since groundwater mining withdraws water faster than it can be replaced, it can reduce the amount of stored groundwater in the area. **18.** Drip irrigation uses less water than traditional irrigation methods.

Real Data

Lake Powell

In this activity, you will determine if Lake Powell is gaining or losing water each year. To start, find the actual annual inflows, or the amount of water flowing into the lake, for 2000–2007. Then, compare these inflows to the minimum outflow, or the minimum amount of water that is being taken out of the lake.

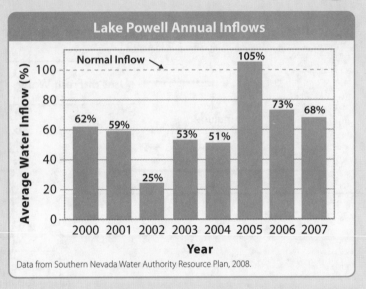

Lake Powell Annual Inflows

Data from Southern Nevada Water Authority Resource Plan, 2008.

Finding Annual Inflows

Use 12 million acre-feet (maf) as 100% of inflow. To find out how much water the percentages in the graph represent, use the percent formula.

$$\frac{\%}{100} = \frac{\text{part}}{\text{whole}}$$

▶ The calculation for 2000 is modeled below:

$$\frac{62}{100} = \frac{x}{12 \text{ maf}}$$

$$.62(12 \text{ maf}) = x$$

$$7.44 \text{ maf} = x$$

Calculate the inflows for 2001–2007. Write your answers in the table.

2000	2001	2002	2003	2004	2005	2006	2007
7.44 maf							

Comparing Inflow and Outflow

According to the Colorado River Compact, the minimum outflow of Lake Powell is 8.23 maf each year. Assuming only 8.23 maf flowed out, calculate if there was a net gain or loss of water each year. Write your answers in the table below.

▶ The calculation for 2000 is modeled at the right: **7.44 maf − 8.23 maf = −0.79 maf**
Lake Powell had a net loss.

2000	2001	2002	2003	2004	2005	2006	2007
−0.79 maf							
loss							

14.3 Water Pollution

Key Concepts

- There are many different kinds of water pollution, each with their own sources and effects.
- It can take decades to clean up groundwater pollution, so every effort should be made to prevent it from occurring.
- Oceans are polluted with oil, toxic chemicals, and nutrients that run off land.
- Government regulation and water treatment are two ways of decreasing the effects of water pollution.

 SKILL BUILDER Vocabulary Preview

Define each vocabulary term in your own words. Then, write yourself a quick note on how you will remember each. One term has been done for you.

Term	Definition	How I Remember
Point-source pollution		
Nonpoint-source pollution	Pollution from many sources spread over a large area	Nonpoint-source pollution comes from many sources. I could *not point* at just one.
Cultural eutrophication		
Wastewater		
Algal bloom		
Pathogen		
Red tide		
Septic system		

SKILL BUILDER Reading Strategy

As you read the lesson, complete the main ideas and details chart.

Main Ideas	Details
Types of water pollution	
Groundwater pollution	
Ocean water pollution	
Controlling water pollution	

Types of Water Pollution

For Questions 1–5, match each type of pollution with the statement that best describes it.

_____ 1. nutrient pollution

_____ 2. toxic chemical pollution

_____ 3. sediment pollution

_____ 4. thermal pollution

_____ 5. biological pollution

a. includes disease-causing agents in the water

b. caused by erosion

c. raises the temperature of the water

d. can cause cultural eutrophication

e. includes heavy metals and toxic organic chemicals

6. **Organize Information** Fill in the flowchart with the terms *increase(s)* and *decrease(s)* to model the process of eutrophication.

Water nutrient levels	→	Aquatic plant growth	→	Decomposition	→	Dissolved oxygen levels

Groundwater Pollution

For Questions 7–11, write True if the statement is true. If the statement is false, replace the underlined word or words to make the statement true. Write your changes on the line.

_____ 7. Groundwater pollution is <u>easy</u> to monitor and clean up.

_____ 8. Groundwater pollution as a result of human activity is <u>widespread</u>.

_____ 9. Pollutants leach through soil and seep into <u>storage tanks</u>.

_____ 10. It can take <u>decades</u> for groundwater to get rid of its contaminants.

_____ 11. Most efforts to reduce groundwater pollution focus on <u>prevention</u>.

Ocean Water Pollution

12. Why is it important to minimize the amount of oil released into the ocean?

_____

13. What is the largest source of oil in the oceans?

_____

14. Why is mercury contamination in the ocean a concern?

_____

_____

15. What causes red tides?

_____

_____

For Questions 16–19, write True *if the statement is true. If the statement is false, replace the underlined word or words to make the statement true. Write your changes on the line.*

_____ **16.** Most oil pollution in the oceans comes from <u>small, nonpoint sources</u>.

_____ **17.** Marine organisms at higher trophic levels contain <u>higher</u> levels of mercury.

_____ **18.** Of the nutrients phosphorus and nitrogen, <u>phosphorous</u> causes the most damage to oceans.

_____ **19.** Reducing <u>oil seepage</u> into coastal waters can lessen the frequency of algal blooms.

Controlling Water Pollution

Complete each statement by writing the correct word or words.

20. The Clean Water Act made it illegal to release _____ from a point source without a permit.

21. Drinking water suppliers _____ water with chemicals and run it through filters before sending it to your tap.

22. _____ includes water from showers, toilets, dishwashers, as well as water used by industry to cool power plants.

14.3 ⊙ SELF-CHECK

Answer the questions to test your knowledge of lesson concepts. You can check your work using the answers on the bottom of the page.

23. List two types of water pollution. _____

24. Describe how The Clean Water Act has reduced point-source pollution in the U.S.

_____

_____

_____

23. List should include two: nutrient pollution, toxic chemical pollution, sediment pollution, thermal pollution, biological pollution 24. The Clean Water Act made it illegal to release point-source pollution without a permit.

Chapter Vocabulary Review

Match each term with its definition.

_____ **1.** reservoir

_____ **2.** nonpoint-source pollution

_____ **3.** desalination

_____ **4.** point-source pollution

_____ **5.** aquifer

_____ **6.** watershed

_____ **7.** wastewater

_____ **8.** fresh water

_____ **9.** runoff

_____ **10.** salinization

_____ **11.** surface water

_____ **12.** well

a. water that flows over land and has not yet been absorbed into the ground

b. water that has been used by people in some way

c. removing salt from seawater

d. pollution that comes from a discrete location

e. water that is relatively pure, with few dissolved salts

f. the area of land that drains water into a river system

g. the buildup of salts in the surface layers of soil

h. a lake that stores water for human use

i. a hole dug into an aquifer to reach groundwater

j. spongelike formation of rock, sand, or gravel that holds water

k. water found on Earth's surface

l. pollution that comes from many sources

Use each vocabulary term in a sentence.

13. Water diversion _____

_____

14. Water table _____

_____

15. Algal bloom _____

_____

EXTENSION Write a paragraph that correctly uses five or more vocabulary terms from the chapter.

Looking for Water... in the Desert

The Law of the River

Defining Colorado River water rights has been—and still is—a fluid process. In 1922, the Colorado River Compact attempted to divide the waters of the Colorado River between seven states: Arizona, California, Colorado, Nevada, New Mexico, Utah, and Wyoming. But, rather than allocate water to each state, the compact divided the entire river basin into two halves: an upper and lower basin. The states in each basin were given rights to 7.5 million acre-feet of water per year to divide among themselves.

Since this compact was signed, additional treaties, compacts, acts, and legal decisions have helped further define who gets to use the river's waters...and how much they get. This cumulative body of laws and court cases is known as the Law of the River. The timeline below summarizes a few of the major components of the Law of the River.

1922
The Colorado River Compact
Divides the Colorado River basin into an upper and lower basin. The states in each basin get rights to 7.5 million acre-feet of water per year.

1974
The Colorado River Basin Salinity Control Act of 1974
Aims to control and improve the salinity of Colorado River water.

1944
Water Treaty with Mexico
Mexico is given rights to 1.5 million acre-feet of water each year.

2003
Colorado River Water Delivery Agreement
Specifies how California's portion of Colorado River water is allocated.

1920   1940   1960   1980   2000

1928
Boulder Canyon Project Aid
Defines how much water each lower basin state has rights to: California, 4.4 million acre-feet; Arizona, 2.8 million acre-feet; and Nevada, 300,000 acre-feet.

1948
Upper Colorado River Basin Compact
Defines how much of the upper basin's water each state has rights to: Colorado, 51.75%; New Mexico, 11.25%; Utah, 23%; and Wyoming, 14%. The small part of Arizona in the upper basin is also given 50,000 acre-feet per year.

Use the information in **The Law of the River** to answer the questions below.

1. List the seven states that signed the Colorado River Compact.

   _____

   _____

2. Describe the outcome of the Boulder Canyon Project Act.

   _____

   _____

   _____

3. Describe the outcome of the Upper Colorado River Basin Compact of 1948.

   _____

   _____

   _____

4. Do you think the Law of the River will change in the future?

   _____

   _____

5. **REVISIT INVESTIGATIVE** PHENOMENON How does the changing nature of water rights relate to the **Investigative Phenomenon**?

   _____

   _____

   _____

   _____

21st Century Skills

Gather into small groups to research the compacts, acts, and court decisions that have helped define water rights to the Colorado River. Compile the results of your research, using a group wiki if possible. Then, present your research to the class.

The 21st Century Skills used in this activity include **Communication and Collaboration, Initiative and Self-Direction,** *and* **Productivity and Accountabilty.**

15 The Atmosphere

Before you read the chapter, answer each question with information you know. After you complete the chapter, re-answer the questions using information you learned.

INVESTIGATIVE PHENOMENON **Does congestion charging work to reduce air pollution?**

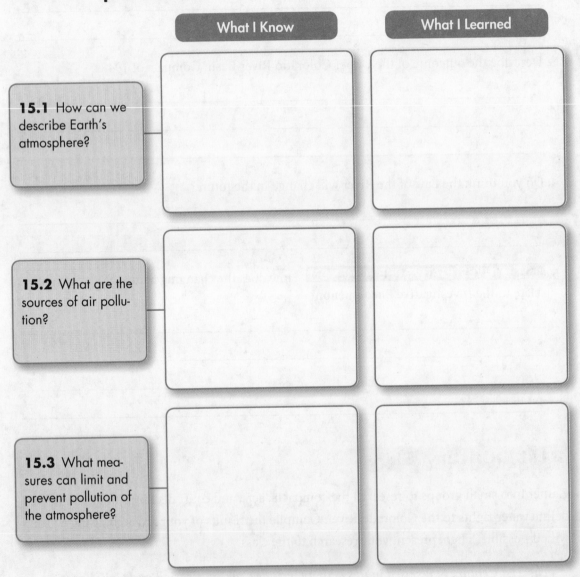

What I Know

What I Learned

15.1 How can we describe Earth's atmosphere?

15.2 What are the sources of air pollution?

15.3 What measures can limit and prevent pollution of the atmosphere?

15.1 Earth's Atmosphere

Key Concepts

 Properties of the atmosphere include its composition, relative humidity, temperature, and air pressure.

 The main layers of the atmosphere are the troposphere, stratosphere, mesosphere, and thermosphere.

 Processes that affect weather in the troposphere include heat transfer and the interaction of air masses.

SKILL BUILDER Vocabulary Preview

Define each vocabulary term in your own words. Then, write yourself a quick note on how you will remember each. One term has been done for you.

Term	Definition	How I Remember
Atmosphere		
Relative humidity		
Air pressure	The force exerted by air on the area below it	I think of how the *air* escapes out of the tire when my bike gets a flat.
Troposphere		
Stratosphere		
Ozone layer		
Mesosphere		

Term	Definition	How I Remember
Thermosphere		
Radiation		
Conduction		
Convection		
Convection current		
Air mass		
Front		

SKILL BUILDER Reading Strategy

Fill in the chart to preview the lesson. Then, write one sentence to explain what you think this lesson will be about.

What is the title of this lesson?	
Which vocabulary words are new for you?	
Which key concept includes the main layers of the atmosphere?	

What does the diagram under the heading, *The Troposphere and Weather* seem to show?	

_____

_____

Properties of the Atmosphere

1. **Organize Information**   Fill in the cluster diagram with the chemical formula and a short description for nitrogen, oxygen, and water vapor. For nitrogen and oxygen, include the approximate percentage of each in Earth's atmosphere.

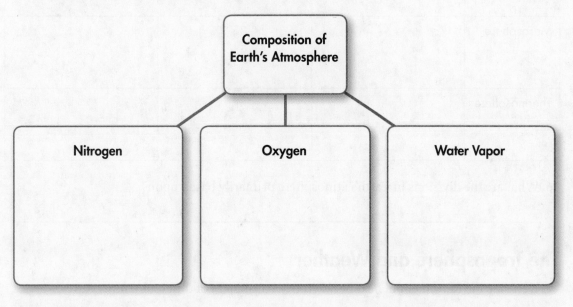

Composition of Earth's Atmosphere

Nitrogen

Oxygen

Water Vapor

2. What does it mean to say that the average daytime relative humidity of a particular city is 31 percent?

_____

_____

3. Explain how a cloud forms.

_____

_____

_____

4. What general statement can be made about the relationship between air pressure and altitude?

_____

Layers of the Atmosphere

5. [Organize Information] Fill in the chart with information about each layer of the atmosphere.

Layer	Distance in Relation to Sea Level	Information About Temperature	Information About the Air
Troposphere			
Stratosphere			
Mesosphere			
Thermosphere			

6. What are the divisions in Earth's atmosphere primarily based upon?

_____

The Troposphere and Weather

7. Describe the movement of heat between two substances of different temperatures.

_____

_____

8. Why does the surface of a black car feel warmer on a sunny day than the surface of a white car?

_____

_____

9. Compare and contrast convection and conduction.

_____

_____

_____

10. Summarize what happens when a colder, drier air mass pushes against a warmer, moister air mass.

_____

_____

_____

_____

11. **Think Visually** Use terms from the word bank to label the diagram.

| cool air | light precipitation | warm air | warm front |

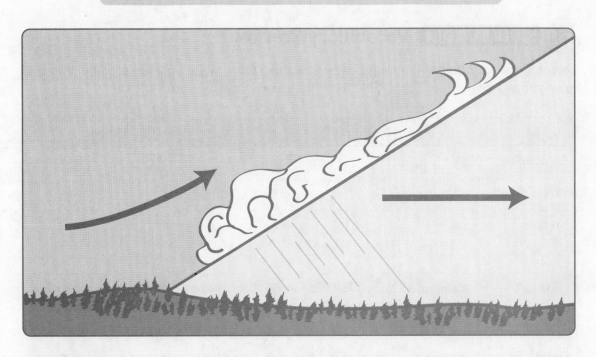

15.1 ○ SELF-CHECK

Answer the questions to test your knowledge of lesson concepts. You can check your work using the answers on the bottom of the page.

12. Which gas makes up most of Earth's atmosphere?

_____

13. What heats the atmosphere?

_____

14. What causes winds and also moves heat through the atmosphere?

_____

12. Nitrogen (N₂) 13. Energy from the sun 14. Convection currents: sinking cool air and rising warm air

15.2 Pollution of the Atmosphere

Key Concepts

 Air pollution can be caused by natural processes and human activities.

 Air pollutants can damage the respiratory system, interfere with the body's uptake of oxygen, and cause cancer.

 Temperature inversions may trap smog close to the surface of Earth, preventing the pollutants from dispersing.

 Acid deposition results when products of combustion combine with water in the atmosphere.

SKILL BUILDER Vocabulary Preview

Define each vocabulary term in your own words. Then, write yourself a quick note on how you will remember each. One term has been done for you.

Term	Definition	How I Remember
Air pollution		
Emission		
Fossil fuel	A carbon-containing fuel that formed millions of years ago from the remains of living things	I remember when our science teacher showed us a plant *fossil* in a piece of coal.
Primary air pollutant		
Secondary air pollutant		
Smog		

Term	Definition	How I Remember
Temperature inversion		
Acid deposition		

Sources of Air Pollution

For Questions 1–5, write True *if the statement is true. If the statement is false, replace the underlined word or words to make the statement true. Write your changes on the line.*

_____ **1.** The particulate matter in emissions such as smoke and soot consist of <u>tiny</u> particles.

_____ **2.** Power plants and factories are examples of <u>nonpoint</u> sources of pollution.

_____ **3.** Most air pollution is the direct or indirect result of the combustion of <u>fossil fuels</u>.

_____ **4.** Fossil fuels are carbon-containing fuels that formed <u>thousands</u> of years ago from the remains of organisms.

_____ **5.** When primary air pollutants react chemically with other substances, they produce new substances called <u>super</u> pollutants.

6. Name three natural processes that contribute to air pollution.

_____

_____

_____

7. How do human activities make natural pollution worse?

_____

_____

8. Compare and contrast primary air pollutants and secondary air pollutants.

_____

_____

_____

_____

How Air Pollutants Affect Your Health

9. Describe two examples of negative effects air pollutants have on the human respiratory system.

_____

_____

_____

10. Why is carbon monoxide particularly harmful for humans to breathe?

_____

_____

_____

11. Why is frequent exposure to car exhaust fumes harmful to the human body?

_____

_____

Smog and Temperature Inversions

12. **Organize Information** Fill in the Venn diagram to compare and contrast industrial and photochemical smog.

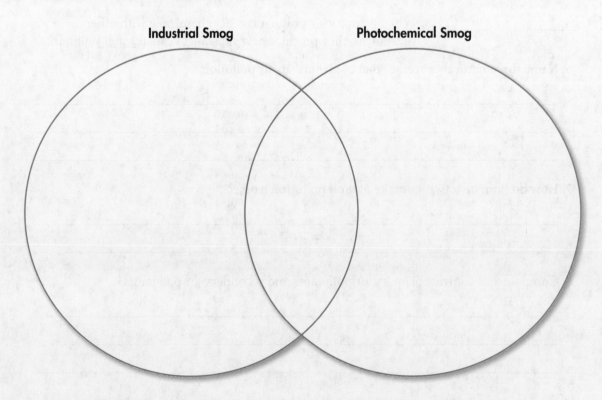

Industrial Smog   Photochemical Smog

13. How do levels of industrial smog compare in developing nations with levels in developed nations? Explain.

_____

_____

_____

_____

_____

14. Explain how a temperature inversion acts to hold air pollutants near Earth's surface.

_____

_____

_____

15. Describe the likely appearance of the air in an industrial city during a temperature inversion.

_____

Acid Deposition

16. **Organize Information** Fill in the cause-and-effect diagram with information on acid precipitation.

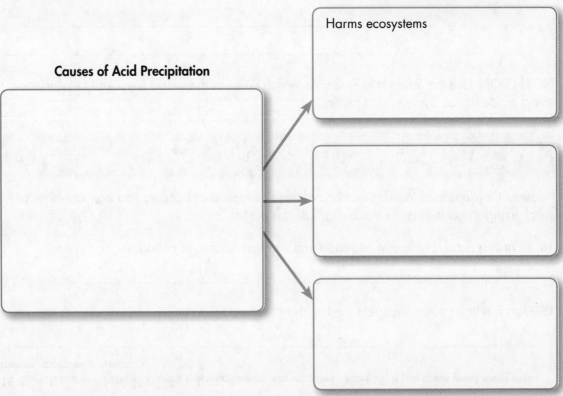

Causes of Acid Precipitation

Effects of Acid Precipitation

Harms ecosystems

SKILL BUILDER Think Visually

17. Draw arrows in the diagram below to show what happens to industrial emissions when a temperature inversion occurs. Label the inversion layer. On the lines below the diagram, describe the effects that the temperature inversion may have on the city's residents.

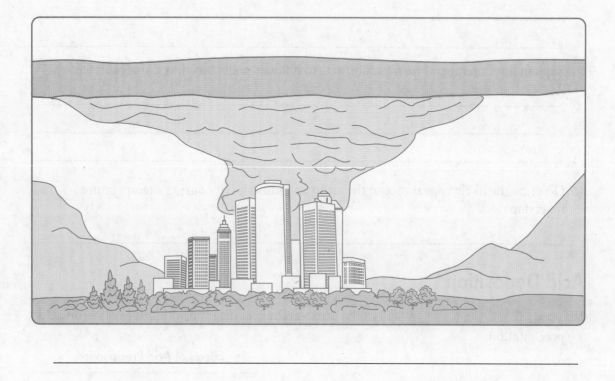

_____

_____

_____

EXTENSION Use the Internet to research which cities in the world frequently experience smog made worse by inversion layers.

15.2 ⬤ SELF-CHECK

Answer the questions to test your knowledge of lesson concepts. You can check your work using the answers on the bottom of the page.

18. Identify a natural source of pollution and a human source of pollution.

_____

19. How might air pollution affect the health of humans who come into contact with it?

_____

18. Sample answer: Natural source: volcano; human source: power plant 19. It can cause great harm to the human respiratory system.

15.3 Controlling Air Pollution

Key Concepts

- The Clean Air Act has provisions that have reduced air pollution in the United States.
- Nations have taken steps to deal with the problem of ozone loss in the stratosphere.

SKILL BUILDER Vocabulary Preview

Define each vocabulary term in your own words. Then, write yourself a quick note on how you will remember each. One term has been done for you.

Term	Definition	How I Remember
Clean Air Act		
Catalytic converter		
Scrubber		
Ozone hole	The area of lowered ozone concentration over Antarctica that occurs every spring	The *O* in ozone makes me think about how a hole in the ozone layer might look.
Chlorofluorocarbons (CFCs)		
Montreal Protocol		

SKILL BUILDER Reading Strategy

As you read the lesson, complete the main ideas and details chart.

Main Ideas	Details
The Clean Air Act	
Ozone: A Success Story	

The Clean Air Act

1. How does the Clean Air Act help safeguard the environment?

_____

_____

2. In what way does the Clean Air Act set standards for air quality in regard to human health?

_____

_____

3. Under the Clean Air Act, which agency sets nationwide standards governing air quality?

_____

4. Have the provisions of the Clean Air Act affected the amount of air pollution in the United States? Explain.

_____

_____

5. Which provision of the Clean Air Act do you believe has had the greatest impact on reduction of air pollution? Explain.

_____

_____

6. **Organize Information** Fill in the diagram with information about the Clean Air Act.

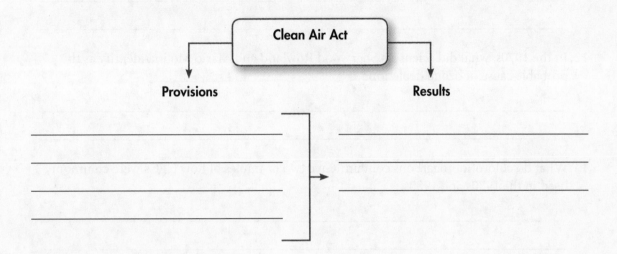

Ozone: A Success Story

For Questions 7–10, circle the letter of the correct answer.

7. Ozone is a pollutant in smog in the
   A. mesosphere.
   B. troposphere.
   C. stratosphere.
   D. thermosphere.

8. Ozone is highly beneficial in the ozone layer of the lower
   A. mesosphere.
   B. troposphere.
   C. stratosphere.
   D. thermosphere.

9. Lowered ozone concentration over Antartica occurs every
   A. fall.
   B. spring.
   C. winter.
   D. summer.

10. Many nations signed the Montreal Protocol in 1987. Since then, the production and use of chlorofluorocarbons has
    A. increased slightly.
    B. decreased slightly.
    C. increased dramatically.
    D. decreased dramatically.

11. Describe how ozone over Antarctica changed during the period from 1975 to 1985.

_____

_____

12. In the 1970s, what did scientists Sherwood Rowland and Mario Molina identify as the probable cause of ozone depletion?

_____

_____

13. What do chlorofluorocarbons contain? Give two examples of how CFCs were commonly used in the 1970s and 1980s.

_____

_____

14. What kinds of health concerns did people have that contributed to the signing of the Montreal Protocol?

_____

_____

15. What do the provisions of the Montreal Protocol focus on? Explain why it was necessary to have an international agreement to address CFCs?

_____

_____

_____

_____

_____

16. What do scientists expect will happen to the ozone concentrations in the near future?

_____

_____

17. Has the Montreal Protocol been a success story? Why or why not?

_____

_____

_____

_____

SKILL BUILDER Reading Strategy

18. Complete the timeline by briefly describing why each year was important to the Clean Air Act or the Montreal Protocol. Write your descriptions in the boxes.

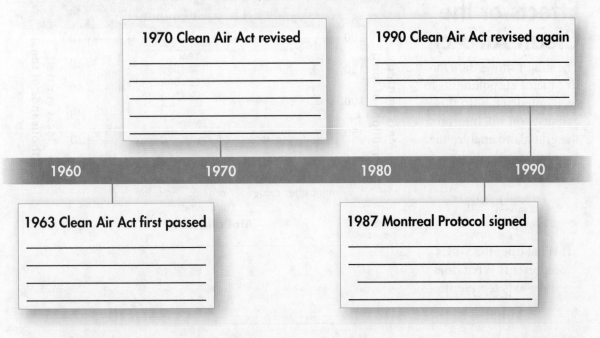

| 1970 Clean Air Act revised | 1990 Clean Air Act revised again |

1960   1970   1980   1990

| 1963 Clean Air Act first passed | 1987 Montreal Protocol signed |

15.3 ⊙ SELF-CHECK

Answer the questions to test your knowledge of lesson concepts. You can check your work using the answers on the bottom of the page.

19. What has the Southern Utes tribe done to preserve air quality in southwestern Colorado, an area rich in natural gas? _____

_____

_____

20. Explain why ozone is considered a pollutant in one layer of the atmosphere, but highly beneficial when located in another layer. _____

_____

_____

19. Tribe leaders have worked with state and local officials to develop an air quality program that monitors the air for pollutants, identifies sources of air pollutants, and inspects industries to make sure they adhere to standards. The Southern Utes are also researching additional air quality control measures. **20.** Ozone in the troposphere contributes to smog. Ozone in the stratosphere is beneficial because it absorbs ultraviolet radiation, which is harmful to humans.

Real Data

Effects of the Clean Air Act

The graph shows data for five major air pollutants in the United States. In this activity, you will interpret the graph and analyze the data by describing the trend shown in the graph.

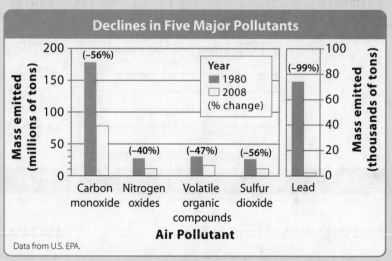

Declines in Five Major Pollutants

Mass emitted (millions of tons)
Mass emitted (thousands of tons)

Year
■ 1980
□ 2008
(% change)

(−56%) Carbon monoxide
(−40%) Nitrogen oxides
(−47%) Volatile organic compounds
(−56%) Sulfur dioxide
(−99%) Lead

Air Pollutant

Data from U.S. EPA.

Interpreting the Graph

1. What does the *x*-axis represent? What does the *y*-axis represent?

_____

_____

2. Study the key. For each pollutant, what does the green bar, white bar, and value in parentheses mean?

_____

_____

_____

Analyzing Data

When a percent change is positive, it indicates an increase. When a percent change is negative, it indicates a decrease.

3. From 1980 to 2008, did the amount of carbon monoxide in the air increase, decrease, or remain the same? _____

4. Notice that all the percent change values on the graph are negative. What does that indicate about levels of the five pollutants in the air during the peiod from 1980 to 2003?

_____

5. Which pollutant showed a greater decrease in emissions from 1980 to 2008: nitrogen oxides or sulfur dioxide? _____

Chapter Vocabulary Review

Match each term with its definition.

_____ 1. convection

_____ 2. temperature inversion

_____ 3. chlorofluorocarbons (CFCs)

_____ 4. front

_____ 5. ozone hole

_____ 6. conduction

_____ 7. fossil fuels

_____ 8. atmosphere

_____ 9. radiation

_____ 10. smog

_____ 11. scrubber

_____ 12. troposphere

_____ 13. relative humidity

_____ 14. acid deposition

a. the atmospheric layer that is nearest Earth's surface

b. an area of lowered ozone concentration over Antarctica

c. the transfer of heat by movement of currents within a fluid

d. a condition in which a layer of cooler air is located beneath a layer of warmer air

e. contain carbon and formed millions of year ago from the remains of organisms

f. the thin layer of gases that surrounds Earth

g. a device attached to factory smokestacks to remove pollutants

h. a boundary between two air masses that differ in temperature and moisture

i. a family of chemical compounds that destroys ozone molecules

j. the transfer of heat directly between two objects in contact

k. the transfer of energy through space

l. a mixture of air pollutants that forms over cities

m. the ratio of water vapor the air contains to the maximum amount it could have at that temperature

n. the settling to Earth's surface of acids formed when pollutants combine with water, oxygen, and other chemicals

Use each vocabulary term in a sentence.

15. relative humidity _____

_____

16. primary air pollutants _____

_____

EXTENSION On a separate sheet of paper, use at least five vocabulary words from the chapter to write a paragraph about the atmosphere.

Charging Toward Cleaner Air in London

Air Pollution

The U.S. Environmental Protection Agency has identified the major air pollutants to include nitrogen oxides, ozone, lead, carbon monoxide, sulfur oxides, and particulates. Nitrogen oxides (NO_x) are a group of highly reactive gases consisting of oxygen and nitrogen. One of the most common nitrogen oxides is nitrogen dioxide (NO_2). Nitrogen oxides harm the human respiratory system, contribute to acid deposition, and are involved in the formation of ground-level ozone.

The map shows the six nations in Europe with the highest NO_x emissions in 2007. At the time, the United Kingdom ranked highest for NO_x emissions, followed by Spain, France, Germany, Italy, and Poland. In an ongoing effort to reduce harmful emissions, European nations have lowered the acceptable emission levels for nitrogen oxides, sulfur dioxides, and other volatile organic compounds. For example, the 1999 Gothenburg Protocol set emission ceilings with the intent of reducing sulfur emission by 63 percent and NO_x emissions by 41 percent by 2010.

The European Union (EU) strives to improve the quality of air through ongoing legislation, cross-border directives, and educational efforts. In March 2001, the EU launched the Clean Air for Europe (CAFE) program to analyze problems related to air pollution and to create a strategic plan for dealing with those problems. In 2005, the EU adopted the Thematic Strategy on Air Pollution, with the aim of decreasing premature deaths from air pollution by

Highest NO_x Emissions in Europe, 2007

Based on data from the European Environment Agency.

40 percent by the year 2020 (that is, 370,000 deaths in 2000 to 230,000 deaths in 2020). To this end, the strategy addressed unified legislation targeting the reduction of particulates and ground-level pollution that travels across political borders.

Some progress in air quality has been accomplished, in particular a reduction in the levels of sulfur dioxide, lead, nitrogen oxides, carbon monoxide, and benzene. However, even with the progress shown, air pollution remains a problem among European nations. Harmful ground-level ozone levels and fine particulates often exceed acceptable limits set by legislation governing air quality in Europe. The EU is working toward a revision of the Gothenburg Protocol to strengthen continued efforts to improve air quality throughout Europe.

Use the information in **Air Pollution** to answer the questions below.

1. Why are nitrogen oxides considered harmful to humans?

   _____

   _____

2. In what way are nitrogen oxides harmful to the environment?

   _____

3. Which six nations in Europe ranked the highest in nitrogen oxide emissions in 2007?
   List the nations from highest in emissions to the lowest.

   _____

   _____

4. Which nation ranked higher in nitrogen oxide emissions than Italy, but lower than France?

   _____

5. How is Europe addressing the problem of harmful emissions, such as nitrogen oxides?

   _____

   _____

6. How does the information in **Air Pollution** affect your answer to the following
   question: How can we ensure everyone has clean air to breathe?

   _____

   _____

   _____

   _____

   _____

21st Century Skills

Work in small groups to brainstorm ideas on how to address air pollution problems in the
United States. Research local air pollution problems by conducting interviews with local officials
and businesses. Focus on the causes of air pollution and develop short and long term solutions to
the problem. Then, create a public policy statement that addresses the problem of air pollution.

*The 21st Century Skills used in this activity include **Critical Thinking and Problem Solving,
Communication and Collaboration,** and **Creativity and Innovation.***

16 Global Climate Change

Before you read the chapter, answer each question with information you know. After you complete the chapter, re-answer the questions using information you learned.

INVESTIGATIVE PHENOMENON **How does climate change impact low-lying areas?**

	What I Know	What I Learned
16.1 Why is the greenhouse effect important for Earth's climate?		
16.2 How can we determine what the atmospheric greenhouse gas levels were in the distant past?		
16.3 How is climate change affecting food availability for both marine and terrestrial organisms?		
16.4 What can we personally do to respond to climate change		

16.1 Our Dynamic Climate

Key Concepts

 The heating of Earth's atmosphere by the sun is influenced by the greenhouse effect, latitude, and sunspot cycles.

 Winds distribute heat and moisture globally.

 Oceans affect climate by transporting heat and absorbing carbon dioxide.

 Global climate may be affected by factors such as topography, volcanic eruptions, regional vegetation, and changes in Earth's orbit.

SKILL BUILDER Vocabulary Preview

Define each vocabulary term in your own words. Then, write yourself a quick note on how you will remember each. One term has been done for you.

Term	Definition	How I Remember
Greenhouse effect		
Greenhouse gas		
Thermohaline circulation	A water movement pattern in which warmer, less salty water moves along the surface of the ocean, and colder, saltier water moves deep beneath the ocean's surface	I know that *therm* refers to heat, and *circulation* refers to the movement of something, so I put the two ideas together and think of movement of water related to heat.
El Niño		
Topography		

Energy From the Sun

1. **Organize Information** Fill in the diagram with three factors that influence the heating of Earth's atmosphere by the sun.

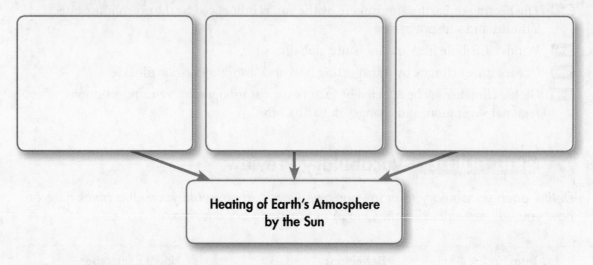

2. What would happen if Earth did not have an atmosphere?

_____

3. What are the two major greenhouse gases?

_____

4. How do greenhouse gases make life on Earth possible?

_____

_____

5. What is the relationship between a geographical location's distance from the equator and climate temperatures?

_____

_____

6. What are the general climate regions on Earth?

_____

7. What is the relationship between sunspots and the energy released by the sun?

_____

8. What is a sunspot cycle?

_____

Wind Patterns in the Atmosphere

For Questions 9–12, write True if the statement is true. If the statement is false, replace the underlined word or words to make the statement true. Write your changes on the line.

_____ 9. Convection currents form from the rising of <u>cool</u> air and the sinking of <u>warm</u> air.

_____ 10. As part of the prevailing wind patterns, cool air moves toward the <u>equator</u>.

_____ 11. When warm, moist air is cooled, water vapor condenses and forms <u>wind</u>.

_____ 12. As winds move over bodies of water, they pick up <u>water vapor</u>, which then falls as precipitation.

13. Describe two ways in which water vapor enters the atmosphere.

_____

_____

The Oceans and Climate

14. Ocean water absorbs carbon dioxide. What effect does this have on the temperature of the atmosphere? Why does it have this effect?

_____

_____

15. Saltier water is denser than water with low salinity. Cool water generally has a greater density than warm water. What effect do these factors have on the movement of ocean water? What is the term for this effect?

_____

_____

16. During El Niño, equatorial winds weaken. What effect does this have on the temperature of surface waters in the eastern Pacific Ocean?

_____

17. Oceans can hold 50 times more carbon dioxide than is found in the atmosphere. Given this fact, why is global warming still occurring?

_____

_____

Other Factors That Affect Climate

18. [Organize Information] Fill in the chart with information about other factors that affect climate.

Factor	Description of the Factor	How the Factor Affects Climate
Topography		
Volcanoes		
Regional vegetation		
Changes in Earth's orbit		

19. Why is the vegetation at the bottom of mountains generally not the same as vegetation found at higher altitudes on mountains?

_____

_____

20. Why does precipitation generally fall on the windward side of mountain ranges?

_____

_____

21. Do volcanic eruptions have long-term effects on climate? Explain.

_____

_____

_____

_____

SKILL BUILDER Think Visually

22. Draw arrows on the diagram to show the direction of each global wind pattern. Then, label the climate zones with terms from the word bank. You may use each word more than once.

| polar | temperate | tropical |

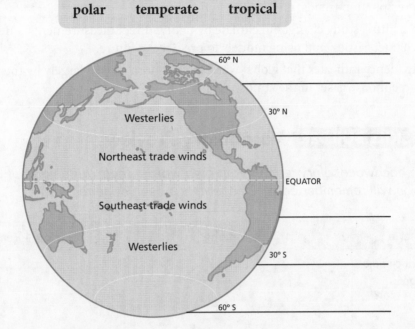

EXTENSION On a separate sheet of paper, draw a diagram that shows wind and precipitation patterns as winds travel from the ocean across coastal mountain ranges.

16.1 ○ SELF-CHECK

Answer the questions to test your knowledge of lesson concepts. You can check your work using the answers on the bottom of the page.

23. Contrast the way solar radiation strikes the poles with the way it strikes the equator.

_____

_____

24. How does the greenhouse effect help warm Earth's atmosphere?

_____

_____

25. What climate-related factors are transported globally by winds?

_____

23. At the equator—directly; at the poles—at an angle and spread out over a larger area than at the equator
24. Greenhouse gases absorb heat from the sun and release it slowly. 25. Heat, moisture

16.2 Climate Change

Key Concepts

- Evidence of global climate change includes rising atmospheric temperature, precipitation trends, melting ice, and rising seas.
- Scientists study changes in climate by taking direct measurements, inferring past climate characteristics, and using models to predict the future.
- Evidence indicates that global warming has been caused largely by the increase in greenhouse gases in the atmosphere.

 SKILL BUILDER Vocabulary Preview

Define each vocabulary term in your own words. Then, write yourself a quick note on how you will remember each. One term has been done for you.

Term	Definition	How I Remember
Global climate change		
Global warming		
Proxy indicator		
Climate model		
Fossil fuel	A fuel that formed millions of years ago from the remains of living things	I remember the color and feel of the leaf fossil my teacher showed me in science class last year.

SKILL BUILDER **Reading Strategy**

As you read the lesson, complete the main ideas and details chart.

Main Ideas	Details
Evidence of a warming earth	
Studying climate change	
Finding the cause of climate change	

Evidence of a Warming Earth

1. What two conclusions has the IPCC made about global climate change?

_____

_____

2. Describe two ways in which precipitation patterns have changed.

_____

_____

3. What changes have scientists noted regarding the size and number of glaciers on Earth?

_____

4. What happens to seawater when it warms? What effect does this have on sea levels?

_____

Studying Climate Change

5. How do scientists study current climate conditions?

_____

_____

6. What are proxy indicators and why are they important to climate scientists?

_____

_____

7. List three types of proxy indicators.

_____

8. How do researchers test the accuracy of climate models?

_____

_____

9. **Think Visually** What does the illustration below show?

_____

_____

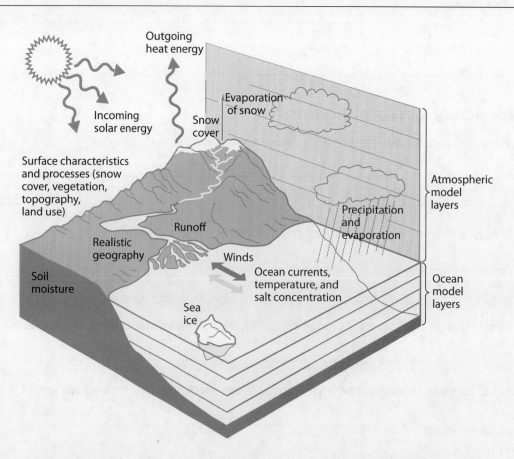

10. What contribution did Charles Keeling make to the understanding of global warming?

_____

_____

Finding the Cause of Climate Change

For Questions 11 and 12, circle the letter of the correct answer.

11. The greenhouse gas considered most responsible for global warming is
   A. methane.
   B. water vapor.
   C. nitrous oxide.
   D. carbon dioxide.

12. Scientists agree that the causes of global warming include all of the following except
   A. industrialization.
   B. forest conservation.
   C. the use of motor vehicles.
   D. increased burning of fossil fuels.

13. Complete the paragraph with terms from the word bank.

fossil fuels	global warming	greenhouse effect	natural gas

Carbon dioxide is the greenhouse gas that is most responsible for _____.
Most scientists agree that the extra carbon dioxide in the atmosphere has come from human

activities. The main source of the extra carbon dioxide is the burning of _____,

such as oil, _____, and coal, for energy. As carbon dioxide in the atmosphere

increases, the _____ increases.

16.2 ◯ SELF-CHECK

Answer the questions to test your knowledge of lesson concepts. You can check your work using the answers on the bottom of the page.

14. According to the IPCC, what is the primary cause of rising seas today? _____

_____

15. Why are proxy indicators important to the study of climate? _____

_____

14. Global warming 15. Sample answer: Scientists must know what climates were like in the past to understand how they are changing today.

16.3 Effects of Climate Change

Key Concepts

 As the atmosphere warms, ecosystems on land and in the ocean are changing, affecting organisms in various ways.

As the atmosphere warms, ecosystems on land and in the ocean are changing, affecting organisms in various ways.

Global climate change is affecting aspects of human life such as farming, forestry, the economy, and health.

Computer modeling predicts that climate change will continue to affect people.

 SKILL BUILDER **Vocabulary Preview**

Define the vocabulary term in your own words. Then, write yourself a quick note on how you will remember it.

Term	Definition	How I Remember
Coral bleaching		

 SKILL BUILDER **Reading Strategy**

Fill in the table to preview the lesson. Then, on the lines below the table, write one sentence to explain what you think this lesson will be about.

What is the title of this lesson?	
What is the vocabulary term for this lesson?	
What do the photos show?	
Choose the caption of one of the photos and identify what it explains.	

_____

_____

EXTENSION On a separate sheet of paper, write five questions that come to mind as you preview this lesson. Answer your questions after you have completed the lesson.

Effects on Ecosystems and Organisms

1. **Think Visually** In each circle of the the cluster diagram, write an effect of climate change on whole ecosystems or individual organisms.

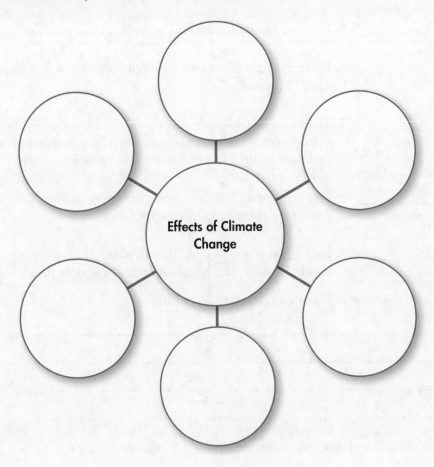

2. Why might early migration be harmful to bird populations?

_____

_____

3. How does the loss of coral reefs affect marine ecosystems and people?

_____

_____

_____

_____

4. What seems to be contributing to coral bleaching?

_____

_____

Impact on People Right Now

For Questions 5–9, write True *if the statement is true. If the statement is false, replace the underlined word or words to make the statement true. Write your changes on the line.*

_____ **5.** Extreme weather is becoming more severe over time.

_____ **6.** Extensive forest fires have resulted partly from <u>shorter</u>, warmer, drier fire seasons.

_____ **7.** The financial consequence of storms is indicated by the amount of money that <u>insurance</u> companies pay to people and companies that have insured their property against weather-related damage.

_____ **8.** Rising property insurance payments may indirectly indicate that storms are <u>decreasing</u> in severity.

_____ **9.** <u>Heat exhaustion</u> is a condition in which the body cannot control its temperature, and body temperature rapidly rises.

10. Summarize the effect of climate change on agriculture.

_____

_____

_____

_____

11. Describe the effect of extended dry conditions on the forestry industry.

_____

_____

_____

_____

12. How will the range of the ticks that carry Lyme disease likely be affected if northern Canada becomes warmer?

_____

_____

13. In the United States, does the majority of the population live in coastal areas or inland areas?

_____

_____

Future Impact on People

14. According to the IPCC report, how will carbon dioxide levels and global temperatures change in the future?

_____

_____

15. **Organize Information** Fill in the cause-and-effect diagram with the correct information about some possible effects of climate change on people.

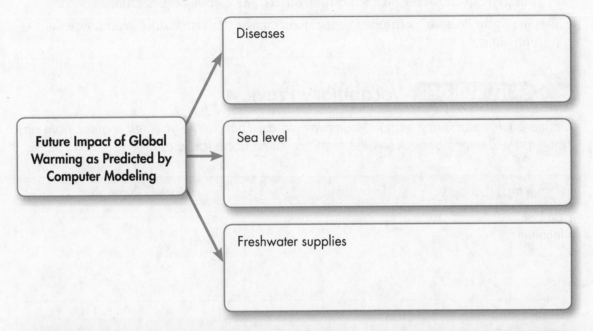

	Diseases
Future Impact of Global Warming as Predicted by Computer Modeling	Sea level
	Freshwater supplies

16.3 SELF-CHECK

Answer the questions to test your knowledge of lesson concepts. You can check your work using the answers on the bottom of the page.

16. How has global climate change affected the Arctic?

_____

_____

17. Explain why increased carbon dioxide in the atmosphere is harmful to ocean ecosystems.

_____

_____

16. Sample answer: Ice sheets are melting, and sea ice is thinning. As a result, polar bears are having difficulty finding food. **17.** The absorption of large amounts of carbon dioxide by ocean waters raises the acidity of the waters, resulting in harm to sea life.

16.4 Responding to Climate Change

Key Concepts

 Ways of reducing the production of greenhouse gases include conserving electricity and finding new ways to produce electricity.

 By choosing more efficient cars, driving less, and using public transportation, people can reduce greenhouse gas emissions.

 Greenhouse gas emissions can also be reduced through improved agriculture and forestry, cap-and-trade policies, carbon offsets, and carbon sequestration.

 The Kyoto Protocol is an agreement among many nations to reduce greenhouse gas emissions.

SKILL BUILDER Vocabulary Preview

Define each vocabulary term in your own words. Then, write yourself a quick note on how you will remember each. One term has been done for you.

Term	Definition	How I Remember
Carbon footprint		
Carbon tax		
Carbon offset	A voluntary payment made when one industry or person, instead of reducing its own greenhouse gas emissions, pays another group or person to do so	I think about how I have to *offset* my time at soccer practice with the same amount of time spent doing homework.
Carbon sequestration		
Kyoto Protocol		

Use and Production of Electricity

1. **Organize Information** Fill in the chart with three ways to conserve energy and three suggestions for alternate sources of electricity.

Ways to Conserve Energy	Alternate Sources of Electricity

2. Why is it important for individuals to reduce their carbon footprints?

_____

_____

Transportation

3. **Think Visually** Use the percentages to correctly fill in the amount of energy lost for each use.

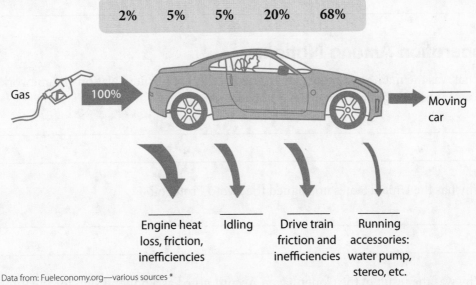

2%   5%   5%   20%   68%

Gas   100% →   → Moving car

Engine heat loss, friction, inefficiencies | Idling | Drive train friction and inefficiencies | Running accessories: water pump, stereo, etc.

Data from: Fueleconomy.org—various sources *

4. Why are vehicles in other nations more efficient than vehicles in the United States?

_____

_____

5. What is one way students could reduce their dependence on cars?

_____

Other Approaches to Reducing Greenhouse Gases

Match each approach to reducing greenhouse gases to the statement that best describes it.

_____ **6.** cap-and-trade

_____ **7.** carbon tax

_____ **8.** carbon offset

_____ **9.** carbon sequestration

a. program in which a government sets a limit on carbon emissions, but allows industries to sell leftover allowances

b. storage system for carbon

c. a fee the government charges polluters

d. voluntary payment made to reduce greenhouse gases

10. How can improved agriculture and forestry help reduce greenhouse gas emissions?

_____

_____

_____

_____

_____

11. What is one identified difficulty with storing captured carbon underground?

_____

Cooperation Among Nations

12. What was the main reason the plan drafted at the 1992 United Nations Framework Convention on Climate Change did not succeed?

_____

_____

13. Why has the United States not signed the Kyoto Protocol?

_____

_____

14. Why was the result of the Copenhagen Accord noted as a hopeful sign for the future?

_____

_____

SKILL BUILDER Organize Information

15. Fill in the chart with terms from the word bank.

> alternative fuels cap-and-trade carbon footprint carbon offset
> Energy Star Program fuel-inefficiency greenhouse gas emissions solar power

Problems	Solutions Developed to Address the Problems

EXTENSION Develop an energy-savings policy for your household. Discuss the advantages and disadvantages of your policy with each household member. Discuss your policy idea in a short presentation to the class.

16.4 SELF-CHECK

Answer the questions to test your knowledge of lesson concepts. You can check your work using the answers on the bottom of the page.

16. Give three examples of mitigation strategies designed to reduce greenhouse gas emissions.

_____

17. Do you think the Kyoto treaty is fair? Compare and contrast why some nations support the

Kyoto treaty while others do not. _____

_____

18. Explain why global cooperation among nations is needed to reduce greenhouse gas

emissions. _____

_____

_____

16. Sample answer: Improving energy efficiency, preventing deforestation, carbon tax. **17.** Answers will vary, but students should include examples such as the following: Nations that don't support the treaty argue there are different requirements for different nations, making the treaty unfair. Supporters say the different requirements are justified since industrialized nations created the greenhouse gas problem. **18.** Because all nations contribute to the release of greenhouse gases, this is a global problem that will require a global effort in developing solutions. Solutions will not work if only a few nations adopt them.

Chapter Vocabulary Review

Use the clues to complete the crossword puzzle. Note that two-word answers have no space between the two words.

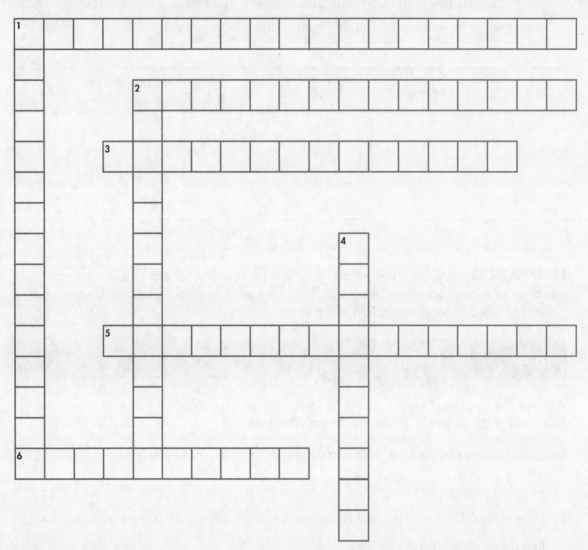

Across

1. storage of greenhouse gases
2. water vapor and carbon dioxide, for example
3. the result of algae in corals dying
5. natural process of trapping heat near Earth
6. surface characteristics of an area

Down

1. amount of carbon dioxide emissions for which each person or group is responsible
2. increase in Earth's average surface temperature
4. source of energy that formed millions of years ago from the remains of living things

EXTENSION On a separate sheet of paper, use chapter vocabulary words to write a paragraph that explains ways in which scientists study climate change.

Ecological Footprints

Carbon Footprints

Your carbon footprint is the amount of carbon dioxide that you cause to be emitted into the atmosphere each year. In this activity, you will learn how to use an online calculator to calculate all or part of the carbon footprint of your household and of your class's households.

Calculating Carbon Footprints

To calculate your individual carbon footprint or that of your household, use an online carbon footprint calculator. Depending on which Web site you use, you may need to enter one or more of the following pieces of information.

• a description of your house or apartment, including the number of bedrooms and the square footage	• your household's annual energy use, such as for electricity and natural gas
• the number of people in your household	• your household's use of energy-saving appliances
• vehicle information	• your household's recycling habits

1. According to the online carbon footprint calculator, what is the approximate carbon footprint of your household?

   _____

2. Describe one way your household could reduce its carbon footprint. Then, use the online calculator to recalculate the carbon footprint. What is your household's new carbon footprint? By how much was the carbon footprint reduced?

   _____

   _____

3. One way of estimating your individual carbon footprint is to calculate your household's carbon footprint and then divide that number by the number of people in your household. How many people are in your household? What is your individual carbon footprint?

   _____

4. Work with a partner. Compare and contrast the online calculators that you each used. What were the differences in the information requested? Is there just one way to calculate a carbon footprint? Explain.

   _____

   _____

Rising Seas May Flood the Maldive Islands

Rising Sea Levels Worldwide

According to the National Centers for Coastal Ocean Science (NCCOS), from 1900 to 2000, sea levels rose worldwide by some 20 centimeters. This is approximately two millimeters per year. The trend in global sea level rise is shown in the graph at right. Scientists predict that global sea levels could potentially rise at double that rate during the twenty-first century.

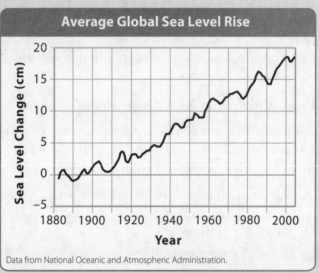

Average Global Sea Level Rise

Data from National Oceanic and Atmospheric Administration.

Coastlines already affected by shoreline retreat will be particularly vulnerable to rising sea levels because of the loss of water-absorbing ecosystems. The Louisiana coast, for example, lost approximately 3058 square kilometers of coastal wetlands in the past 100 years. Rising sea levels pose a threat to the well-being of island nations, such as the Maldives, the Philippines, and Japan, as well as to coastal populations throughout the world. Coastal flooding can destroy homes and businesses, and negatively effect coastal ecosystems. Significantly, the mixing of seawater and fresh water is harmful to aquatic organisms and compromises drinking-water supplies for people.

Approximately 60 percent of the world's population lives at a distance of no more than 60 kilometers from the sea. Large coastal populations are found in many nations, including China, Egypt, India, and the United States. Besides New Orleans, other important seaport cities include Boston, New York, and Miami.

According to a 2009 report issued by the U.S. Global Change Research Program, of particular concern are an increase in the size and shifting of "dead zones" off the coasts of Oregon and Washington. These "dead zones" are areas where the sustainability of marine life that once existed there is compromised due to the depletion of oxygen levels within the zone. Scientists believe these "dead zones" are the direct result of deepening water levels along the Pacific coastlines.

As sea levels rise, governments around the world are looking for ways to mitigate the consequences of global warming. Importantly, agreements among nations, such as the Kyoto Protocol and the 2009 Copenhagen Accord, serve to bring worldwide attention to the devastating effects of rising sea levels and other problems associated with global warming.

Use the information in **Rising Sea Levels Worldwide** to answer the questions below.

1. Why are governments of island nations, such as the Maldives, particularly concerned about rising sea levels? _____

_____

_____

2. Aside from the potential for major flooding of homes and businesses, describe another problem associated with rising sea levels. _____

_____

3. Describe the trend shown on the graph.

_____

4. Why are marine "dead zones" of particular interest and concern for scientists?

_____

_____

_____

5. **REVISIT INVESTIGATIVE** PHENOMENON How does the information in Rising Sea Levels Worldwide affect your answer to the **Investigative Phenomenon:** "How does climate change impact low-laying areas?"

_____

_____

_____

21st Century Skills

Work in small groups to select and research a region of the United States, such as the Gulf of Mexico or the Chesapeake Bay, that is likely to be affected by rising sea levels. A good source of information is the U.S. Geological Survey. Create a multimedia presentation about the region, such as its population, major cities, industries, and ecological characteristics, including estuaries. Predict the effects of rising sea levels on the coastal region. Support your predictions with evidence from your research.

*The 21st Century Skills used in this activity include **Communication and Collaboration, Information Literacy,** and **Information, Communication, and Technology (ICT) Literacy.***

17 Nonrenewable Energy

Before you read the chapter, answer each question with information you know. After you complete the chapter, re-answer the questions using information you learned.

INVESTIGATIVE PHENOMENON **What effect does the use of nonrenewable energy resources have on the environment?**

	What I Know	What I Learned
17.1 What is energy and how is it used?		
17.2 How did fossil fuels form, and how are they obtained and used?		
17.3 What problems are associated with fossil fuel use?		
17.4 What are the advantages and disadvantages of nuclear energy?		

17.1 Energy: An Overview

Key Concepts

🔑 Energy, which is the ability to do work, can be classified as either kinetic or potential.

🔑 Forms of energy include mechanical energy, electrical energy, thermal energy, electromagnetic energy, chemical energy, and nuclear energy.

🔑 Human society uses renewable and nonrenewable energy resources in industry, transportation, commerce, and residences.

SKILL BUILDER Vocabulary Preview

Define each vocabulary term in your own words. Then, write yourself a quick note on how you will remember each. One term has been done for you.

Term	Definition	How I Remember
Energy		
Kinetic energy		
Potential energy		
Combustion		
Energy efficiency	An expression of how much of the energy put into a system actually does useful work	I know that to be *efficient* means to do something in the best way possible without wasting too much time or energy.

Term	Definition	How I Remember
Renewable energy		
Nonrenewable energy		
Electricity		

What is Energy?

For Questions 1–4, complete each statement by writing the correct word or words related to energy.

1. Energy is the ability to do _____ or cause a _____.

2. Energy is necessary to change the position, _____, or _____ of something.

3. When a diver stands at the top of a platform, before the diver starts moving, the diver has _____ energy.

4. As the diver pushes off from the platform toward the water, the diver has _____ energy.

5. Give an example of a process that requires energy, and explain why it requires energy.

_____

_____

Forms of Energy

6. Explain the energy conversion(s) that take place during combustion.

_____

_____

7. What are the two main products of the combustion of methane and other fossil fuels?

_____

8. A vehicle must have energy to run; however, not all the energy the vehicle is supplied is used to perform the intended work. What happens to some of the energy that is not converted to motion?

_____

For Questions 9–14, match each form of energy with the statement that best describes it.

_____ 9. mechanical energy

_____ 10. electrical energy

_____ 11. thermal energy

_____ 12. electromagnetic energy

_____ 13. chemical energy

_____ 14. nuclear energy

a. found in the bonds that hold atoms together

b. waves from the sun or in a microwave oven

c. associated with the motion and position of an object

d. involves forces within atoms

e. used to power computers

f. results in an object becoming warmer if the particles in the object begin to move faster

Sources and Uses of Energy

For Questions 15 and 16, circle the letter of the correct answer.

15. Which is an example of a nonrenewable resource?

   A. sun

   B. moving water

   C. nuclear energy

   D. heat from deep within Earth

16. Which is a secondary source of energy?

   A. coal

   B. wind

   C. wood

   D. electricity

17. Identify the four major sectors of the economy that consume energy.

_____

18. How does the quantity of energy used in developed nations compare with the quantity used in developing nations?

_____

19. Contrast energy use in developed nations and developing nations.

_____

_____

SKILL BUILDER **Organize Information**

20. Complete the cluster diagram. Continue adding ovals and filling them with facts and details that relate to energy.

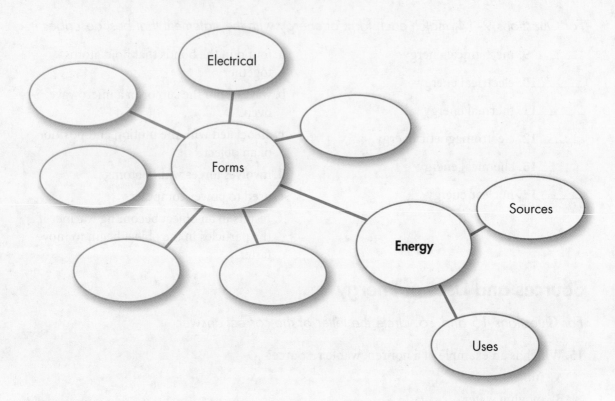

Electrical		
Forms		Sources
	Energy	
	Uses	

17.1 ◉ SELF-CHECK

Answer the questions to test your knowledge of lesson concepts. You can check your work using the answers on the bottom of the page.

21. Explain the difference between potential and kinetic energy. _____

_____

22. What are three examples of ways you use electromagnetic energy?

_____

_____

23. List five examples of renewable energy resources. _____

_____

21. An object has potential energy because of its position or shape, while kinetic energy is the energy an object has due to its motion. 22. Sample answer: Powering the microwave, warming myself in the sun, powering the radio 23. Possible answers: Sun, wind, moving water, wood, heat from deep within Earth

17.2 Fossil Fuels

Key Concepts

- Fossil fuels formed from the remains of organisms that lived millions of years ago.
- Coal, which is used mainly to generate electricity, is obtained by mining.
- Petroleum, which is obtained by drilling, is a major source of energy and is used to make a variety of products.
- Natural gas yields a large amount of energy and is less polluting than other fossil fuels.
- The supply of fossil fuels is limited.

 SKILL BUILDER Vocabulary Preview

Define each vocabulary term in your own words. Then, write yourself a quick note on how you will remember each. One term has been done for you.

Term	Definition	How I Remember
Strip mining		
Subsurface mining	Typically, the practice of digging shafts deep into the ground to find and remove a mineral	*Sub–* can mean "below," so *subsurface* mining occurs below Earth's surface.
Petroleum		
Petrochemicals		
Oil sands		
Oil shale		
Methane hydrate		

SKILL BUILDER **Reading Strategy**

As you read the lesson, complete the main ideas and details chart.

Main Ideas	Details
Fossil fuels formed from the remains of ancient organisms.	
Coal is mined from the ground and used mainly to generate electricity.	
Petroleum is drilled from the ground and used as the source for fuel and other products.	
Natural gas is extracted from the ground and used as a source to produce heat for homes and businesses.	
Fossil fuel use continues to rise, and the supply of easily obtainable fossil fuels will likely eventually run out.	

EXTENSION Research fossil fuels in your state. Are there any deposits of coal, oil, or natural gas? If not, discover which state nearest your state has deposits of coal, oil, or natural gas. Create a poster presentation that explains where these deposits are located, whether the quantity in the location is abundant, and how the production of the fossil fuel impacts the environment and economy of the state.

How Fossil Fuels Form

1. **Organize Information** Complete the flowchart to describe how fossil fuels form.

| | Sediments settle on top of the dead organisms. | |

2. How does the formation of oil differ from the formation of coal?

_____

_____

_____

3. Do all types of coal have the same energy value? Include examples in your response.

_____

_____

Coal

For Questions 4–6, complete each statement by writing the correct word or words.

4. Beginning in the 1300s, Native Americans of the Hopi Nation used coal to
_____, _____, and _____.

5. _____ of the world's energy is provided by coal.

6. The main use of coal is to generate _____.

7. Compare and contrast strip mining and subsurface mining.

_____

_____

_____

_____

8. State four advantages of coal use as compared to use of other fossil fuels.

_____

_____

_____

Oil

9. How are petrochemicals used?

_____

_____

10. Explain how scientists use sound waves to find oil deposits.

_____

_____

_____

11. Identify and briefly describe the process that makes crude oil usable. Name the type of place where this process occurs.

_____

_____

12. ⬚ (Organize Information) Use the Venn diagram below to compare primary extraction and secondary extraction of oil.

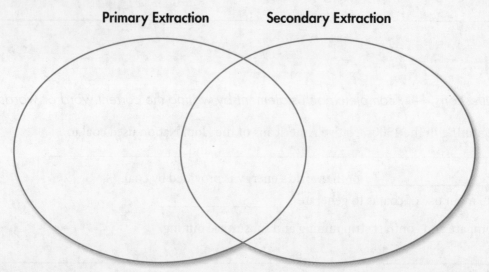

Primary Extraction   **Secondary Extraction**

Natural Gas

For Questions 13–16, write True is the statement is true. If the statement is false, replace the underlined word to make the statement true. Write your changes on the line.

_____**13.** Natural gas is <u>more</u> polluting than coal or oil.

_____**14.** Natural gas produces a <u>small</u> amount of energy.

_____**15.** Natural gas is sometimes found <u>above</u> coal deposits.

_____**16.** About half the homes in the United States use natural gas for <u>heating</u>.

17. Identify four products that are made with natural gas.

_____

The Supply of Fossil Fuels

18. Why are energy experts concerned about the supply of fossil fuels?

_____

19. What are three drawbacks of alternative sources of fossil fuels?

_____

_____

_____

For Questions 20–22, match each alternative source of fossil fuel with the statement that best describes it.

_____20. oil shale

_____21. oil sands

_____22. methane hydrate

a. can be burned like coal or processed to extract liquid petroleum

b. icelike solid(s) located in the deep ocean floor and made up of molecules of methane within a crystal network

c. contain(s) bitumen and generally removed through strip mining

17.2 ⊙ SELF-CHECK

Answer the questions to test your knowledge of lesson concepts. You can check your work using the answers on the bottom of the page.

23. How do fossil fuels form? _____

_____

24. How does natural gas compare to other fossil fuels for energy production and pollution?

_____

_____

25. Describe the trend in world consumption of fossil fuels during the past several decades.

_____

23. They form during millions of years from the remains of once-living things that have settled to the bottom of a body of water and then been subjected to pressure. 24. Compared to other fossil fuels, natural gas produces a large amount of energy and less pollution. 25. The use of all types of fossil fuels has increased.

17.3 Consequences of Fossil Fuel Use

Key Concepts

- The burning of fossil fuels causes pollution that affects human health and the environment.
- Mining and drilling for fuels can endanger people and change ecosystems in harmful ways.
- Since fossil fuels are unevenly distributed in the world, many nations need to depend on foreign sources.
- To save fossil fuels and limit the damage they cause, we need to conserve energy.

 SKILL BUILDER Vocabulary Preview

Define the vocabulary term in your own words. Then, write yourself a quick note on how you will remember it. One term has been done for you.

Term	Definition	How I Remember
Acid drainage		
Energy conservation	The limiting of energy use	When you *conserve* something, you save it for the future. Energy *conservation* helps fossil fuels last into the future.

Pollution From Fossil Fuels

1. **Organize Information** Fill in the cause-and-effect diagram with information about how fossil fuel use affects health and the environment.

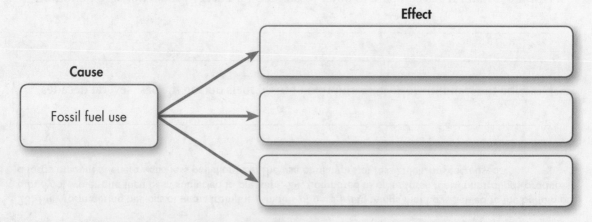

Cause

Fossil fuel use

Effect

2. Explain how burning coal and oil pollutes the air.

_____

_____

3. Other than through huge oil spills, how can oil cause water pollution?

_____

_____

_____

Damage Caused by Extracting Fuels

4. Complete the following paragraph with terms from the word bank.

acid drainage	coal dust	ecosystems	soil erosion	technology

The _____ required to remove fossil fuels from the ground is very

expensive. The removal process can endanger people and harm _____.

For example, strip mining can cause the release of harmful chemicals in a process called

_____. Coal mining is one of the world's most dangerous occupations.

Miners risk injury or death from collapsing mines. In addition, they inhale _____,

which can cause respiratory disease. Strip mining is not as dangerous for humans as

underground coal mining, but it can cause extreme habitat damage and _____.

5. How can mountaintop removal be worse for the environment than strip mining?

_____

_____

_____

6. Why do scientists disagree about whether the oil industry in Prudhoe Bay has negatively
affected the region's caribou?

_____

_____

7. Discuss the two major scientific opinions related to the possible effects of drilling for oil
on the Arctic National Wildlife Refuge.

_____

_____

_____

_____

Dependence on Foreign Sources

8. To what extent does the United States depend on foreign sources of fossil fuels? Which type of fossil fuel is plentiful in the United States?

_____

_____

9. Identify three ways the United States can reduce its dependence on foreign oil.

_____

_____

10. Name four nations, other than those in the Middle East, from which the United States now imports large amounts of oil.

_____

Energy Conservation

For Questions 11–13, write True is the statement is true. If the statement is false, replace the underlined word or words to make the statement true. Write your changes on the line.

_____**11.** Transportation accounts for <u>one half</u> of oil use in the United States.

_____**12.** Drivers in European nations pay <u>higher</u> gas taxes than those paid in the United States.

_____**13.** Energy conservation is the practice of <u>increasing</u> energy use to meet goals.

14. **Organize Information** In the cluster diagram below, identify at least four ways you and your family can conserve energy. You can add more ovals to the diagram if you want to identify more than four ways.

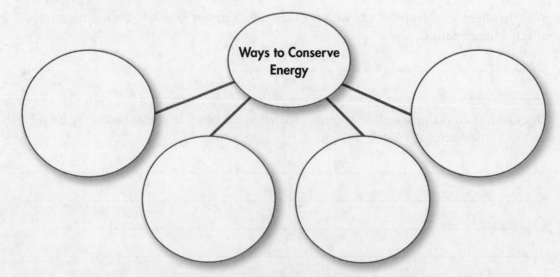

SKILL BUILDER Organize Information

15. Use what you learned in Lesson 3 to complete the chart below. In the right column, list at least two main points for each topic. Then, write a summary of the entire lesson.

Topic	Notes
Pollution from fossil fuels	
Damage caused by extracting fuels	
Dependence on foreign sources	
Energy conservation	
Summary	

17.3 SELF-CHECK

Answer the questions to test your knowledge of lesson concepts. You can check your work using the answers on the bottom of the page.

16. What are two reasons coal mining is a dangerous occupation?

_____

17. What are two main goals of energy conservation?

_____

16. Mines can collapse, and exposure to coal dust can cause respiratory illness. 17. To make fossil fuels last longer and to limit environmental damage

17.4 Nuclear Power

Key Concepts

 The process of nuclear fission releases energy.

 In a nuclear power plant, nuclear fission is used to generate electricity.

 Nuclear power does not create air pollution, but its problems include risk of accidents and disposal of wastes.

 Nuclear fusion has advantages over fission, but the technology does not yet exist to use fusion to generate power.

SKILL BUILDER Vocabulary Preview

Define each vocabulary term in your own words. Then, write yourself a quick note on how you will remember each. One term has been done for you.

Term	Definition	How I Remember
Nuclear energy		
Nuclear fission	The splitting of an atom's nucleus into two two smaller nuclei	A *fissure* is a break, so I remember that *fission* breaks a nucleus apart.
Nuclear reactor		
Meltdown		
Nuclear waste		
Nuclear fusion		

SKILL BUILDER Reading Strategy

Preview the lesson and use what you learn in your preview to complete the chart below. Read the questions in the left column. Write your answers in the right column. Then, on the lines below the chart, write one sentence to explain what you think this lesson will be about.

What is the title of this lesson?	
What are the vocabulary terms for this lesson?	
What are the key concepts for the four main sections of this lesson?	
What do the photos depict?	
What do the diagrams seem to show?	

_____

_____

Nuclear Energy

1. What are two examples of unstable atoms that can be used for nuclear fission?

_____

2. **Organize Information** Fill in the flowchart to describe the process of nuclear fission.

Generating Electricity

3. What type of fuel is used in a nuclear power plant?

_____

4. **Think Visually** Label the diagram with the captions below.

> **Electricity is generated.**
> **Water cools steam, changing it to liquid water.**
> **Nuclear fission occurs.**
> **Steam is produced.**

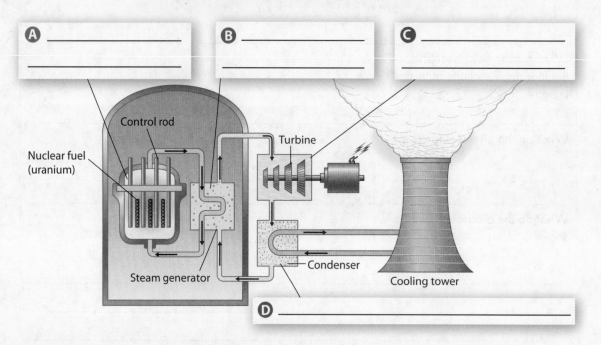

Ⓐ _____

Ⓑ _____

Ⓒ _____

Ⓓ _____

Benefits and Costs of Nuclear Power

5. List three examples of costs and three examples of benefits for nuclear power.

_____

_____

_____

6. What is the main benefit of storing all nuclear waste at a single site?

_____

_____

_____

_____

7. Why did the federal government end its support of Yucca Mountain as a site for long-term storage of nuclear waste?

_____

_____

Nuclear Fusion: The Future?

8. Complete the following paragraph with terms from the word bank.

energy	nuclear fission	nuclei	sun

Nuclear fusion reactions generate the energy released by the _____.

The process of nuclear fusion is essentially the opposite of _____. Nuclear

fusion involves two atomic _____ that are joined, or fused. This releases a

tremendous amount of _____.

9. Why isn't nuclear fusion currently in use?

_____

_____

17.4 SELF-CHECK

Answer the questions to test your knowledge of lesson concepts. You can check your work using the answers on the bottom of the page.

10. What is nuclear fission?

_____

_____

11. What are two main drawbacks of nuclear power?

_____

_____

12. What are the potential benefits of producing energy through nuclear fusion?

_____

_____

10. The separation of an atom's nucleus into two smaller nuclei 11. The risk of accidents and the management of nuclear waste disposal 12. Lack of air pollution, limited radioactive waste, use of water as a fuel

Chapter Vocabulary Review

Use each vocabulary term in a sentence.

1. Renewable energy _____

_____

2. Nonrenewable energy _____

_____

3. Strip mining _____

_____

4. Subsurface mining _____

_____

5. Petroleum _____

_____

6. Acid drainage _____

_____

7. Energy conservation _____

_____

8. Nuclear energy _____

_____

9. Nuclear waste _____

_____

10. Methane hydrate _____

_____

11. Oil shale _____

_____

EXTENSION On a separate sheet of paper, make a crossword puzzle that uses as many of the chapter's vocabulary terms as possible. Write clues for the terms. Exchange your puzzle with another student. Each of you should then complete the other student's puzzle.

Ecological Footprints

Oil Consumption

In this activity, you will calculate the amount of oil used per day and per year by different groups of people.

Calculating Daily Oil Use

In the United States, each person uses an average of 3 gallons of oil per day. To find the gallons of oil used per day by a group of people, multiply the number of people by 3.

- In 2010, there were approximately 309 million people in the United States.

▶ The calculation of the gallons of oil used per day by the people in the United States in 2010 is modeled at the right:

gallons used per day	**=**	**number of people in U.S.**	**×**	**daily use by 1 person**
	=	309 million	×	3 gallons
	=	927 million gallons		

1. Record the number of people in your class, hometown, and state. Then, calculate the gallons of oil used per day for each group. Write your answers in the table.

	Population	Gallons of Oil per Day	Gallons of Oil per Year
You (or the average American)	1	3	
Your class			
Your hometown			
Your state			
United States	309 million	927 million	

Data from Energy Information Administration, Official Energy Statistics from the U.S. Government.

Calculating Yearly Oil Use

▶ To find the gallons of oil used per year, multiply the amount used per day, 3, by the number of days in a year, 365: **3 × 365 = 1095 gallons.**

2. Calculate the gallons of oil used per year by each group in the table. Write your answers in the table. _____

3. The average person in a developing country uses about 0.2 gallon of oil per day. How much oil does the average person in a developing country use in a year? About how much more than this does the average person in the United States use in a year?

_____

Oil or Wilderness on Alaska's North Slope?

Polar Bear Den Sites in the 1002 Area

The 1002 Area is a section of Alaska's Arctic National Wildlife Refuge that may, in the future, be opened for oil development, provided that both the United States Senate and the House of Representatives vote to do so. Many people, however, object to using this area to obtain oil. One major concern is the possibility of damage to the area's ecosystem and its animal populations. Polar bears (*Ursus maritimus*) are one animal species that can be found in the 1002 Area. Every winter in the 1002 Area, some female polar bears of the Beaufort Sea populations build dens in which they give birth to their young. Female bears and their cubs stay within the dens until springtime, when they travel to the seacoast.

Scientists captured some female bears belonging to the Beaufort Sea populations and attached radio transmitters to these bears. The scientists then used the radio transmitters to track these bears and determine where they built their dens. The map shows the locations in which radio-collared females built dens between 1981 and 2001. Study the map and answer the questions on the following page.

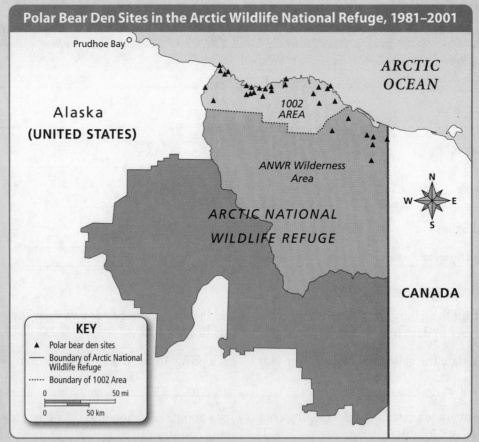

Adapted from U.S. Fish and Wildlife Service

Use the information in **Polar Bear Den Sites in the 1002 Area** to answer the questions below.

1. In the map, how many polar bear dens are located within the 1002 Area? How many polar bear dens are located outside the 1002 Area? _____

2. Does the map show the locations of all the polar bear dens that were built between 1981 and 2001? Explain your answer. (*Hint:* Did scientists track the movement of all the polar bears in the Beaufort Sea population?)

_____

3. Based on the distribution of polar bear dens, how do you think the overall polar bear population would be affected by drilling in the 1002 Area? _____

_____

_____

4. Some people suggest drilling in the winter to avoid caribou calving season, which occurs in the summer. Polar bears, however, give birth to their young in the winter. How do you think decision makers should decide which time of year to drill?

_____

_____

_____

_____

5. **REVISIT INVESTIGATIVE PHENOMENON** The 1002 Area is thought to be a rich source of petroleum reserves. Do you think there should be drilling for oil in this area—or do you think the area should be maintained as a wilderness preserve? Explain.

_____

_____

_____

21st Century Skills

Use Internet and library resources to research opinions and actions from a U.S. senator or representative from your state related to drilling in the Arctic National Wildlife Refuge or another part of the country. Then, write a letter to him or her explaining why you agree or disagree with the position.

*The 21st Century Skills used in this activity include **Critical Thinking and Problem Solving, Media Literacy, Initiative and Self-Direction,** and **Productivity and Accountability.***

18 Renewable Energy Alternatives

Before you read the chapter, answer each question with information you know. After you complete the chapter, re-answer the questions using information you learned.

INVESTIGATIVE PHENOMENON **Do the benefits of renewable energy outweigh the costs?**

What I Know	What I Learned

18.1 How can we use the heat from the Earth to both warm and cool our homes?

18.2 How can the movement of water be used to generate electricity?

18.3 How does both solar and wind energy depend upon radiation from the sun?

18.4 How can a reaction that produces water also generate electricity?

18.1 Biomass and Geothermal Energy

Key Concepts

- Alternative energy resources are needed to replace fossil fuels, reduce air pollution, and reduce the emission of greenhouse gases.
- Energy derived from biomass is used for cooking, heating, powering motor vehicles, and generating electricity.
- Steam and hot water produced by geothermal energy can be used for generating electricity and for heating.

 SKILL BUILDER Vocabulary Preview

Define each vocabulary term in your own words. Then, write yourself a quick note on how you will remember each. One term has been done for you.

Term	Definition	How I Remember
Biomass energy		
Biofuel		
Biopower	Electricity that is generated by the combustion of biomass	Because *bio* refers to living things, *biopower* is power, such as electricity, produced from living or once-living things.
Geothermal energy		
Ground source heat pump		

The Reasons for Alternative Energy

1. List four natural sources of renewable energy. _____

_____

2. Describe three benefits of renewable energy sources. _____

_____

_____

_____

3. **Organize Information** In the concept map below, give three reasons why renewable energy resources will keep growing rapidly.

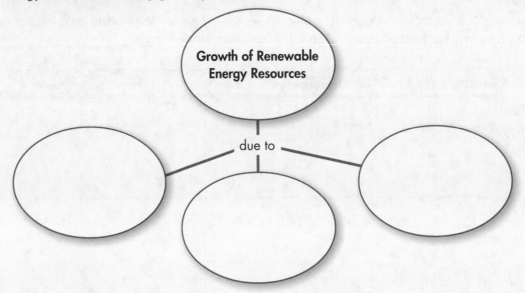

Biomass Energy

4. Complete the following paragraph with terms from the word bank.

biodiesel	biofuels	biopower	ethanol	methane	wood

In developing nations, _____, charcoal, and manure are forms of biomass that provide much of the energy used for heating, cooking, and lighting. In developed nations, many vehicles use liquid fuels, called _____, that come from biomass sources. One such fuel is _____, which is produced in the United States, primarily from corn. _____, which is produced from vegetable oil, is another one of these fuels. Waste biomass from the timber industry and farms is burned to generate electricity; electricity generated from biomass is called _____. In addition, the decomposition of biomass in landfills produces _____, which can also be burned to generate electricity.

5. Explain why the combustion of biomass releases no net carbon into the atmosphere.

_____

_____

_____

6. Identify two disadvantages of using biomass as a source of energy.

_____

_____

_____

_____

Geothermal Energy

For Questions 7–11, complete each statement by writing the correct word or words.

7. Geothermal energy is produced from a combination of high pressure and the breakdown

of _____ underground.

8. In a geothermal _____, steam from below ground turns the blades of a turbine, which makes a generator produce electricity.

9. In some places, hot _____ is piped directly to buildings from underground.

10. A benefit of geothermal energy is that it creates less air pollution than combustion of

_____.

11. A negative aspect of geothermal energy is that some projects can trigger massive shaking

in the form of _____.

12. Describe how a ground source heat pump works.

_____

_____

_____

_____

13. Explain why geothermal energy sources may not always be truly sustainable.

_____

_____

_____

_____

SKILL BUILDER Organize Information

14. Fill in the cluster diagram with terms from the word bank.

| biopower | burning wood | geothermal power plant |
| ground source heat pumps | ethanol and other fuels |

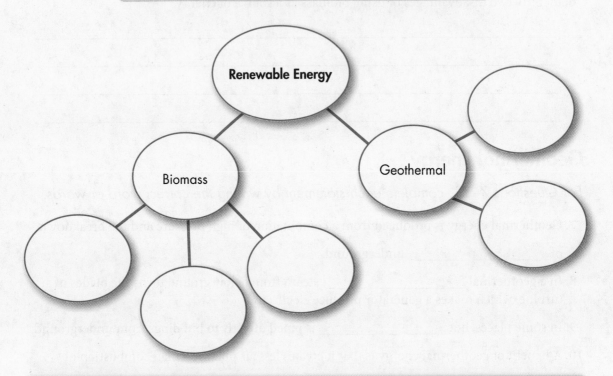

18.1 ◯ SELF-CHECK

Answer the questions to test your knowledge of lesson concepts. You can check your work using the answers on the bottom of the page.

15. Why is the replacement of fossil fuels by renewable energy sources highly probable?

_____

_____

16. Explain whether ethanol is a renewable alternative to gasoline.

_____

_____

15. Because fossil fuels are a nonrenewable energy resource, they will someday run out. In addition, the combustion of fossil fuels causes pollution. **16.** It is a renewable alternative only if the corn from which ethanol is made can be continuously grown and processed faster than the ethanol is used. If not, ethanol is not truly a renewable resource.

Real Data

Biodiesel

The graph at the right represents how much pollutant emissions are reduced when two types of biodiesel fuel, B20 and B100, are used instead of petroleum-based diesel fuel. In this activity, you will interpret the graph and use the information to compare and contrast the two types of biodiesel fuel.

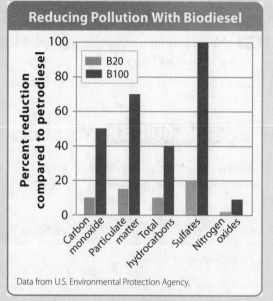

Reducing Pollution With Biodiesel

Data from U.S. Environmental Protection Agency.

Interpreting the Graph

1. Describe what the light bars and the dark bars represent.

_____

_____

2. What is the vertical axis label? What does it mean, and how is it represented in the graph?

_____

_____

_____

Calculating Pollution Reduction

▶ Suppose a car that uses petrodiesel releases 940 pounds of carbon per year. The method for calculating the amount of carbon monoxide released if B20 is used is modeled below.

Step 1	Use the graph to find the percent reduction of carbon monoxide for B20. Write the percent as a decimal.	**10% = 0.1**
Step 2	Find the number of pounds by which carbon monoxide emissions are reduced. To do this, multiply the decimal by the original amount of carbon monoxide emitted.	**0.1 × 940 = 94 pounds**
Step 3	Subtract the amount of pollution reduction from the original amount.	**940 – 94 = 846 pounds**

So, by using B20 instead of petrodiesel, the car would release 846 pounds of carbon monoxide each year, rather than 940 pounds.

3. By what percentage are carbon monoxide emissions reduced if B100 is used instead of petrodiesel? How much carbon monoxide would the car release per year if B100 is used?

_____

18.2 Hydropower and Ocean Energy

Key Concepts

- The movement of river water can be used to generate electricity.
- Hydropower is nonpolluting and relatively inexpensive, but dams can harm ecosystems and disrupt people's lives.
- The movement of tides and ocean thermal energy can be used to generate electricity.

SKILL BUILDER Vocabulary Preview

Define the vocabulary term in your own words. Then, write yourself a quick note on how you will remember it. One term has been done for you.

Term	Definition	How I Remember
Hydropower		
Tidal energy	The use of the movement of tidal water to generate electricity	I form a mental picture of tidewater rising rapidly and powerfully on a beach.
Ocean thermal energy conversion (OTEC)		

Generating Electricity with Hydropower

1. How does hydropower compare to other renewable energy sources in terms of the quantity Americans use?

_____

2. Describe the sequence of steps involved in using water stored behind dams to generate electricity.

_____

_____

_____

3. **Organize Information** In the concept map below, explain the run-of-the-river approach to generating hydropower. Include one advantage and one disadvantage of this approach.

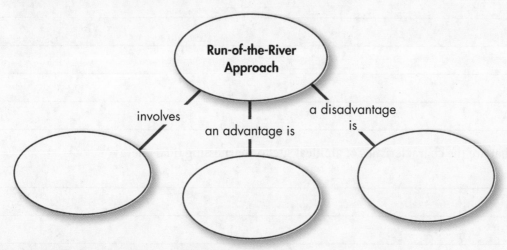

Benefits and Costs of Hydropower

For Questions 4–7, complete each statement by writing the correct word or words.

4. Because nothing is burned, hydropower does not _____ the atmosphere.

5. Hydropower dams can provide electricity and may control _____.

6. When they change the flow of rivers, hydropower dams drastically change _____ and reduce fish populations.

7. China's _____ provides enough hydroelectric power to replace dozens of coal or nuclear plants, but it has forced the relocation of more than 1 million people.

8. How has the Aswan High Dam changed the soil in Egypt? How has this affected agriculture?

_____
_____
_____

9. Summarize the costs and benefits of hydropower.

_____
_____
_____
_____
_____
_____

Energy From the Ocean

10. Describe one process of producing electricity from the movement of tides.

_____

_____

_____

_____

_____

11. What are the characteristics of an ideal site for harnessing tidal energy?

_____

_____

_____

12. What are the costs and benefits of using tidal energy to generate electricity?

_____

_____

_____

13. ▧ **Organize Information** Complete the flowchart to show one approach of ocean thermal energy conversion (OTEC).

```
┌─────────────────────────────────────────┐
│ Warm surface water circulates around     │
│ pipes containing gases that boil at      │
│ temperatures lower than water's boiling  │
│ point.                                   │
└─────────────────────────────────────────┘
                    │
                    ▼
┌─────────────────────────────────────────┐
│                                          │
│                                          │
│                                          │
└─────────────────────────────────────────┘
                    │
                    ▼
┌─────────────────────────────────────────┐
│                                          │
│                                          │
│                                          │
└─────────────────────────────────────────┘
```

14. Why are there no OTEC facilities today that provide electricity to consumers?

_____

_____

SKILL BUILDER Organize Information

15. Fill in the Venn diagram with characteristics that compare and contrast hydropower and tidal power.

Hydropower   **Tidal Energy**

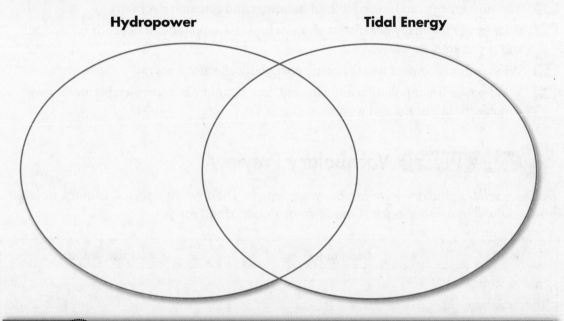

18.2 ◯ SELF-CHECK

Answer the questions to test your knowledge of lesson concepts. You can check your work using the answers on the bottom of the page.

16. Briefly explain how rivers can generate electric power.

_____

_____

17. Why is the growth of hydropower unlikely?

_____

_____

18. Why are there few power plants that use tidal energy to generate electricity?

_____

_____

16. The moving river water turns a turbine, causing the turbine to spin; this turns a generator and produces electricity. **17.** Most of the places along rivers that are good for the production of hydropower have already been dammed. **18.** There are relatively few locations where the difference between high and low tide is sufficient to enable the generation of electricity.

18.3 Solar and Wind Energy

Key Concepts

- The sun's energy can be used to heat buildings and generate electricity.
- Solar power has many benefits, such as its limitless supply, but it depends on weather and is currently expensive.
- Wind turbines convert wind's kinetic energy into electrical energy.
- Wind power is nonpolluting and efficient, but its supply is unpredictable and it may damage the landscape and wildlife.

 SKILL BUILDER **Vocabulary Preview**

Define each vocabulary term in your own words. Then, write yourself a quick note on how you will remember each. One term has been done for you.

Term	Definition	How I Remember
Passive solar heating		
Active solar heating		
Flat-plate solar collector		
Photovoltaic (PV) cell	A device that converts solar energy directly into electricity	I know that *photo* refers to light, and a *volt* is a measurement of electricity.
Concentrating solar power (CSP)		
Wind turbine		
Wind farm		

SKILL BUILDER Reading Strategy

Before you read the lesson, fill in the first column of the KWL chart below with information you already know about solar energy and wind energy. Fill in the second column with information you want to know about these topics. After you have read the lesson, fill in the third column with information you have learned.

	I Know	I Want to Know	I Learned
Solar energy			
Wind energy			

Harnessing Solar Energy

For Questions 1–4, write True if the statement is true. If the statement is false, replace the underlined word or words to make the statement true. Write your changes on the line.

_____ **1.** Greenhouses use <u>active</u> solar heating to collect the sun's energy.

_____ **2.** Flat-plate solar collectors, or solar panels, provide a method for <u>passive</u> solar heating.

_____ **3.** In a <u>photovoltaic cell</u>, sunlight striking a silicon plate begins a process that creates an electric current.

_____ **4.** Concentrating solar power (CSP) is a technology that uses <u>turbines</u> to focus sunlight in order to generate electricity.

5. Describe two features of a house that would promote passive solar heating.

_____

_____

_____

_____

Benefits and Costs of Solar Power

6. **Organize Information** Fill in the table with information about the benefits and costs of solar power. Provide at least three examples of each.

Benefits of Solar Power	Costs of Solar Power

Harnessing Wind Power

7. Explain how wind energy is considered an indirect form of solar energy.

_____

_____

For Questions 8–10, circle the letter of the correct answer.

8. Which of the following is NOT a part of a wind turbine?

A. blades

B. mirrors

C. gearbox

D. generator

9. To create electricity, wind blowing into a turbine turns

A. towers that maintain farms.

B. drains that irrigate wetlands.

C. blades that connect to a gearbox.

D. generators that are placed underground.

10. Offshore wind farms are becoming more common because they

A. are less expensive to build, due to materials.

B. are economical to maintain, due to location.

C. produce more power, due to stronger winds.

D. produce wind farms, due to higher elevations.

Benefits and Costs of Wind Power

11. Complete the following paragraph with terms from the word bank.

efficient	electricity	migrating birds	noisy	pollution

There are advantages and disadvantages to production and use of wind power. It does

not cause _____, as the combustion of fossil fuels does. Wind power is

also very _____ because wind turbines produce much more energy than

they use. However, some communities do not want wind turbines nearby because they

can be _____ and unattractive. Their rotating blades can be a danger

to _____ and other wildlife. In addition, wind turbines cannot produce

_____ when there is no wind.

12. Which two nations produce the highest percentage of wind power in the world?

_____

13. How does the cost of wind farms compare to the cost of plants powered by fossil fuels?

_____

_____

18.3 ◯ SELF-CHECK

Answer the questions to test your knowledge of lesson concepts. You can check your work using the answers on the bottom of the page.

14. Describe how photovoltaic cells work. _____

_____

_____

_____

15. Identify the role of the sun in the production of wind power.

_____

_____

14. The plates of a PV cell are made primarily of silicon. When sunlight strikes the plate that is rich in electrons, it knocks some electrons loose. These electrons are attracted to the other plate. The flow of electrons from one plate to another generates electricity. **15.** The sun's unequal heating of air masses causes winds to blow. The winds are then harnessed to produce electricity.

18.4 Energy From Hydrogen

Key Concepts

 Hydrogen fuel can be produced from the breakdown of water or other hydrogen-containing compounds.

 Fuel cells are used to generate electricity.

SKILL BUILDER Vocabulary Preview

Define each vocabulary term in your own words. Then, write yourself a quick note on how you will remember each.

Term	Definition	How I Remember
Electrolysis		
Fuel cell		

Producing Hydrogen Fuel

For Questions 1–6, complete each statement by writing the correct word or words.

1. The chemical breakdown of hydrogen-containing compounds requires an input of

   _____.

2. _____ is a process that breaks water down into the gases hydrogen and oxygen.

3. The most common way to obtain hydrogen today is to extract it from _____, which is a component of natural gas.

4. The breakdown of methane to obtain hydrogen has the drawback of also releasing

   _____, a greenhouse gas.

5. Hydrogen can be stored and _____ from one place to another.

6. For hydrogen to become a useful vehicle fuel, scientists must determine how to

   _____ it into a smaller volume.

7. What is the chemical equation for the reaction that occurs during electrolysis?

_____

8. What is the chemical equation for the reaction that occurs during the breakdown of methane?

_____

9. Compare and contrast the production of hydrogen through electrolysis and through the breakdown of methane.

_____

_____

_____

_____

10. List three benefits and three costs of using hydrogen as a fuel.

_____

_____

_____

_____

Fuel Cells

11. What is the purpose of creating a reaction in a fuel cell?

_____

12. How does a fuel cell differ from electrolysis?

_____

_____

13. What is the chemical reaction that takes place inside a fuel cell?

_____

14. How is electricity produced in a fuel cell?

_____

_____

_____

_____

15. Name one way fuel cells are being used.

_____

_____

16. Explain how increased use of fuel cells would increase the energy independence of the United States.

_____

_____

_____

_____

_____

_____

_____

17. **Think Visually** The diagram below shows a fuel cell. In the spaces following the diagram, describe what is indicated by each letter. The first one has been done for you.

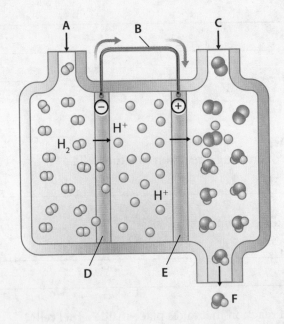

A Hydrogen enters the side of the electrode with the negative terminal

B _____

C _____

D _____

E _____

F _____

SKILL BUILDER Organize Information

18. Fill in the graphic organizer with terms from the word bank.

| breakdown of methane | electricity | electrolysis | fuel cell | oxygen | water |

```
  (            )        (            )
         \              /
          \    produce /
           \          /
        ( hydrogen gas )
               |
          that can be
          combined with
               |
        (            ) — inside a — (            )
                                         |
                                    to produce
                                         |
              (            ) — and — (            )
             as a waste              to power
              product                vehicles
```

EXTENSION Use Internet and library resources to learn more about other ways fuel cells can be used, in addition to powering motor vehicles. Add the information you find to the graphic organizer above.

18.4 ○ SELF-CHECK

Answer the questions to test your knowledge of lesson concepts. You can check your work using the answers on the bottom of the page.

19. List three methods, current and proposed, of producing hydrogen fuel. _____

_____

20. State the most common use of fuel cells. _____

_____

19. Electrolysis, breakdown of methane, use of algae **20.** Fuel for vehicles, such as cars, buses, and space vehicles

Chapter Vocabulary Review

Match each term with its definition.

_____ **1.** biomass energy

_____ **2.** geothermal energy

_____ **3.** hydropower

_____ **4.** ocean thermal energy conversion (OTEC)

_____ **5.** photovoltaic (PV) cell

_____ **6.** concentrating solar power (CSP)

a. use of the energy of moving water to produce electricity

b. a device that converts solar energy directly into electricity

c. produced from materials that make up living organisms

d. use of mirrors to focus sunlight to generate electricity

e. a process that changes the heat energy in seawater to electricity

f. produced from heat deep below Earth's surface

Write a sentence that distinguishes between the two terms or shows the relationship between the two terms.

7. Biofuel, biopower _____

_____

8. Active solar heating, flat-plate solar collector _____

_____

9. Wind turbine, wind farm _____

_____

10. Electrolysis, fuel cell _____

_____

_____

11. hydropower, biopower _____

_____

EXTENSION On a separate sheet of paper, write a short paragraph to describe the benefits of renewable energy—as compared with the use of fossil fuels. Use at least one vocabulary term from each lesson in this chapter in your paragraph.

Germany's Big Bet on Renewable Energy

Renewable Energy in Germany and the United States

In Germany, it is government policy to obtain 20 percent of the nation's electricity from renewable sources by 2020. German law also requires utilities to buy the power produced by wind, solar, hydro, or other alternative energy producers at prices that are higher than market value.

The German government has been very active in pushing the nation toward a renewable-energy future. In 2007, Germany was first in production of energy from solar power, and it also ranked near the top in the production of wind energy; more than 14 percent of the nation's energy came from renewable sources. By 2009 Germany's big bet had made it a world leader in the use of renewable energy resources. What was happening in the United States?

The Road to Renewables

In 2008, while Germany was in the lead, the United States obtained less than 10 percent of its energy from renewables. Furthermore, much of that was hydropower that had been in place for many years. Although the U.S. government also supported the growth of renewable energy and did provide some incentives, these incentives did not equal those of Germany. Still, renewable-energy producers hoped the U.S. Congress would act to make more subsidies available, and to require that renewables produced a specific amount of the nation's electricity in the future.

The U.S. Congress is moving in that direction. In 2009, the House of Representatives passed a bill mandating that 20 percent of electric power come from renewable energy, attaining energy efficiency by 2020. Similar measures are anticipated from the Senate.

Meanwhile, individual states in the United States have been acting on their own. By 2009 about half of the states had established requirements for production of a specific amount of energy as of a specific date. Experts state, however, that renewable resources would likely grow faster if the United States follows Germany's lead and the federal government adopts renewable energy mandates that spur expansion.

For example, largely as a result of new tax credits and other incentives in the federal economic stimulus program in 2009, U.S. wind-energy capacity grew by 39 percent that year. This meant that wind was on the way to supplying almost 2 percent of the electricity needs of the United States by 2010. The federal incentives were limited, however. Supporters of renewables look forward to long-term government policies to boost the use of renewables.

What is the prospect of renewables in the United States? Wind is likely to provide most of the future growth in the renewable sector in the United States. Our nation has great wind-power potential, especially in the Great Plains and the mountains of the West. Solar potential is also growing. The shift away from fossil fuels will continue as renewable sources, including wind and solar power, help solve problems such as polluted air, dependence on foreign oil, and the need to decrease greenhouse gas emissions.

Use the information from **Renewable Energy in Germany and the United States** to answer the questions below.

1. In 2007, how did Germany compare with the United States in terms of the production of

renewable energy? _____

_____

2. What accounted for the differences in renewable energy production between Germany

and the United States? _____

_____

_____

3. Infer why U.S. state governments created their own renewable energy mandates.

_____

_____

_____

4. **REVISIT** **INVESTIGATIVE** PHENOMENON   How would the United States benefit from the

increased use of renewable energy resources? _____

_____

_____

_____

21st Century Skills

Work with a partner to research the push for greater renewable energy capacity in the United States. Respond to these questions in a computer slide show for the class: What is the status of legislation establishing renewable energy mandates? What incentives are available? What is the trend in use of wind, solar, biomass, and other renewable sources?

*The 21st Century Skills used in this activity include **Creativity and Innovation, Communication and Collaboration, Information Literacy, Media Literacy,** and **Information, Communicationf, and Technology (ICT) Literacy.***

19 Waste Management

Before you read the chapter, answer each question with information you know. After you complete the chapter, re-answer the questions using information you learned.

INVESTIGATIVE PHENOMENON **What can we do with old landfills?**

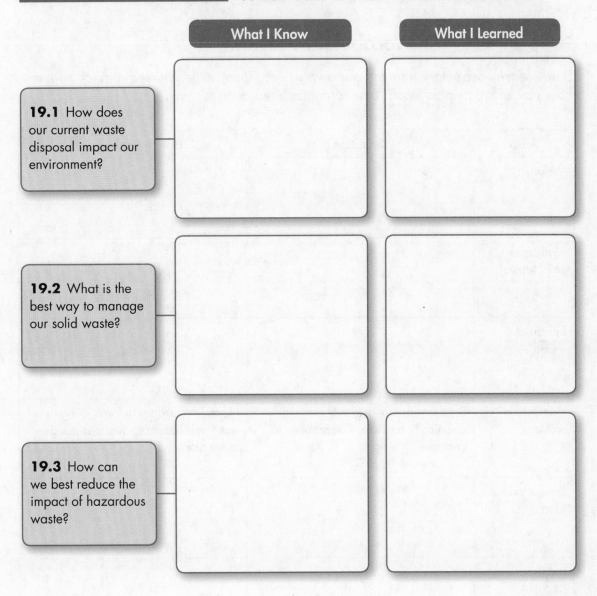

What I Know	What I Learned
19.1 How does our current waste disposal impact our environment?		
19.2 What is the best way to manage our solid waste?		
19.3 How can we best reduce the impact of hazardous waste?		

19.1 Municipal and Industrial Waste

Key Concepts

- The three main categories of waste include municipal solid waste, industrial waste, and hazardous waste.
- Current solid waste disposal methods are based on ancient practices of dumping, burying, or burning waste.

SKILL BUILDER Vocabulary Preview

Define each vocabulary term in your own words. Then, write yourself a quick note on how you will remember each. One term has been done for you.

Term	Definition	How I Remember
Waste		
Municipal solid waste		
Industrial waste		
Hazardous waste	Solid or liquid waste that is toxic, chemically reactive, flammable, or corrosive	I know *hazardous* means "dangerous," so *hazardous waste* is dangerous waste.
Sanitary landfill		
Leachate		
Incineration		

What Is Waste?

For Questions 1–6, complete each statement by writing the correct word or words.

1. Every person in the United States generates about _____ of trash per year.

2. _____ is the largest component of U.S. municipal solid waste.

3. Pens, disposable cameras, and paper coffee cups are examples of _____ goods.

4. In the 1970s, nondurable goods made with _____ became widely available.

5. The EPA classifies _____ waste as waste that is neither hazardous nor municipal solid waste.

6. _____ accounts for about 97 percent of the 7.6 billion tons of waste generated by U.S. industrial facilities every year.

7. Where does industrial waste come from?

_____

_____

_____

8. Where does wastewater come from?

_____

_____

_____

9. Why do you think companies wrap their products in so much packaging—and what can consumers do to reduce the amount of packaging companies use?

_____

_____

_____

_____

_____

_____

10. What effect has the widespread availability of plastic products had on the environment?

_____

_____

_____

Methods of Solid Waste Disposal

11. **Organize Information** Fill in the table to compare and contrast the three methods of solid waste disposal.

	Open Dumps	Sanitary Landfills	Incinerators
Benefits			
Drawbacks			

12. What does NIMBY stand for, and how does it relate to where landfills are located?

_____

_____

_____

_____

13. Explain how people can use the gas that is generated by landfills.

_____

_____

14. Describe technologies scientists have devised to mitigate emissions from incinerators.

_____

_____

_____

SKILL BUILDER Think Visually

15. Label the diagram of a sanitary landfill using terms from the word bank. Below the diagram, briefly describe where the solid waste in landfills come from.

| aquifer | compacted impermeable clay | gravel | plastic liner | soil | solid waste |

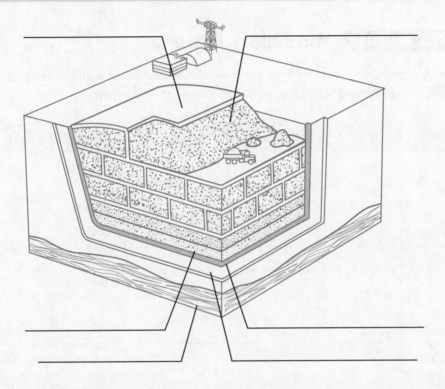

_____

_____

EXTENSION On the diagram, draw a methane gas recovery well, leachate collection pipes, and a leachate treatment system connected to the leachate collection pipes.

19.1 SELF-CHECK

Answer the questions to test your knowledge of lesson concepts. You can check your work using the answers on the bottom of the page.

16. In the United States, what does municipal solid waste mainly consist of?

_____

17. How do most industrialized nations today dispose of their wastes?

_____

16. Paper, yard debris, food scraps, and plastics 17. They bury waste in landfills or burn it in incinerators.

19.2 Minimizing Solid Waste

Key Concepts

🔑 One of the best ways to manage solid waste is to reduce the amount we generate.

🔑 The amount of waste can also be reduced by composting and recycling.

SKILL BUILDER **Vocabulary Preview**

Define each vocabulary term in your own words. Then, write yourself a quick note on how you will remember each. One term has been done for you.

Term	Definition	How I Remember
Source reduction		
Biodegradable		
Composting		When I see *composting*, I think of *decomposition*, or breaking down into basic parts.
Recycling		
Material recovery facility (MRF)		

SKILL BUILDER Reading Strategy

Before you read the lesson, fill in the first column of the KWL chart with what you already know about minimizing solid waste. Fill in the second column with what you want to know about this topic. After you have read the lesson, fill in the third column with what you have learned.

I Know	I Want to Know	I Learned

Waste Reduction

1. What are the benefits of reducing the amount of waste we generate?

_____

_____

2. How can plastic grocery bags damage the environment?

_____

_____

3. What can consumers do to convince companies to produce quality goods that last a long time, rather than using poorly made or nondurable goods?

_____

_____

_____

4. Describe financial incentives used by some local and state governments to convince consumers to reduce waste.

_____

_____

5. Complete the following paragraph with terms from the word bank.

> **biodegradable** **durable** **nondurable** **packaging**
> **plastics** **source reduction** **waste**

There are many steps people can take to reduce _____ in their lives every day. People can achieve _____ by buying items that use less _____ and by buying _____, rather than _____ goods. They can also support the ban of certain _____, such as those used to make grocery bags, that are not _____ and therefore will not break down naturally. Another way to reduce waste is to return glass bottles to stores or collection facilities instead of throwing them away.

Waste Recovery

6. **Organize Information** Fill in the boxes of the cycle diagram with short descriptions of the three steps in the recycling process.

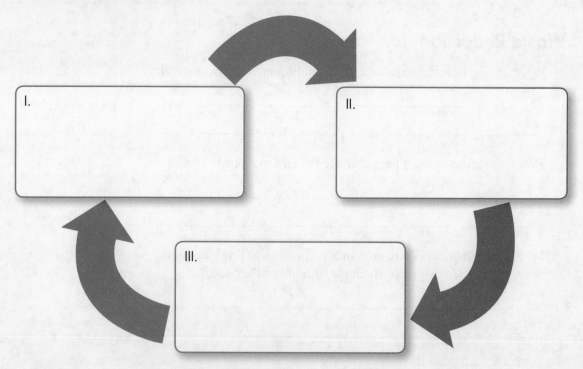

7. Describe the process of composting, and list two uses for compost.

_____

_____

_____

8. How can municipalities and businesses benefit by recycling?

_____

_____

9. Why is it important for consumers to buy products made with recycled materials whenever possible?

_____

_____

_____

_____

10. Name one limit of recycling.

_____

_____

_____

19.2 ◯ SELF-CHECK

Answer the questions to test your knowledge of lesson concepts. You can check your work using the answers on the bottom of the page.

11. Why does reusing items make sense environmentally and economically?

_____

_____

_____

12. Have bottle bills been successful? Explain. _____

_____

_____

13. Describe what happens during the second step of the recycling loop.

_____

_____

_____

11. Used items often work as well as and are less expensive than new ones. If you buy used items, you keep them out of a landfill, and you save the resources that would be used to manufacture a new item. 12. Yes, they have. Bottle bills are among the most successful recent state legislation. They greatly cut down on litter and decrease waste. 13. At material recovery facilities (MRFs), workers and machines sort collected recyclables and prepare them for reprocessing by cleaning and shredding them.

19.3 Hazardous Waste

Key Concepts

 Waste that is ignitable, corrosive, chemically reactive, or toxic is considered to be hazardous waste.

 Both industry and the private sector produce hazardous wastes.

 There are three main ways to dispose of hazardous waste—landfills, surface impoundments, and injection wells.

 Radioactive waste is particularly dangerous to human health and is persistent in the environment.

 Hazardous waste is regulated and monitored, but illegal dumping is a problem.

SKILL BUILDER Vocabulary Preview

Define each vocabulary term in your own words. Then, write yourself a quick note on how you will remember each. One term has been done for you.

Term	Definition	How I Remember
E-waste		
Surface impoundment		
Deep-well injection		
Radioactive waste		
Superfund	A cleanup program developed to address U.S. sites polluted with hazardous waste from past activities	When I see *super*, I think of the *super* effort required to help people and the environment by cleaning up polluted sites.

What Is Hazardous Waste?

For Questions 1 and 2, write True *if the statement is true. If the statement is false, replace the underlined word to make the statement true. Write your changes on the line.*

_____ 1. <u>Hazardous</u> waste may be liquid, solid, sludge, or gas.

_____ 2. Reactive substances are chemically <u>stable</u> and sometimes react with other compounds.

3. List three examples of ignitable hazardous waste.

_____

_____

4. Why is it difficult to safely dispose of corrosive substances?

_____

Sources of Hazardous Wastes

5. How can organic compounds harm humans and animals?

_____

_____

6. What are heavy metals, and how do they get into the environment?

_____

_____

_____

_____

Disposal of Hazardous Waste

Match each method of hazardous waste disposal with the statement that best describes it.

_____ 7. landfill

_____ 8. surface impoundment

_____ 9. deep-well injection

a. designed to keep waste deep underground

b. most common method of dealing with hazardous waste

c. water and waste mixed and placed into a pit

10. Is surface impoundment a permanent storage solution? Explain.

_____

_____

_____

Radioactive Waste

11. Organize Information Fill in the table to compare and contrast high-level and low-level radioactive waste.

Radioactive Waste	High-Level	Low-Level
Sources		
Characteristics		

12. Why are radioactive wastes difficult to dispose of safely?

_____

_____

Hazardous Waste Regulation

13. How and why do some companies improperly dispose of their hazardous waste?

_____

_____

_____

For Questions 14 and 15, complete each statement by writing the correct word or words.

14. Resource Conservation and Recovery Act (RCRA), the EPA sets standards by which states are to manage _____.

15. The Comprehensive Environmental Response Compensation and Liability Act (CERCLA) established a program known as the _____ to clean up hazardous waste sites.

SKILL BUILDER Think Visually

16. Which method of waste disposal is represented by the diagram below? Explain whether or not this type of facility can be used for radioactive waste disposal.

_____

_____

_____

_____

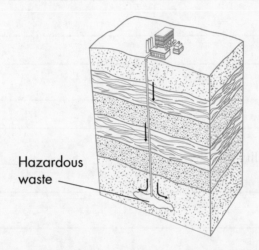

Hazardous waste

EXTENSION On the diagram, show how an injection well could fail.

19.3 SELF-CHECK

Answer the questions to test your knowledge of lesson concepts. You can check your work using the answers on the bottom of the page.

17. List the characteristics of hazardous waste. _____

_____

_____

18. Why is it so difficult to clean up hazardous waste sites? _____

_____

able for this purpose.
health. **18.** Sample answer: Cleanup is very expensive and can take many years. Funds are not always avail-
rosive, ignitable, reactive, and toxic. Some are radioactive. They harm human, animal, and environmental
17. Hazardous wastes can be liquid, solid, sludge, or gas. They can come from many sources. They are cor-

Chapter Vocabulary Review

Write a definition for each of the following terms.

1. Waste _____

_____

2. Composting _____

_____

3. Radioactive waste _____

_____

4. Incineration _____

_____

5. Material recovery facility (MRF) _____

_____

6. E-waste _____

_____

Use each vocabulary term in a sentence.

7. Superfund _____

_____

8. Leachate _____

_____

9. Biodegradable _____

_____

10. E-waste _____

_____

EXTENSION Research the current state of the CERCLA or Superfund program, and write a short report on the topic. Your report should include at least one vocabulary term from each lesson in the chapter.

Ecological Footprints

Municipal Solid Waste Production

In this activity, you will calculate the amounts of municipal solid waste (MSW) produced daily and yearly by your class, your state, and the United States using three different rates: the U.S. average, the rate for high-income nations, and the world average rate.

Groups Generating Municipal Solid Waste	Population	Per Person MSW Generation Rates					
		U.S. Average (lb)		High-income Nations (lb)		World Average (lb)	
		Day	Year	Day	Year	Day	Year
You	1	7.56	2759	2.64	963.6	1.47	536.65
Your Class							
Your State							
United States (tons)							

Data from Simmons, P., et al. 2006. The State of Garbage in America. **BioCycle**. 47:26

Calculating MSW Generation

To calculate the amount of MSW generated daily by your class, multiply the number of people in your class by the daily average.

▶ For example, if there are 28 students in your class, the daily MSW generation based on the U.S. average is 28 × 7.56 lb = 211.7 lb.

To calculate the amount of MSW generated yearly by your class, multiply the number of people in your class by the yearly average.

▶ If there are 28 students in your class, the yearly MSW generation based on the U.S. average is 28 × 2759 lb = 77,252 lb.

1. Calculate the amounts of MSW generated daily and yearly by your class. Write your answers in the table.

2. Use this same process to calculate daily and yearly MSW generation for your class based on the rates for other high-income nations and the world. Then, find the population of your state. Repeat each step to calculate the MSW for your state using each of the rates.

Converting Pounds to Tons

When you calculate MSW generation for the entire population of the United States, you will convert the amount of MSW from pounds (lb) to tons.

1 ton = 2000 lb

▶ In 2010, there were about 309 million people in the United States, which equals 2,336,040,000 pounds of MSW per day. The example at right shows the conversion of 2,336,040,000 pounds to tons.

$$2{,}336{,}040{,}000 \text{ lb} \times \frac{1 \text{ ton}}{2000 \text{ lb}} = 1{,}168{,}020 \text{ tons}$$

3. Calculate the MSW production for the United States, in pounds, using each of the three rates.

Transforming New York's Fresh Kills Landfill

Capping the Mounds

In 1948, the City of New York opened Fresh Kills Landfill on Staten Island, not knowing that over the years, the landfill would collect 150 million tons of solid waste. Eventually, the city decided to close Fresh Kills. In 1997, two of the landfill's giant trash mounds were capped. After 2001, the landfill was closed to waste shipments, and it was anticipated the other two mounds of waste would be capped between 2010 and 2014.

Layers of Protection

It is a time-consuming process to cap Fresh Kills. The process of capping such a large landfill is accomplished in phases. The work has to be thorough, so public and environmental health will not be threatened.

Six layers are applied to the landfill to accomplish the purpose.

- The first layer is made up of soil placed over the solid waste.

- This *soil barrier layer* is graded to prevent erosion and provide drainage. Moving upward, the second layer, or *gas vent layer*, is made up of mixed materials. This layer is engineered so that landfill gases will move toward vents or extraction wells.

- The third layer, or *hydraulic barrier*, is comprised of impermeable plastic. This important layer performs several functions. It keeps water out of the layers beneath, and it stops landfill gases from escaping into the atmosphere.

- The fourth layer, a *drainage layer*, is engineered to drain water from the layers of soil above.

- The fifth layer is the *barrier protection layer*, which is made of soil and is at least 61 centimeters (24 inches) thick. This layer is designed to protect the layers beneath from temperature changes and precipitation that could cause the layers

to crack or shift. The barrier protection layer also collects water.

- The sixth, topmost layer is the *planting soil layer*, which must be at least 15 centimeters (6 inches) thick. Different kinds of plants, including trees, are planted in this layer to help prevent soil erosion.

Landfill caps provide important protection for the environment, but additional systems are in place at Fresh Kills to further prevent pollution. The leachate management system collects and treats leachate as it is drained from the capped mounds. The Fresh Kills site also has a system that collects landfill gases, such as methane and carbon dioxide. Pipes deep in the landfill shunt the gases to extraction wells. Some of the collected gases are burned, and the rest of the gases are processed for use as an energy source. Monitoring wells at various locations within the site helps to ensure that pollution is not seeping into the environment.

The city of New York is required to maintain and monitor the capped landfill mounds for 30 years. After 30 years, planners assume the waste in the mounds will be thoroughly decomposed. Plans for the Fresh Kills Park will depend on the landfill caps and the leachate and landfill gas collection systems to provide a safe and sturdy base for the many uses designers have envisioned for the park.

Use the information in **Capping the Mounds** to answer the questions below.

1. List the six layers—beginning with the bottom layer—involved in capping the waste mounds at Fresh Kills Landfill. _____

_____

2. What roles do the additional leachate management and gas collection systems play at Fresh Kills? _____

_____

_____

3. Do you think New York should stop monitoring and maintaining the Fresh Kills landfill after 30 years have passed? Explain. _____

_____

_____

_____

4. **REVISIT** **INVESTIGATIVE** PHENOMENON What could New York residents have done to reduce the volume of waste in the Fresh Kills Landfill? Use the information provided in the article to explain how the choices of people across the country, as consumers and waste producers, affect our environment. _____

_____

_____

_____

_____

21st Century Skills

Work in small groups to find out more about the closing of the Fresh Kills landfill. Utilize Internet resources to explore the topic. Investigate ways technology makes it possible to maintain and monitor landfills. After reading more about Fresh Kills, construct a model of the landfill caps. Present your group's model to the class, and explain what you learned about the process.

*The 21st Century Skills used in this activity include **Critical Thinking and Problem Solving, Creativity and Innovation, Communication and Collaboration,** and **Information, Communication and Technology (ICT) Literacy.***